Business as unUSUAL

RADICAL IDEAS FOR CITIES

JULIAN BOLLETER

*This book is for Richard Weller.
Mentor, colleague, friend...
Legend.*

Reviews of

BUSINESS AS UNUSUAL:
RADICAL IDEAS FOR CITIES

Julian Bolleter's Business As Unusual *is never didactic and always wryly good-humoured. It's brimming with concepts and arguments, more than enough for an imaginative reader to change their mind multiple times about what's best for our cities and where urban design and policy should be heading. It could be the update on Hugh Stretton's* Ideas for Australian Cities *we've been waiting for over the last 55 years.*
David Nichols, Professor in Urban Planning, Melbourne School of Design Faculty of Architecture Building and Planning.

Business As Unusual: Radical Ideas for Cities challenges the stale conventions of urban planning instead offering bold, visually engaging alternatives to the status quo. Dr Julian Bolleter explores forgotten ideas, unconventional theories, and radical design strategies to break free from the restrictive planning ideologies shaping Australia's urbanizing territories. Packed with provocative insights and hand-drawn diagrams, this field guide invites planners, designers, policymakers, and frustrated city-dwellers to reimagine urban life beyond business-as-usual 'density and compactness fix all problems.' If you've ever wondered whether our cities could be something more—something more sustainable, diverse, and livable—this book is your blueprint for change.
Alan M. Berger, Norman B. and Muriel Leventhal Professor of Advanced Urbanism Department of Urban Studies and Planning, Massachusetts Institute of Technology.

The need for radical thinking in urban design is clear, but how to make radical change realistic rather than idealistic? With both theoretical depth and diagrammatic thinking, this highly accessible book stimulates new thinking about what is possible for even the most unsustainable of urban landscapes.
Kim Dovey, Chair of Architecture and Urban Design, Faculty of Architecture, Building & Planning, University of Melbourne.

True to form, Julian Bolleter has delivered the perfect combination of provocation, insight, creativity and entertainment. A 'must read' for those who need cheering up from the realities of BAU urbanism.
Professor Josh Byrne, Dean of Sustainable Futures, Faculty of Humanities, Curtin University

Business As Unusual *is packed with ideas that are fresh, bold, and thought-provoking. Business as usual is failing our cities. But, as this book powerfully reminds us, our cities are the result of choices. We could choose a different future for our cities, away from the treeless car-dependent urban fringe developments that typifies BAU. If they are to be more liveable, better-connected places with smaller ecological and carbon footprints, we must. If BAU is in part a failure to imagine a better alternative for our cities, then* Business As Unusual *encourages us to think differently and boldly. Not every idea in this book is intended to be practical or even to everyone's taste. Still, each provocation offers a kernel of hope of potential alternatives that could take us beyond the soulless suburbia that defines so much of our urban form.*
Brad Pettitt, Greens Member of the Western Australian Legislative Council

Contents

Preface	9
Introduction	11
Body: Alternative Urbanisms	21
Bunnings-Lite Urbanism	22
Car-Phobic Urbanism	28
Charter Urbanism	34
Deregulation Urbanism	38
Donga Urbanism	44
Dumb Urbanism	48
Edible Urbanism	52
Effluent Urbanism	58
Enlightenment Urbanism	62
Eternal Urbanism	66
Fair-Go Urbanism	72
Hamlet Urbanism	78
Incentive Urbanism	82
Inside Out Urbanism	88
Island Urbanism	94
Kibbutz Urbanism	98
Lifeboat Urbanism	104
Laneway Urbanism	108
Modern Urbanism	112
National Park Urbanism	118
Nature-Play Urbanism 2.0	122
Radburn Urbanism	128
Resignation Urbanism	134
Shame Urbanism 2.0	140
Supergraphic Urbanism	144
Symbolic Urbanism	150
Tax-Break Urbanism	154
Tinder Urbanism	158
Undercover Urbanism	164
Woollies-Lite Urbanism	168
Conclusion: Towards Business as Unusual	174
Acknowledgements	178
Bibliography	180

Preface

The day-to-day life of the harried mid-career academic involves teaching, hustling for research funding, and navigating the highs and lows of journal paper publication (and rejection). In the urban planning and design arena, the latter two pursuits lend themselves to analysing existing planning approaches and suggestions for policy tweaks to improve outcomes. All important work. However, it is unfortunate that more ideas-led propositional work is hard to successfully pitch to serious academic journals and research funding agencies like the Australian Research Council ('You want us to pay you taxpayer's money to sit around and draw stuff?'). The result is that many planning academics understandably spend their time in a critical or analytical mode, too encumbered with their own theoretical baggage to venture alternatives (and possibly not wanting to open themselves up to critiques such as they have doled out to students for years). This book of urban diagrams emerged out of frustration with this critical mode of academic work and as a necessary counter-reaction to quotidian (and funded) academic work. Generally, diagramming would proceed with no planned outcome, just the quietly insistent thought that the form of our cities is not preordained; things *could* be different. The alternative urbanisms that emerged each evoke a little world where the unusual reigns, just for a moment. I hope you enjoy your tour.

JULIAN BOLLETER
Perth, Australia
2025

INTRODUCTION: ESCAPING THE CAGE OF IDEOLOGY

> *How is it we are persuaded that there is no alternative? Why is it that we often seem to be such helpless puppets of the institutional and imaginative worlds we inhabit?*[1]
> **David Harvey**

The dream runs out of steam

How our world evolves is not the preordained result of some self-evident progression.[2] The past reinforces a simple but pertinent lesson that things will be different. That change will come is certain.[3] Younger generations will likely witness the 'radical destabilization of life on Earth, apocalyptic fires, epic flooding, and hundreds of millions of refugees fleeing regions made uninhabitable by extreme heat or permanent drought'.[4] Indeed, due to climate change alone, our cities will be unimaginably different one hundred years from now.

Reflecting on the unfolding crisis, a spate of recent books catalogue the cascading decline of Australian cities, with evocative titles such as *Breaking Point: The Future of Australian Cities*[5], *City Limits: Why Australian Cities are Broken and How We Can Fix Them*[6], and *Killing Sydney: The Fight For a City's Soul* to name just a few.[7] Indeed, despite the enviable liveability Australian suburbs have offered, the Australian dream of a quarter-acre lot is running out of steam. Climate stresses, such as bushfires, extreme heat, drought and water insecurity, have all impacted our suburban idyll.[8] Moreover, there is a growing divide between people who live near the city centres and those who live on the outer fringes (Figure 1). These cohorts encounter our cities very differently.[9] For those on the far-flung fringe, scarce job opportunities affect their ability to build a career, and marathon commutes are expensive, punishing and diminish the time and energy for connecting with family and friends.[10] Meanwhile, our cities insidiously nibble away at fragile fringing ecosystems. So, what solutions do contemporary planning approaches offer?

Densification drives

Much of the current planning for Australian cities tends to adopt a myopic focus on the compactness of development as an answer to our problems. As Elizabeth Farrelly wonderfully evokes, 'betraying us with reductivism'.[11] Indeed, policymakers offer the compact city as a panacea to our stubborn reliance on cars, indulgent overconsumption and increasing societal alienation.[12] Characterised by high-density development around mass transit and urban growth boundaries delineating urban extents,[13] by the early 2000s, all Australian capital cities had adopted planning guidelines based on the precepts of the compact city.[14] As it stands, all these cities have targets for housing delivered through densification.[15] Transit oriented development (TOD) theory underpins this concerted drive for densification and proposes that development around public transport nodes will reduce energy use because of more compact and efficient built forms, and proximity to mass transit systems, workplaces and services.[16]

However, the result of decades of densification drives (in some cases) has been the rise of 'parallel universes', one occupied by urban policymakers and their neat networks of TODs along train lines, the other by the realities of the 'increasingly complex, dispersed, residentially differentiated suburban metropolitan areas most Australians live in'.[17] Indeed, a yawning gulf exists between policy aspiration and the reality of urban development[18] and housing and travel patterns.[19] Applying TOD ideology in all capital cities has proven challenging,[20] and despite such policies being operational for up to fifty years,[21] Australia's sprawling cities remain some of the lowest density on the planet.[22]

Where planning has enabled density, the results are patchy. Exemplars of liveable, green and egalitarian living exist, such as the Nightingale model, which arose as an architect-led, limited-profit variant of considered medium-density housing in Melbourne.[23] In such projects, architects work directly with a cohort of local buyers (and soon-to-be residents) to craft a bespoke design offering affordability and the desired urban lifestyle.[24] At the other end of the spectrum are surging numbers of developer-led apartment projects in inner-city areas.[25] According to some, this 'rapid escalation in apartment construction is little more than a frenzy of speculative investment by purchasers who have no intention of actually living in the apartment they have bought'.[26] Indeed, negative impacts of certain aspects of apartment living are evident, e.g., shoddy construction, crowding, lower liveability (particularly for children) and loss of urban green space (Figure 2).[27]

Research has generally found that compact cities save energy, emissions and help take the pressure of peri-urban biodiversity.[28] Nonetheless, some questions remain.[29] Despite the promise of the imagined compact city, the literature does not fully support the assumption that merely cranking up urban density will predictably alter travel patterns.[30] A pertinent criticism is that the complex interwoven relationship between land use and uptake of mass transit is being crudely reduced to a sole criterion: urban density.[31] Sure, lower densities may encourage car use, but accessibility and income are important factors that shouldn't be overlooked.[32] Not surprisingly, the compact city can also trigger indirect energy consumption elsewhere through behavioural responses referred to as the 'rebound effect'.[33]

Figure 1: There is a growing divide between people who live near the city centres and those who live on the outer fringes.

Researchers in Finland have found that above a particular density threshold, the energy consumption of residents rises due to more leisure-related travel by car or plane.[34] If such dynamics are significant, *some* residents in dense urban areas may expend more energy than suburbanites.[35]

Of course, anyone who has driven along the fringes of Australian cities and seen the environmental devastation that goes hand-in-hand with suburban expansion would concede that compact city models are surely the way forward. However, we must be careful about assumptions that policymakers can use density alone as a crude lever to lessen environmental impact and deliver urban liveability. As author and planner Peter Seamer explains, 'one of the biggest mistakes made in city planning is to oversimplify the nature of a problem, and to presume that changing one thing will make all the difference'.[36]

Path dependency

 All systems of domination work by enveloping us in their narrative and superstitions in such a way that we cannot see beyond them. Taking a step or two back, finding a way to inspect them from the outside, allows us a glimpse of how imperfect they are.[37]
Yanis Varoufakis

So why the tunnel vision view of density as the panacea for our suburban malaise? In urban planning,[38] encompassing policy frameworks and previous professional and educational experiences guide decision-making. The result can be path-dependent planning systems locked into existing patterns of thinking.[39] Prevailing theory also often forms a kind of conceptual straitjacket. For example, while offering a sensible basis for urban planning practice, the current hegemony of the compact city movement (promulgated by the Congress for New Urbanism and adherents to Smart Growth and Green Urbanism) also smothers other ways of thinking. The British comedian John Cleese said: 'Everybody has theories. The dangerous people are those who are not aware of their own theories.'[40] That is, they are unconscious of the theories on which they operate. Such is the dominance of compact city ideology that many involved in planning and designing cities are unaware of how it shapes and, in some cases, limits their thinking.

Once entrenched, certain planning ideologies (including the rules that result) can be very fiddly to unpick.[41] An invisible and institutionalised substrate of regulations shapes almost every building or street. These regulations orchestrate the city's system and the lives it contains in a self-reinforcing dynamic.[42] A lack of what psychologists' call 'conceptual distance' compounds this dynamic. Indeed, when immersed in a project, its intricacies surround urban planners. Therefore, it is tempting to make only minor modifications to business as usual (BAU) practices. In essence, these planners become prisoners of their own paradigms.[43] As influential economist John Maynard Keynes evoked, 'the difficulty lies, not in the new ideas, but in escaping from the old ones'.[44] Indeed, it is because planners are so well-informed and enmeshed in the status quo that they struggle to imagine alternatives and the unrealised potential they may yield.[45]

Beyond path dependency, an unswerving commitment to harmony within the capitalist social order also diminishes the potential for radical innovation in planning.[46] In this way, urban planning cannot transcend capitalist society's social and property relations; instead, it is contained by and exhibits those same relations.[47] Indeed, the neoliberalist ideology promoted by the dominant class serves urban planning's material interests well. In turn, they have internalised this ideology to such a degree that they are willing to work within a system they might otherwise consider unjust.[48] A central theme, repeated ad nauseam, is that any alternatives to the apparent 'common-sense' of the free market are to be mercilessly 'mocked out of existence'.[49] In this way, neoliberalism is oblivious to, and at worst, coercively controlling of 'other' ways of thinking, including those ventured by planners with an alternative mindset.[50]

Figure 2: The fast escalation in apartment construction is partly a frenzy of speculative investment by buyers who have little intention of living in the apartments they have bought.

The result is that radical ideas about Australian cities have become almost unthinkable. The expectations of what urban planners can achieve have been drastically curtailed, 'leaving us with the cold, hard truth that without utopia, all that remains is a technocracy'.[51]

Methods

 There are no non-radical options left before us. Imagination is the only thing we have that is – or could be – radical enough to get us through.[52]
Naomi Klein

I have developed this book's urban proposals through techniques that help us transition to an 'outsider perspective', where we see the familiar with fresh eyes and approach problems from unexpected angles. The first of these techniques is 'assumption reversal'. In assumption reversal, innovators upturn commonly accepted notions to open up other ways of thinking. For example, upturning the planning orthodoxy that policymakers should graft urban density onto train stations allows us to consider alternatives, such as urban density around schools (for instance), which has been previously overlooked. Of course, the result will not necessarily be workable, but disrupting conventional thinking can catalyse new ideas and associations.[53] The second technique is 'recombinant innovation' in which innovators fuse two ideas from divergent fields (otherwise known as 'ideas sex'). Recombinant innovation often yields surprising results because it bridges between domains, opening up fertile terrain to explore.[54] For example, in urban planning, we could consider fusing two previously discrete entities, such as a national park and a city, to produce a 'national park city', which poses intriguing questions as to whether you could administer a city with the same attentiveness to biodiversity as found in the management of national parks.

The proposals in this book also embody a speculative mode of design exploration that generates and tests urban ideas through sketching and diagramming, and (on a good day) exposes new ways of thinking.[55] But how does this differ from conventional design processes? The key difference is the sketching and diagramming conducted for this book[56] I generally undertook without a particular goal in mind. Instead, I only evaluated the utility of the specific urban proposal after the drawing progressed. Rather than a classical model of scientific discovery, this approach embodies the idea that innovation is often the product of serendipity. In other words, in tinkering without a grand plan, you find something you are not looking for, which then proves transformative and even changes the world (such as Alexander Fleming's chance discovery of penicillin).[57] As philosopher Francis Bacon noted, the most significant advances are the least predictable, those 'lying out of the path of the imagination'.[58]

The urban proposals herein also draw on some distinctly unfashionable theories. Proposals derive from much-criticised contemporary planning theories, such as Landscape Urbanism,[59] long discarded theories (e.g., Modernism), theories that planners and designers have not previously brought to bear on urban planning (e.g., degrowth theory), as well as trawling through the archives for long-forgotten, dusty and sometimes dangerous ideas, all to penetrate past BAU practice.

One such unfashionable thread is utopianism. While not utopias, the urban proposals herein share the tendency to combine the architectural and social that was typical of the ideal cities of the nineteenth and twentieth centuries (e.g., Ebenezer Howard's Garden City or Frank Loyd Wright's Broadacre City). Indeed, behind any proposal for the 'good city' is some model of social organisation.[60] In those ideal cities – and many of the urbanisms herein – the proposed revolution in spatial form is an outward expression of an inner revolution in social structure.[61] While it is prudent to be cautious about the relationship between urban form and social conditions, it seems unnecessarily downplayed in contemporary urban planning and design.[62] Indeed, this is an age of realism (if not pessimism).[63] As Bregman explains, 'Utopias are attacked on three fronts: futility (it's not possible), danger (the risks are too great), and perversity (it will degenerate into dystopia).'[64] This outright rejection of utopianism has the adverse effect of constraining the 'free play of the imagination in the quest for alternatives'.[65] As David Harvey neatly puts it: 'The problem is that without a vision of utopia, there is no way to define the port to which we might want to sail.'[66]

What this book is not

At the risk of sounding overly defensive (and to pre-empt the likely critics), it is important to state what this book is *not*. Firstly, it is not a manual for implementing sustainable cities. Instead, I intend it as a conversation starter to open up fertile areas of opportunity through design experimentation, not close them down with detailed policy prescriptions. Incremental improvement in existing ways of planning cities is vital but well covered elsewhere.[67] The book is also not a manifesto for a shiny, new urban planning movement. Instead, I intend to counterbalance existing BAU planning practices. Moreover, while the urban proposals combine the architectural and social to some degree, this book is also not a manifesto setting out an alternative socio-political vision for Australian society. In other words, the proposals in this book tend to focus on the symptoms of capitalism rather than the overarching causes, and I note the limits of design in precipitating widespread social change.

A guide to alternative urbanisms herein

The book comprises an alphabetised list of proposed 'urbanisms', each of which evokes an alternate 'Australian Dream' and embodies a different way of dwelling in Australian cities. The result is a noisy cabinet of curiosities that deliberately eschews an overarching narrative.[68] The documentation of these urbanisms comprises two hand-drawn diagrams comparing the current condition and a possible alternative accompanied by the proposal's name, intended site, scale (street block, the neighbourhood or the larger district), method of generation (recombinant innovation or assumption reversal) and thematic relevance to other urbanisms ventured. I explain each urbanism in a brief, digestible way, describing the problems the proposal tackles and the potential it offers. The urbanisms were posted on LinkedIn and the worthiest (or most entertaining) commentary that ensued is also included. Where appropriate. commentary has also been drawn from related surveys.

I targeted the proposals towards the two primary development fronts: new suburbs on the far-flung fringes of our cities (Figure 3)[69] and existing middle-ring suburbs undergoing urban densification (Figure 4).[70] Credible projections from the Australian Bureau of Statistics anticipate Australia's population will double (or even triple) by 2101.[71] Most of this growth will occur across these two arenas. Critics will no doubt assert that we should be curtailing new suburban development completely (good luck with that). However, urban densification shoe-horned into existing urban areas alone could never accommodate this population surge entirely. Therefore, while some proposed urbanisms in this book are denser than their BAU counterparts, density is not the sole focus.

The twenty-first century will witness more urbanisation than all human history, suggesting we are amidst a once-off opportunity to profoundly reshape our cities. To rise to this challenge, we need diverse urban dreams to address the social, cultural and environmental issues that have bedevilled BAU development to date. Simply put, we need business-as-*un*usual solutions.

Figure 3: New compact suburbs on the far-flung fringe.

Figure 4: A middle-ring suburb undergoing urban densification.

BODY:
ALTERNATIVE URBANISMS

Bunnings-Lite Urbanism

Inequality is vital for capitalism to flourish. As environmental activist Rob Hopkins explains, 'it is a model that thrives by imagining us as isolated consumers, cultivating a desire for things we do not need and a sense of inadequacy if we fail to attain them, promulgating the myth that the route to happiness is through the accumulation of "stuff".'[72] However, the myths of materialism, possessiveness and individualism that claim worldly goods lead to happiness often result in a bitter harvest of isolation and inadequacy.[73] Inadequacy arises because we do not perceive the value of possessions in absolute terms. Our brains constantly adjust the idea of what we need to feel fulfilled.[74] They compare what we possess now to what we possessed yesterday, what we might own next and, most importantly, what our friends have.[75] While a new kitchen benchtop (possibly) makes you happier in the short term, it won't deliver long-term happiness, and most of the boost you feel will seep away within a year.[76] This unfortunate tendency is aptly referred to as the 'treadmill theory', which ventures that the richer you become, the more you benchmark yourself against other rich people and 'the faster the wheel of desire spins beneath your feet so that you end up feeling as though you have not made any progress'.[77] Life on the treadmill causes us to strive slavishly for more, failing to make us happy in the longer term and further depleting an exhausted planet.[78]

So, what is a better route to long-term happiness? Happiness flows from those activities and states that relate to our deep need to feel connected to other people.[79] Moreover, living contentedly requires recognising that we do not truly own anything: our cordless drills, iPhones, our homes or new kitchen benchtops. Zen teacher Jack Kornfield reminds us that happiness does not come 'through possession but rather through our capacity to open, and to move and be free in life'.[80] Indeed, sharing enriches our lives and deepens our connections with others; it is not a burden but a gain.[81] Ignoring for a moment the happiness and connectedness that comes with sharing, it is also the logical response to our current crisis of overconsumption.[82] Indeed, rewiring our hearts and minds toward the sharing paradigm is the 'most critical task for urban governance and urban futures in the twenty-first century'.[83]

Card-carrying New Urbanists Andres Duany and Elizabeth Plater-Zyberk note, 'The suburb is the last word in privatization, perhaps, even its lethal consummation... and it spells the end of authentic civic life'.[84] But does this need to be the case? Could we incubate a more collective mentality through suburban design? Sure. Much of the stuff we consume is technically 'necessary' but seldom used. Householders use tools like lawnmowers and drills every few months for 10 minutes and they gather dust for the rest of the year.[85] Of course, manufacturers and retailers want everyone to accumulate a shed full of such 'home essentials' (drills, leaf blowers, lawn mowers, ladders; Figure 5). But, a more rational and communitarian approach would be residents constructing communal sheds in suburban streets where they can store equipment as needed – much like a Facebook 'buy nothing' group minus big tech and with more social interaction. Local governments could support the roll out of shed projects like these with accompanying apps for easy user coordination (Figure 6).[86] So, what about communal street sheds for sharing those tools you (almost) never use? What about street shed parties on a Saturday night in late summer, as if collecting experiences were more important than things?

(With apologies to Bunnings)

Commentary

Joshua
I'm sorry, mate, I like my tools. I like that they sit there for months, or I may never even use them. No one can borrow them, and I will not share them. But one day, I will need them.

Ehsan
This has been one of the best posts I have seen on LinkedIn.

Warren
Love it. My shed and garage contents would support a whole street just by themselves!

Figure 5: The Saturday morning tide of home-improvers flock into a Bunnings warehouse. Manufacturers and retailers want everyone to accumulate a shed full of 'home essentials'.

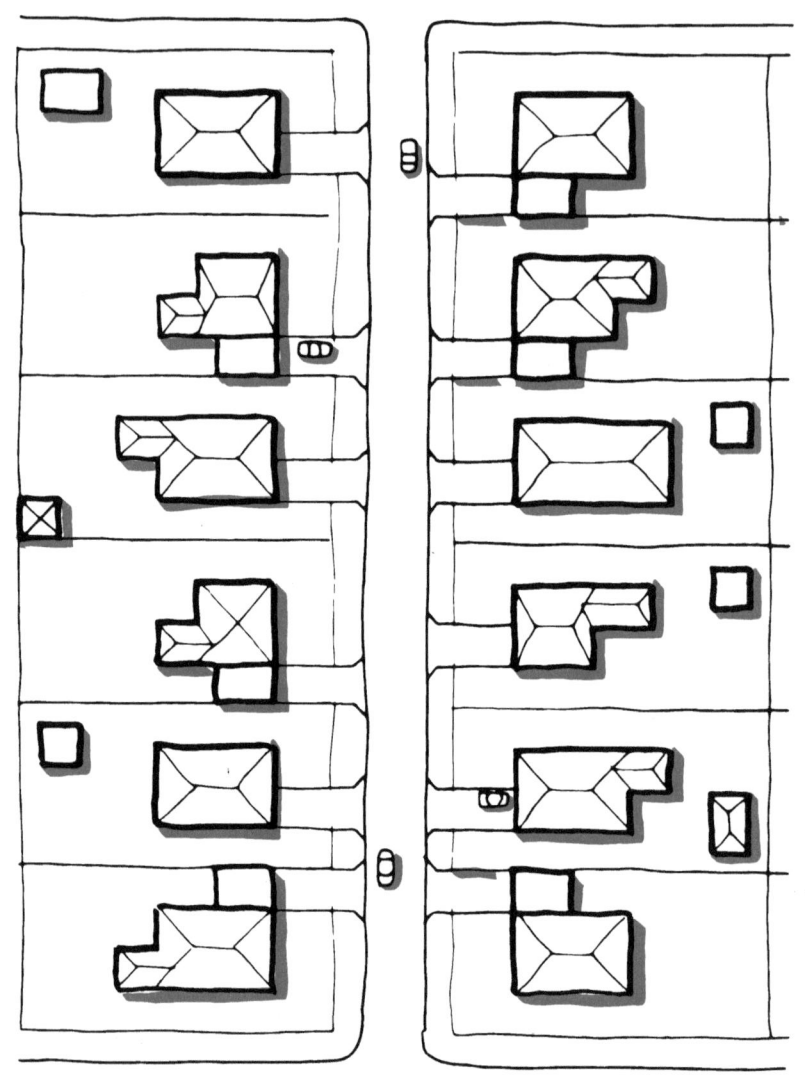

BAU: Urbanism

Figure 6: Bunnings-Lite Urbanism
Site: Existing suburbs
Scale: Street block
Method: Recombinant innovation (Facebook 'buy nothing' group + toolshed
Relates to: Woollies-Lite Urbanism, Kibbutz Urbanism

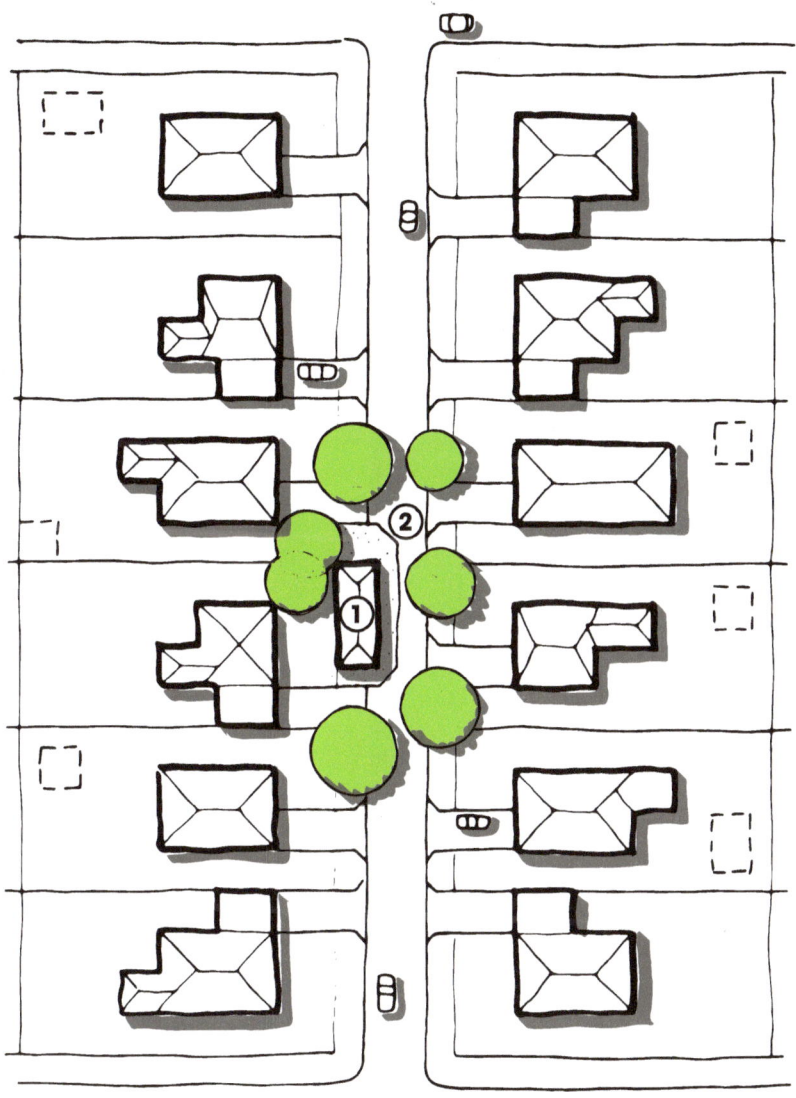

BAUn: Bunnings-Lite Urbanism

Legend:
1. Communal street shed
2. Roadway narrowing

Car-Phobic Urbanism

> *Behind our prioritisation of the 'going' over the 'being' lies an overweening impatience, a focus on efficiency and a near-universal obsession with utility.*[87]
> **Elizabeth Farrelly**

The streets of the late nineteenth and early twentieth centuries were nothing like today's. Most were dirt or cobbles and while they people still used them to get around, they were not the exclusive dominion of the car.[88] Instead, horse-drawn carriages, trams, cyclists and pedestrians all shared and animated the street. As Canadian tech journalist Paris Marx explains, 'People could walk in the street, linger for a conversation, or buy something from a vendor. It was even a space where children could play, especially on the side streets.'[89] As one writer in the 1920s in London wrote, 'The street is the cradle of the new-born babe, and the nursery of the toddler, and the playing field of the elementary school child; and running wild in it is responsible for much of the vitality and the wit and the insatiable curiosity that are found animating every grown-up London crowd.'[90]

Fast-forward a century, and cars consume vast space in the city and its streets.[91] Asphalt, a byproduct of the oil refining process, has coated vast swathes of the planet, 'Asphalt is what cities wear.'[92] Our cities have moulded themselves to the 'needs' of cars, and in doing so, they have morphed into 'planned preserves for countless herds of these four-wheeled creatures, Serengetis for cars and trucks'.[93] Ruthlessly applied road design standards have led to such asphalt expanses; (figure 7) however, the origins of these standards can be arcane. Indeed, back in the 1950s, the width of North American streets in residential areas related to the prospect of nuclear war with the Soviets. Gloomy policymakers believed that wide streets would make cleaning up the radioactive remnants with bulldozers easier in the aftermath of a war.[94]

Back to reality, studies have revealed that most people drive not according to the signposted speed limits but according to how 'safe' they intuitively feel the road is. In other words, we drive as fast as road layouts implicitly tell us to drive. The result is that drivers in the USA kill four times as many pedestrians on expansive, over-engineered suburban streets than on the narrow streets of traditional inner-city neighbourhoods because roomy roads make driving fast feel safe.[95] Globally, the death toll of the automobile is astronomical. Indeed, cars kill an estimated 1.3 million people every year[96] – a city of the dead the size of Adelaide annually.

A city can rightfully discourage driving by reducing parking and narrowing roads to add shared paths that are more pedestrian and bike friendly.[97] However, ultimately, a city can be friendly to people or friendly to cars,[98] and most Australian cities have chosen the latter option. But what if we revoked the 'assumed right' of private vehicles to 'destroy a city'?[99] What if we questioned destroying so much 'being there' to achieve so little in the way of 'going there'?[100]

In response, this proposal asks what neighbourhoods would look like if getting somewhere else in a car wasn't our planning priority (Figure 8). What if we went from pedestrian-friendly to car-phobic layouts? What if we didn't just limply encourage people to get out of their cars but made daily driving difficult? The byproduct could be more intricate, intimate and interesting neighbourhoods easily serviced with micro-mobility vehicles such as e-bikes, e-scooters, e-skateboards and electric neighbourhood vehicles – with shared cars (automated or otherwise) relegated to fringing carparks. Modernist messiah Le Corbusier dismissed the medieval complexity of traditional European cities, decrying, 'The Pack-Donkey's Way is responsible for the plan of every continental city, including Paris, unfortunately.'[101]

Long live the donkey.

Commentary

Keith
The question I want every urban designer to ask is, 'If an alien anthropologist were to fly over this development to write their PhD, what would they decide it says about our society?' In most cities in this country, they would determine that the automobile is the primary resident and that the humans both worship the automobile as a God and are its slaves. Let's start confusing alien PhD students by changing our cities so that humans, especially children, are the primary focus.

Shane
My mobility and health do not support cycling or extended walking. Community members such as myself are forgotten in the dream of a young, fit and mobile population.

Figure 7: Our cities have moulded themselves to the demands of cars.

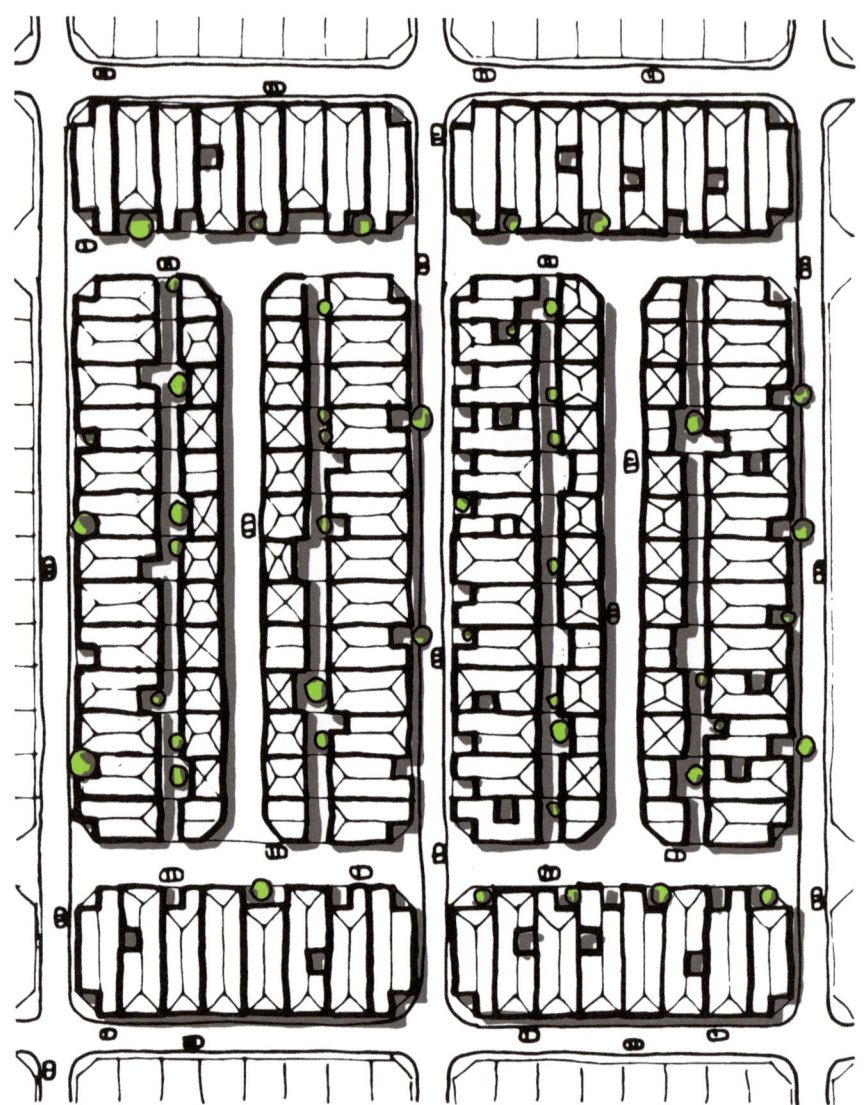

BAU: Urbanism

Figure 8: Car-Phobic Urbanism
Site: New suburbs
Scale: Neighbourhood
Method: Assumption reversed: 'Cars have an inherent right to the city'
Relates to: Symbolic Urbanism

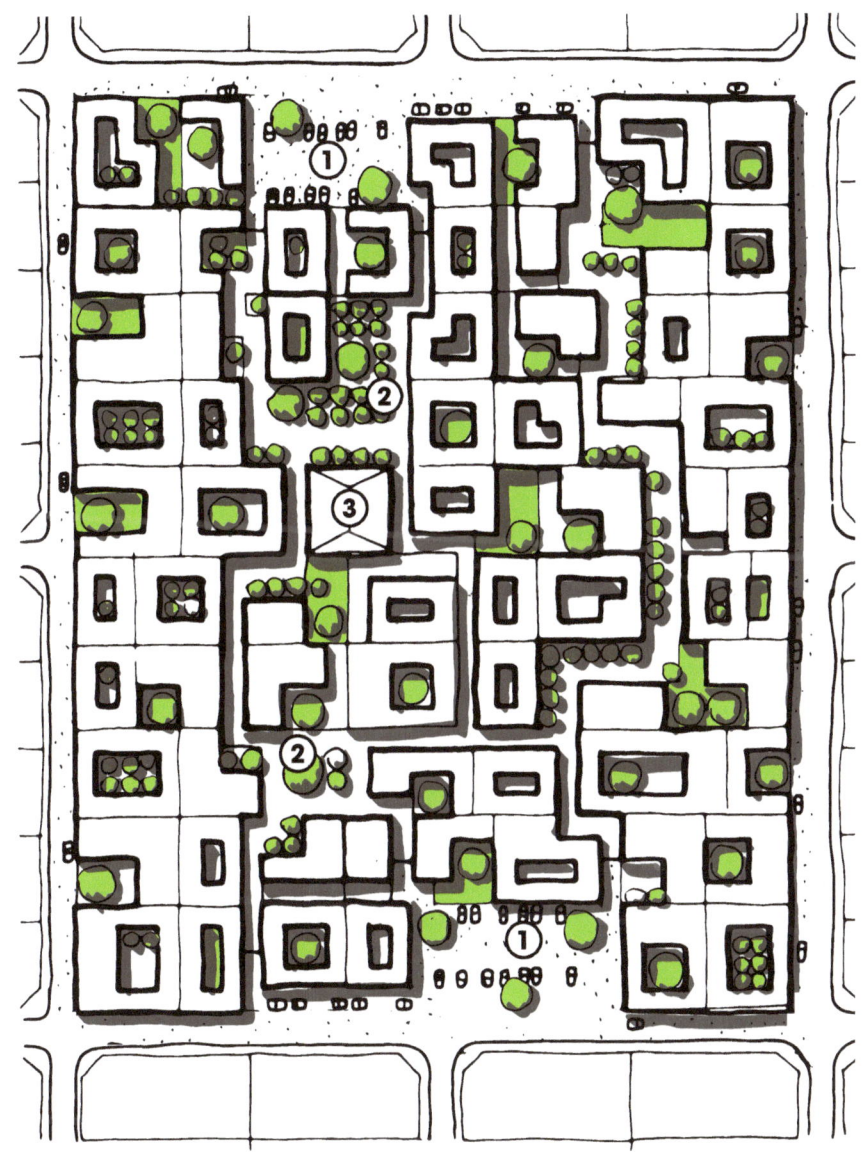

BAUn: Car-Phobic Urbanism

Legend:
1. Communal carparks
2. Pedestrianised laneways
3. Communal facilities

Charter Urbanism

British author Matthew Syed explains that the most innovative societies tend to proactively incubate dissent instead of those constrained by rigid regulatory frameworks that demand conformity.[102] So, what governance models that incubate dissent could facilitate urban innovation?[103] One potential candidate is the charter city governance model, which derives from Hong Kong. Historical accidents made the British-administered Hong Kong a freshly minted system for political and institutional rules in China, and many Chinese people were keen to opt in to the opportunities offered. Inspired by this example, the Chinese government kicked off the construction of Shenzhen, implementing market rules based on those that prevailed in booming and bustling Hong Kong.[104] Spinning off such examples, US economist Paul Romer has proposed charter cities in the Global South as politically autonomous regions that are free from the crippling constraints of corrupt and sclerotic national legal frameworks.[105] Smaller-scale siblings of charter cities are Free Trade Zones, Export Processing Zones or Special Economic Zones, which have evolved into models for new cities.[106] These zones have become 'spaces of exception' where regular rules are relinquished and where governments bestow preferential treatment on them to be competitive internationally.[107]

But what alternative charter zone approaches could we experiment with that are less concerned with economic competitivity? One example is Christiania. In 1971, eager liberty-seekers flocked to Christiania, the self-declared 'free city' in Copenhagen. Its stated anti-authoritarian mission was 'to be a self-governing society, self-sustaining and aspiring to avert psychological and physical destitution'.[108] Another is Frestonia, a heterogeneous group that occupied decrepit dwellings owned by the Greater London Council on Freston Road in London. The mix of artists and activists creatively responded to the announcement of the demolition of their dwellings. Collectively, the group declared independence from the UK and adopted the surname Bramley in response to a policy in which the Greater London Council had to rehouse family members together.[109] Closer to home, the Principality of Hutt River was an informal micronation in Western Australia's mid-west region, proclaimed in 1970 when farmer Leonard Casley declared his farm a sovereign state in response to apparently draconian wheat production quotas implemented by the then government.[110]

These experiments were sometimes short-lived, but this proposal poses the question, could we orchestrate selected zones of our cities to operate under their own charter (free from the strangling effects of existing governance) to experiment with loosening or tweaking regulatory frameworks and alternative urban layouts and housing types (Figure 9)? Cutting-edge companies often harness diversity by using 'shadow boards', which consist of younger people who counsel executives on critical decisions, 'thus lifting the conceptual blinkers that can attach to age'.[111] These proposed charter zones could undertake the same function as shadow boards in opening up opportunities that existing governance systems may be blind to by giving a voice to young people (for instance) who haven't absorbed the same particular cultural and intellectual paradigm as middle-aged urban planners.[112]

Commentary

Robert
This is great. But it's worth acknowledging that all Charter Cities are based on labour, tax, environmental or privacy exemptions (and encourage growth through allowing exploitation).

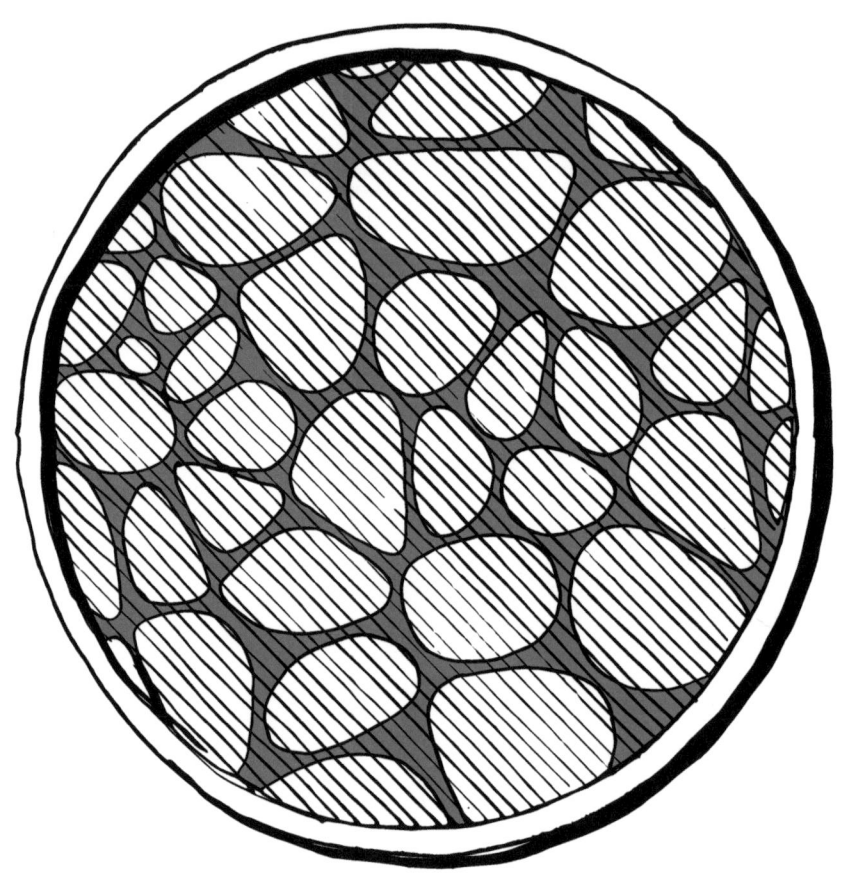

BAU: Urbanism

Figure 9: Charter Urbanism
Site: Existing suburbs/new suburbs
Scale: Neighbourhood
Method: Assumption reversal (Assumption reversed: 'Cities should have consistent, top-down, regulatory frameworks')
Relates to: Deregulation Urbanism

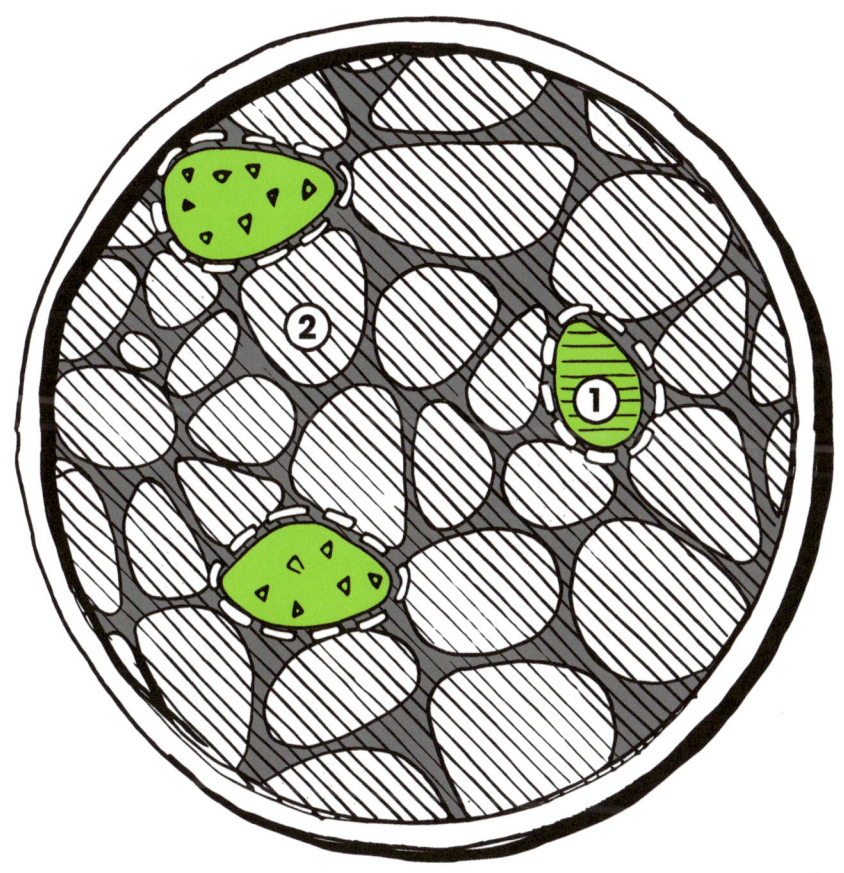

BAUn: Charter Urbanism

Legend:
1. Charter zones
2. Existing regulatory context

Deregulation Urbanism

 The desire of the state is always to order the city, linked to a demand for images of law and order. Order on the streets works to legitimate the state, it signifies a strong state, while disorder on the streets tends to signify political disorder, signifying weakness.[113]
Kim Dovey

Policymakers use regulatory zoning as the weapon of choice for achieving urban order. This process involves carving up cities into zones (typically using designations such as 'industrial', 'commercial' or 'residential') and setting detailed stipulations on how that zoned land can be utilised. This practice of segregating uses by zones is the legacy of the Industrial Revolution's 'dark satanic mills', which were genuine hazards to public welfare.[114]

Historically, many suburban zoning regulations in Australian had social, hygienic and aesthetic objectives. Minimum dwelling sizes restricted those with minimum incomes; minimum garden sizes encouraged young families with kids.[115] Bans on pubs were not instigated because their residents didn't like beer but because they were perceived to attract hooligans to the neighbourhood.[116] As social historian Graeme Davison explains, this logic of avoidance structured the Australian suburb; the determination to flee the city's 'vice, ugliness and violence', and a countervailing logic of attraction, the desire to 'embrace the virtue, health, beauty and peace of the countryside'.[117]

While most would recognise zoning's key role in creating a functional city, critiques that planners want to separate everything as a 'toddler separates peas from potatoes on the plate' plague zoning.[118] Indeed, by separating central business districts and residential suburbs, planners separated commerce from domesticity and inadvertently (or otherwise) gender from gender. Moreover, the residential suburb that emerged from restrictive zoning practices was, for many people, too spacious, clean, safe, conventionally virtuous and sanctimonious.[119] As Australian poet Louis Esson declared in 1910:

> The suburban home must be destroyed. It stands for all that is dull, and cowardly and depressing in modern life. It endeavours to eliminate the element of danger in human affairs. But without danger, there can be no joy, no ecstasy, and no spiritual adventures. The suburban home is a blasphemy. It denies life. Young men, it would save from wine and young women from love. But love and wine are eternal verities. They are moral. The suburban home is deplorably immoral.[120]

In this vein, critics view planners as stiflers unsettled by the 'unknown and the uncontrolled',[121] whose stiff and unyielding environments suppress people's freedom to act and suffocate informal social relations.[122] While too little order generates mayhem and fear, too much is stifling.[123] Consider contemporary Western Australia, which has eight different levels of planning control, and where it has taken as long as twenty-three years for local plans to be updated to reflect changes to city or state-wide plans.[124]

Of course, the comprehensive planning of urban settlements is comparatively recent. In traditional, 'unplanned' settlements without such top-down planning, residents' daily needs, religious beliefs, way of life and available local building materials all drove growth patterns.[125] Urban fabric accreted from the accumulation of informal, private actions. Rulers limited public actions to major urban elements such as city walls, arteries and civic buildings.[126]

With this history in mind, this proposal poses the question: what is the potential for loosening the stranglehold of zoning regulation in street scale 'demonstration projects' in our suburbs? In terms of built form, this could mean permitting multi-family dwellings where planning currently prohibits them and rolling back rigid building codes, minimum lot sizes, maximum density, minimum setbacks and other hurdles to development, all of which could improve housing affordability.[127]

Such changes could also open opportunities for small family businesses or restaurants to run from suburban houses or container modules. For willing families, such buildings should have the capacity to be workplaces – for making clothing, running a repair shop or engaging in other forms of non-harmful, light industry (Figure 10).[128] Moreover, artists need places that are adaptable, cheap and capable of evolving quickly with their needs, all of which could be enabled in a deregulated suburb (Figure 11).[129] In the public domain, undesigned, unregulated 'loose-fit' spaces[130] free of top-down programming could afford a variety of functions and enable informal, spontaneous and unplanned uses of the public realm.[131] Supporting these uses could be points of access to water and power for running activities, such as a for a community kitchen.[132] Could releasing planning's grip on our suburbs unleash their chaotic, creative potential?

Commentary

Peter
The stranglehold of zoning regulation in our suburbs is stifling. We'll look back in 50 years and wonder why planners were so hell-bent on micromanaging whilst everything in the world was changing so rapidly.

Rob
This works if citizens are sympathetic to their neighbours/surroundings. It would lead to a much more diverse, interesting and heterogenous urbanity. However, people are dicks. They would use this freedom to exploit the commons for their own personal gain.

Figure 10: Marooned houses in an industrial area offer a glimpse of a deregulated suburb where houses could have the capacity to be workplaces.

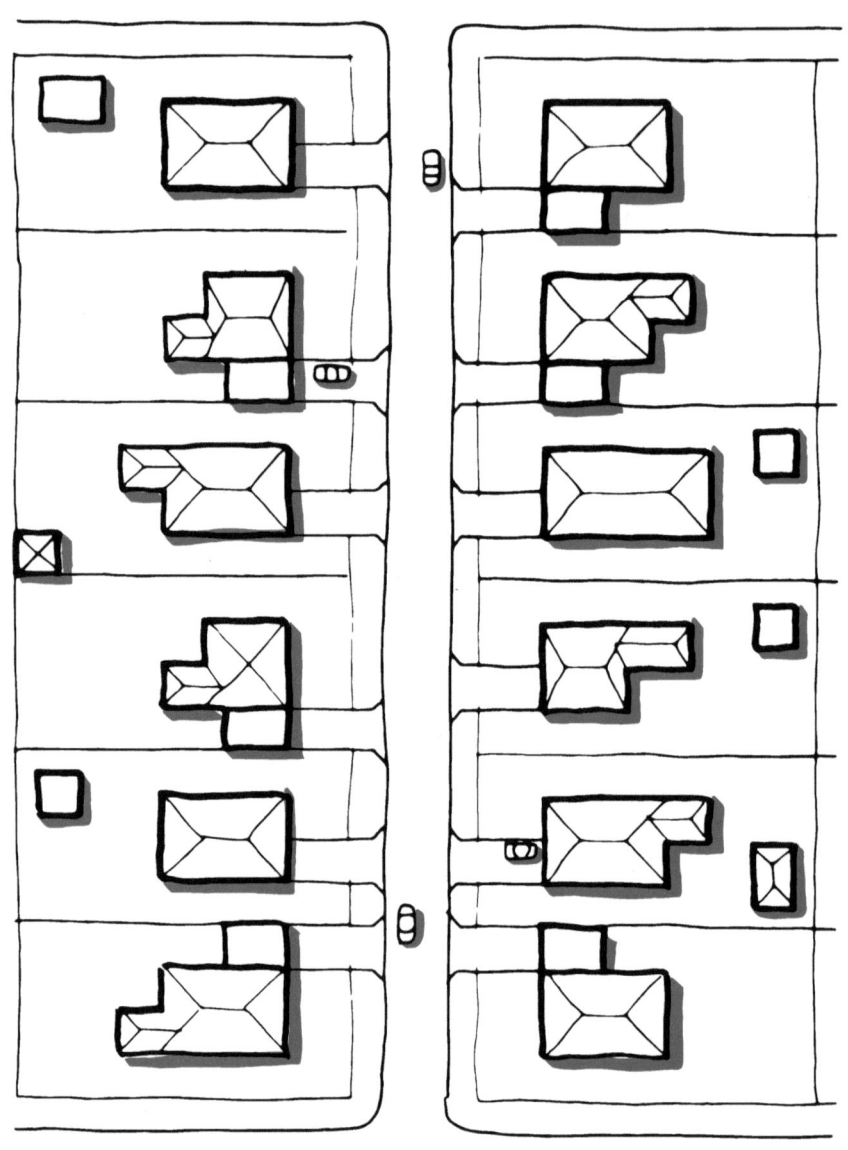

BAU: Urbanism

Figure 11: Deregulation Urbanism
Site: Existing suburbs
Scale: Street block
Method: Assumption reversal (Assumption reversed: 'Suburbs should be heavily regulated to avoid conflict')
Relates to: Charter Urbanism

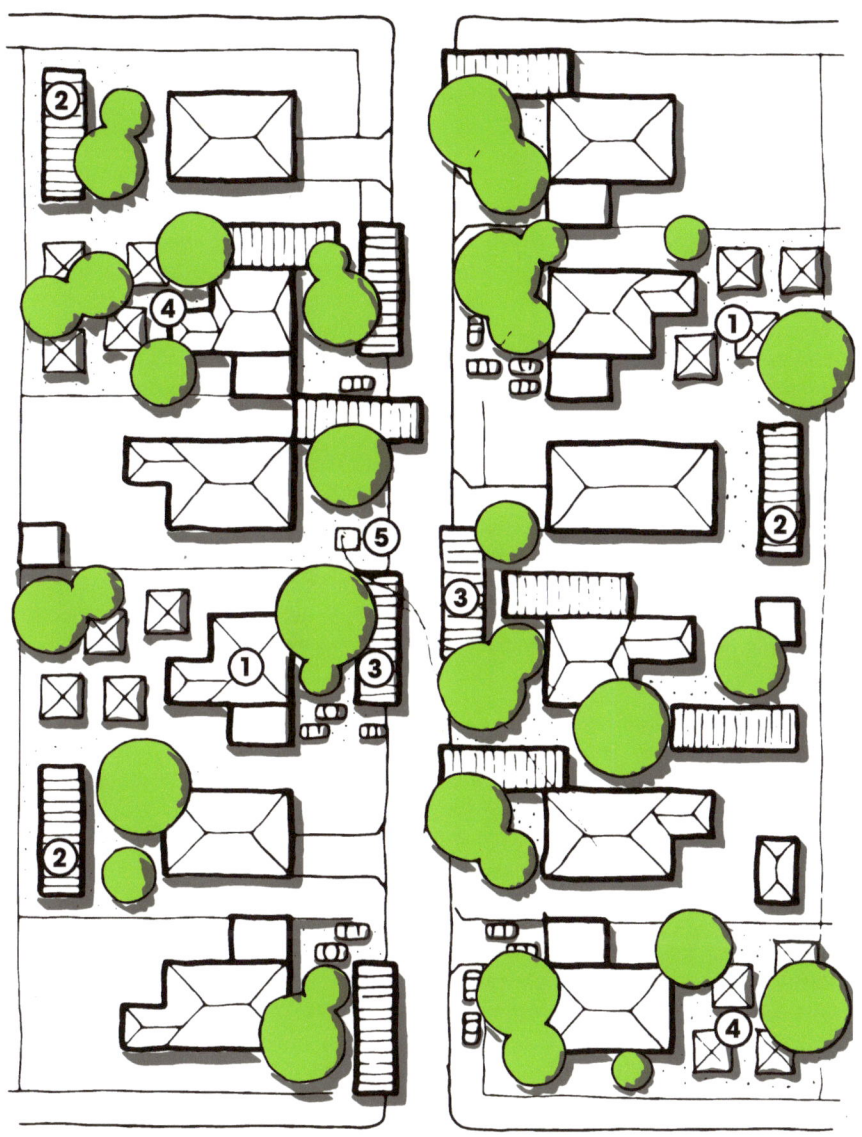

BAUn: Deregulation Urbanism

Legend:
1. Restaurant
2. Light industry
3. Artist studio
4. Pub
5. Fire pit

Donga Urbanism

> *The power of temporary and tactical urbanism is that it shifts the ontology of the city from being towards becoming; it opens a space of possibility.*[133]
> **Kim Dovey**

Our pressing societal and environmental challenges demand swift and decisive responses. Yet, as urban design academic Kim Dovey notes, 'our cities are hard to reshape. The built environment is a heavy, fixed thing that is slow and expensive to change.'[134] Indeed, once developers and builders have constructed an urban area, urban design thinking is locked in; the values of one moment in history are frozen in time.[135] Pragmatically, the construction of heavy-masonry buildings also results in massive emissions. Indeed, the global production of concrete is responsible for around 8 per cent of annual carbon dioxide emissions globally (about twice that of air travel).[136]

Lightweight modular construction, however, offers the potential to alleviate such emissions and slash the cost of housing. The advantage of using modular construction to create affordable prefab housing is that builders can construct units off-site and quickly stack them into place, making building affordable housing faster and cheaper.[137] A further benefit of modular, lightweight urbanism is its potential for innovation and flexibility in relation to future conditions. As Kim Dovey explains:

> *It turns the city into a testing ground where new forms of thinking can be implemented without the danger of permanent failure. Urban design is not a science, and the city does not have the controlled conditions of a laboratory. Yet, our cities are littered with the permanent remains of failed urban design experiments based on flawed thinking. Lightweight urbanism could enable us to increase the scope of experimentation and speed up the learning process.*[138]

Moreover, such a lightweight building method could achieve a characteristic of flexible cities: incomplete form. Incompleteness may seem like the foe of 'real' cities, but it offers a built-in capacity for personalization and adaptation.[139] Rather than completed dwellings, houses could comprise lightweight modules that residents eventually fit out, expand and add to (for instance, when an unplanned child arrives). This could reduce upfront costs, lead to diversity and engender a true sense of ownership among the residents.[140] Such a process shifts from the futile fiction of building forever and, instead, building in a way that recognises that people have continually changing desires and life circumstances.[141]

Urban planners consider fly in, fly out (FIFO) camps with lightweight modular dongas for accommodation beneath contempt as examples of 'urbanism'(Figure 12). However, this proposal poses the question: What if we delivered urban infill with donga dwellings to allow experimentation with alternate layouts and lifestyles adapted to the uncertainties of our times? Rather than units being constructed in China and shipped worldwide, such modular housing could be built by local companies or cooperatives (Figure 13).[142] Could the humble donga be the saviour of our cities?

Figure 12. FIFO camps and their dongas are regarded as beneath contempt as examples of 'urbanism.' Image by Eden Nguyen (Shutterstock asset ID: 386315631)

Commentary

Tuan
Yeah, I don't see this ever happening here in Australia or Europe, where planning control is too rigid, maybe in Southeast Asia and other parts of the world where urbanism still grows more organically.

Estelle
Yes! It also means orienting buildings to environmental conditions and maximising solar gain rather than following a strict human-made-up land division!

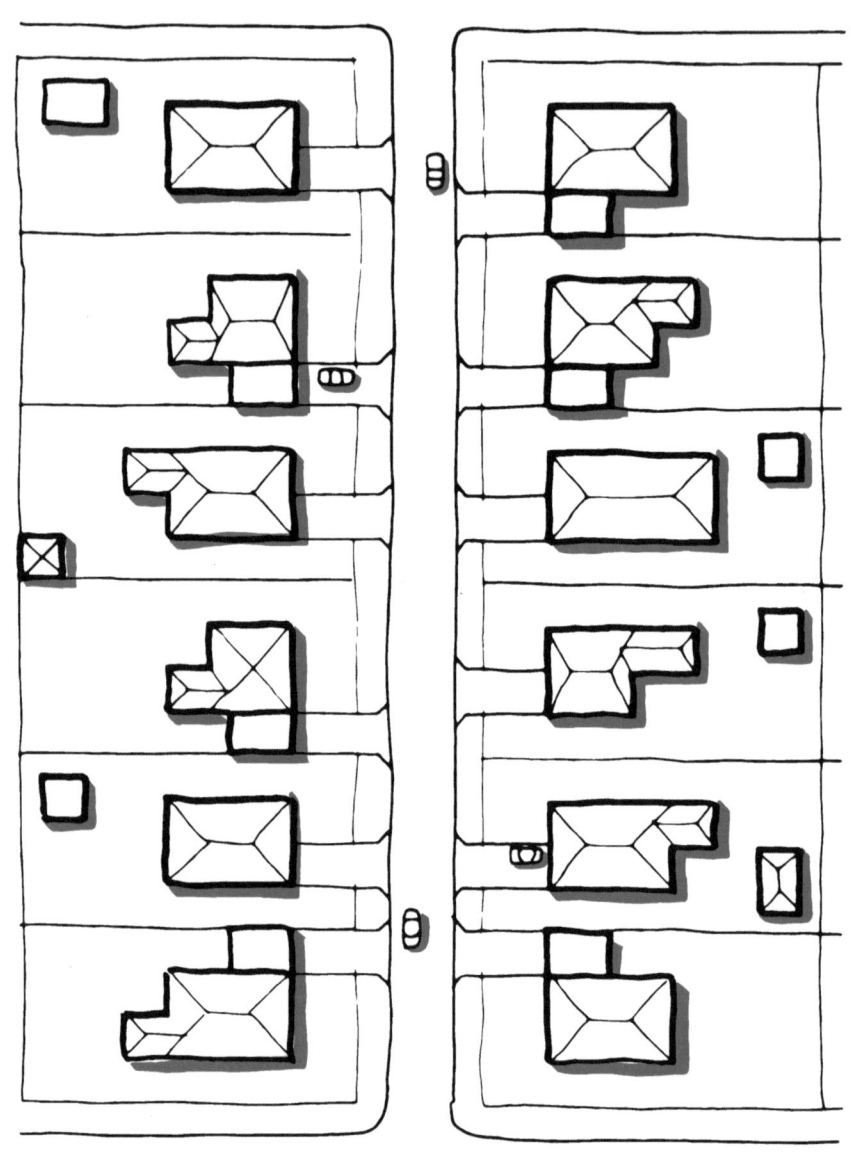

BAU: Urbanism

Figure 13: Donga Urbanism
Site: Existing suburbs
Scale: Street block
Method: Recombinant Innovation (fly in, fly out camp + suburb)
Relates to: Deregulation Urbanism

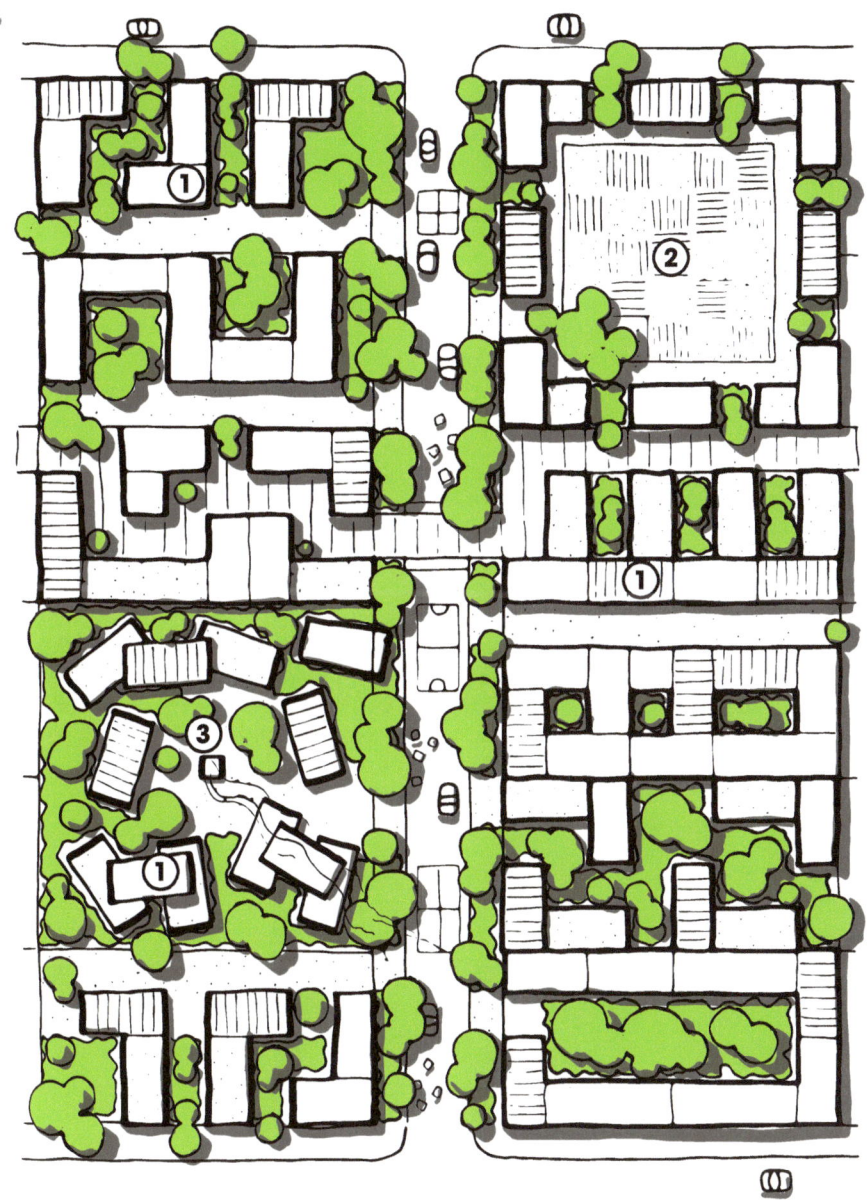

BAUn: Donga Urbanism

Legend:
1. Donga dwellings
2. Urban farm
3. Communal gathering area

Dumb Urbanism

 Cutting ourselves off from the internet, switching off our phones, using cash instead of plastic may help for a while, but they are no solution. Unless we band together... we shall never reclaim our own minds from its grip.[143]
Yanis Varoufakis

Proponents assert that smart city tech helps policymakers devise solutions for urban improvement and provides residents with the 'resources they need to find happiness, fulfilment, and prosperity'.[144] Indeed, planting sensors throughout a city and its buildings, and wiring them to a dashboard can take the city's 'pulse'. This digital infrastructure allows operators to monitor and manage everything from energy and water use, waste, temperature, traffic patterns and security.[145] Techno-utopian thinking underpins such innovations and tends to characterise urban areas not connected to the Internet of Things and feeding central dashboards as not smart or, more to the point, just plain dumb.[146]

However, the maxim that 'technology will solve our problems' ignores that technology, while potentially helping us manage current challenges, undoubtedly spawns a host of new issues.[147] Take smart phones and tablets for example. Research has found that, outside of school and work, Australians are on screens at home a staggering 40 hours per week – more than most full-time jobs.[148] This situation will only worsen as the number of devices connected to the internet grows by 140 per cent, reaching 50 billion worldwide by 2030.[149] Digital technologies are beginning to blindly overrun the experiential world,[150] and urban lives are now experienced as much through digital interfaces and representations as embodied experience.[151]

Of course, such concerns are not novel. In the 1960s, American historian Lewis Mumford said of suburban TV addiction, 'the end product is an encapsulated life, spent more and more within the cabin of darkness before a television', which he gloomily predicted, 'would completely demoralize mankind and lead to nuclear holocaust'.[152] While this might have been slightly overstated, the problems of screen addiction are evident. Rachel Clements, a clinical psychologist, explains, 'It definitely has an impact on mental health, in terms of low mood, ability to get through difficult situations, having someone to talk to, to debrief with.'[153] These problems were compounded by COVID-19 lockdowns, which deepened our reliance on online communications to connect with social networks.[154] However, research identifies that people who use social media daily are 11 per cent more likely to feel lonely (with loneliness, in turn, increasing the risk of premature death by up to 30 per cent).[155]

Given these issues, what could be the benefits of periodically decoupling technology from residential neighbourhoods in our cities? Could select residential neighbourhoods be 'turned off' one day a month to allow people to reconnect with their families, friends (real ones), neighbours and the natural world – much like successful weekly car-free days in Jakarta or Bogota (Figure 14)? Appropriately authorised municipalities could carve out these ephemeral islands of digital silence via a series of powerful mobile phone jammers that can disable all 4G, 5G and wi-fi frequencies within a specified radius, such as used in many jails (yes, I realise this comparison is not likely to be a compelling selling point). For the welfare of the broader populace, governments in tandem with residents should implement a revolution against the damaging side effects of techno-utopianism. Down with 'smart cities', up with Dumb Urbanism. Well, for at least one day a month.

Commentary

K M
To me, it's a bit harsh to restrict users from using what they have the right to use. But maybe it's time to engage people digitally with outdoor activities to encourage them to go outside and explore. Design innovation is required, and we need to explore the integration of outdoor/physical activities with digital activities. For example- using physical movement-based VR games, interacting with augmented reality, etc.

Damien
This one is sure to upset. Nice one JB.

Chris
Love it! But I will run it past my teenager on the weekend and see what she thinks :)

Aaron
Julian for Mayor.

Rob
Connectivity and the devices are not the problem, the media itself is...

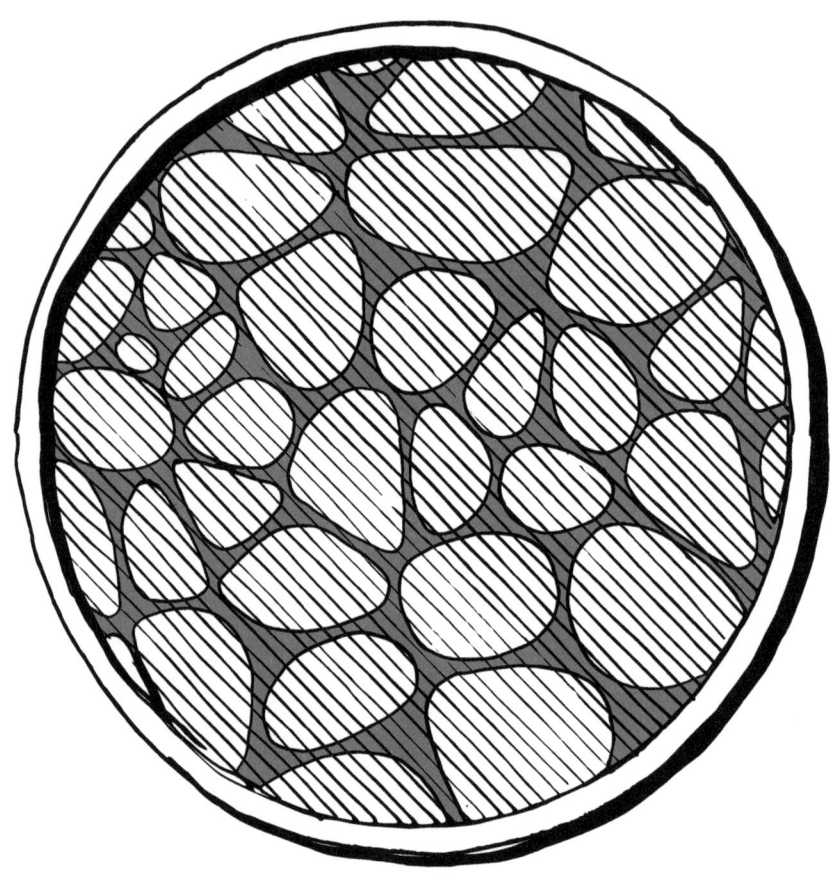

BAU: Urbanism

Figure 14: *Dumb Urbanism*
Site: *Existing suburbs/new suburbs*
Scale: *Neighbourhood*
Method: *Assumption reversal (Assumption reversed: Constantly digitally connected cities are 'smart' cities)*
Relates to: *Charter Urbanism*

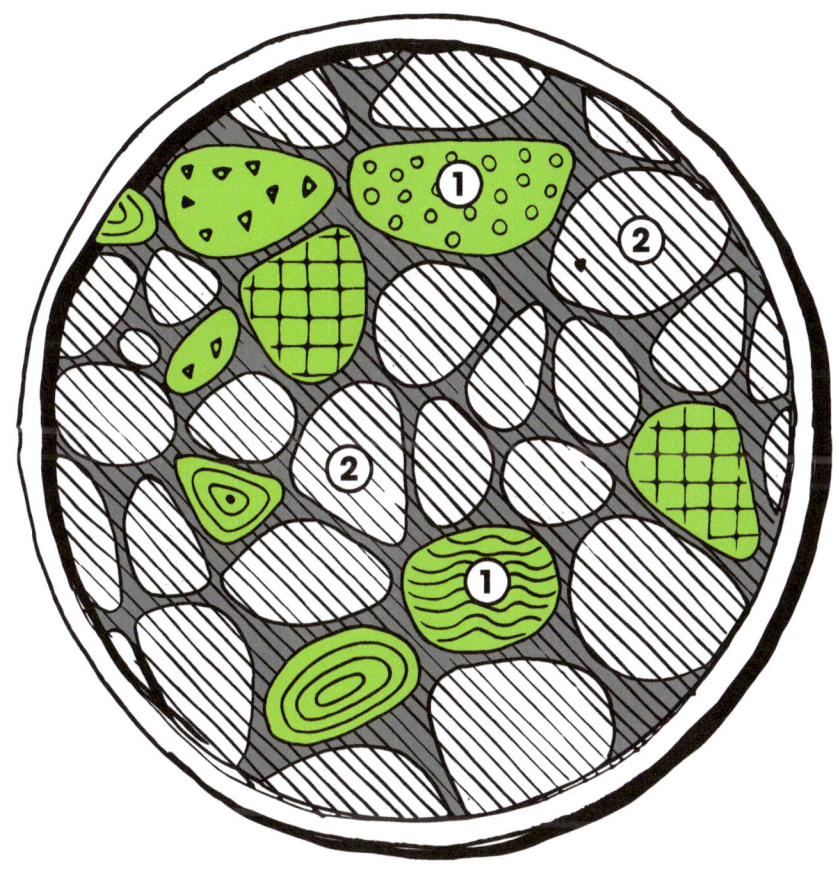

BAUn: Dumb Urbanism

Legend:
1. Turned-off neighbourhoods
2. Turned-on neighbourhoods

Edible Urbanism

 It is true that city people – consumers in general – want all the advantages of efficient agriculture but do not always acknowledge what efficiency requires.[156]
Don Watson

In Australia, farming has degraded 70 per cent of arable land, and soils are eroding faster than they can be replaced. Moreover, suburban development on the fringe of Australia's cities steadily nibbles into once fertile 'salad bowls' (Figure 15).[157] Worries about urban food security are increasing accordingly. Indeed, modelling of Melbourne has shown that continued urban sprawl will curtail the city's agricultural areas from providing 40 per cent of total needs to around 18 per cent by the middle of the 21st century.[158] In response, many metropolitan plans propose to 'draw a line' on this ravenous expansion. Such policies include Melbourne's and Hobart's urban growth boundaries, greater Sydney's metropolitan rural area and Adelaide's environment and food production areas.[159] While well-intentioned, these policies are generally too little too late and can struggle in the face of mounting pressures to roll out housing.

One result is the ostracism of our cities from the agricultural systems that 'nourish' them. As Australian author Don Watson explains, most food shoppers 'interest stops at the supermarket, as if the food were made out the back'. People know little and care less about the origins of their food.[160] Indeed, we are 'sustained' by heavily processed food with many origins, loaded with salt, sugar and fat, putting us on the fast track to the emergency department.[161] Another reason for the relative secrecy about where our food comes from is that we rely on a vast monocultural agricultural system that generally drives out the biodiversity that underpins our 'culture and connection to the world',[162] hardly a compelling selling point in the supermarket aisle.

Of course, the desire to reconnect urbanites with the process of food production through urban farming is hardly novel. As New Urbanist leader Andres Duany wonderfully evoked, urban 'agriculture is the new golf'.[163] However, when we attempt communal urban farming, it tends to be in leftover fragments of space that are inconvenient to access and not central to our daily lives. With a nod to the US city Savannah's famous grid of public squares set out in 1733,[164] why not disperse communal food gardens throughout new suburbs for growing organic fruit and vegetables, replete with polytunnels, orchards and buzzing with biodiversity? Surrounding the squares could be medium-density housing (taking the pressure off peri-urban salad bowls), with local restaurants selling organically grown food whose distance from paddock to plate could measure not in food miles but food metres (Figure 16). The boost to the local economy could be significant[165] while stripping profits from the domineering duopoly of Coles and Woolworths.

Some studies propose that transforming the urban environment to counter the rise in obesity is misguided and that the focus should be on diet instead.[166] But couldn't we do both?

Commentary

Sarah
Indeed. Since when has a complex human behaviour been the purvey of one variable? Layers. Do it all.

Figure 15: Suburban developments on the fringe of Australia's cities are steadily nibbling into once fertile 'salad bowls' (or in this case a 'wine bowl')

BAU: Urbanism

Figure 16: *Edible Urbanism*
Site: *New suburbs*
Scale: *Street block*
Method: *Recombinant innovation (suburb + urban farm)*
Relates to: *Woollies-Lite Urbanism, Hamlet Urbanism*

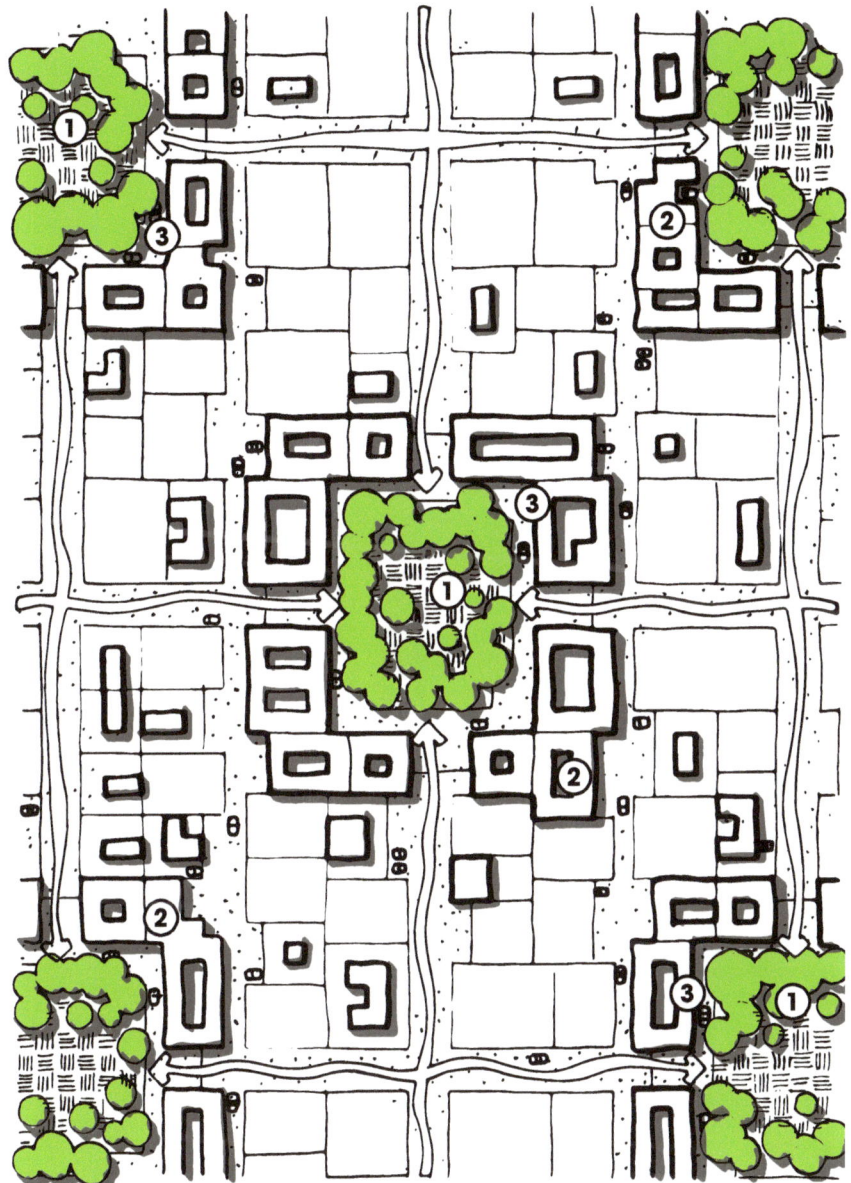

BAUn: Edible Urbanism

Legend:
1. *Urban farms*
2. *Medium-density housing*
3. *Restaurants*

Effluent Urbanism

 The city digests, defecates, and procreates using the same organ, its sewers.[167]
Rob Giblett

In the early days of Australian cities, poorly drained cesspits and open and stagnant sewers leaching into rivers made cities notoriously malodorous, incubating typhoid outbreaks and related deaths.[168] By the 1880s, public health experts had discovered that simple sanitation measures, such as separating sewage from drinking water, could uplift public health. All it needed was 'a bit of plumbing, but public plumbing requires public works, and most importantly, public money'.[169] This hurdle was evident in 1898 when Perth's doctors petitioned parliament on the need for a deep sewerage system to little effect.[170] Indeed, less than one-fifth of households in Perth were sewered by the Great War.[171] By the early 1970s, officials reported that over half a million houses in Australia's capital cities were still unsewered, having only septic tanks.[172]

While utilities have now connected most houses in urban Australia to a wastewater treatment plant, the history of disease emanating from sub-par sewage systems has led to a perception that treated wastewater is best out of sight and mind. This enduring attitude sees cities pump drinkable water from wastewater treatment processes into the ocean in a worrying waste of an increasingly rare resource. Nonetheless, as Australian cities begin to run dry, reuse of treated wastewater from sewage treatment plants may become necessary – if not for drinking water, then at least for agriculture.[173] Indeed, our ancient forebears diverted sewers to agricultural land for more than three thousand years,[174] and wastewater treatment plants in contemporary Israel provide irrigation water for adjacent agriculture.[175] Moreover, treatment processes chemically transform the residual 'waste' products (such as nutrients, sludge and biogas) into valuable products, such as fertilisers.[176]

Nonetheless, policymakers in Australia continue to frame a city's sewers and wastewater treatment infrastructure as the 'underside of the city', which should be cloaked with anonymous green buffers (Figure 17).[177] This tendency is not new; it goes largely unknown that the sewers were as central as the boulevards in Haussmann's nineteenth-century modernisation of Paris.[178] Or that the Australian Dream and its allotment area of a quarter of an acre was not conceived on the merits of amenity. Instead, experts believed it to be a suitable size to cope with the waste flows on-site in a septic system.[179]

In response, this proposal asks if we could visibly express this vital infrastructure in the structure of new urban districts. Could we encircle appropriate sewage treatment plants in well-connected areas with a green armature that can grow food and provide urban cooling and amenity to fringing apartment dwellers, particularly in times of increasing heat stress and drought?[180] (Figure 18)

Figure 17: Anonymous green buffers cloak a sewage treatment plant.

Commentary

Dan
Interesting idea julian bolleter. Perhaps a slightly less controversial starting point would be to consider how we can better capture and utilise storm water run off...

Damien
With up to 50% of Perth water coming from desal (once the 3rd plant is running), we are putting too many eggs in the desal basket and exposing ourselves to security issues

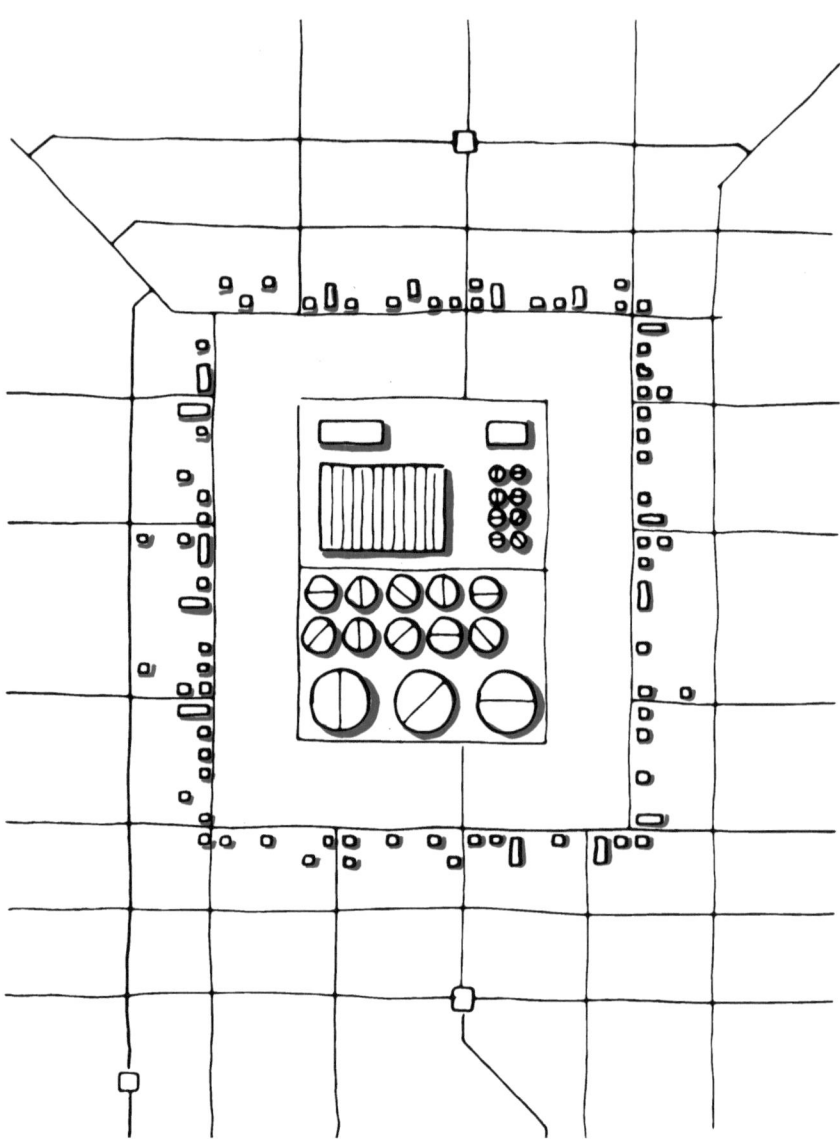

BAU: Urbanism

Figure 18: Effluent Urbanism
Site: New suburbs
Scale: Neighbourhood
Method: Assumption Reversal: 'Sewage treatment plants should be cloaked with anonymous buffers.'
Relates to: Edible Urbanism

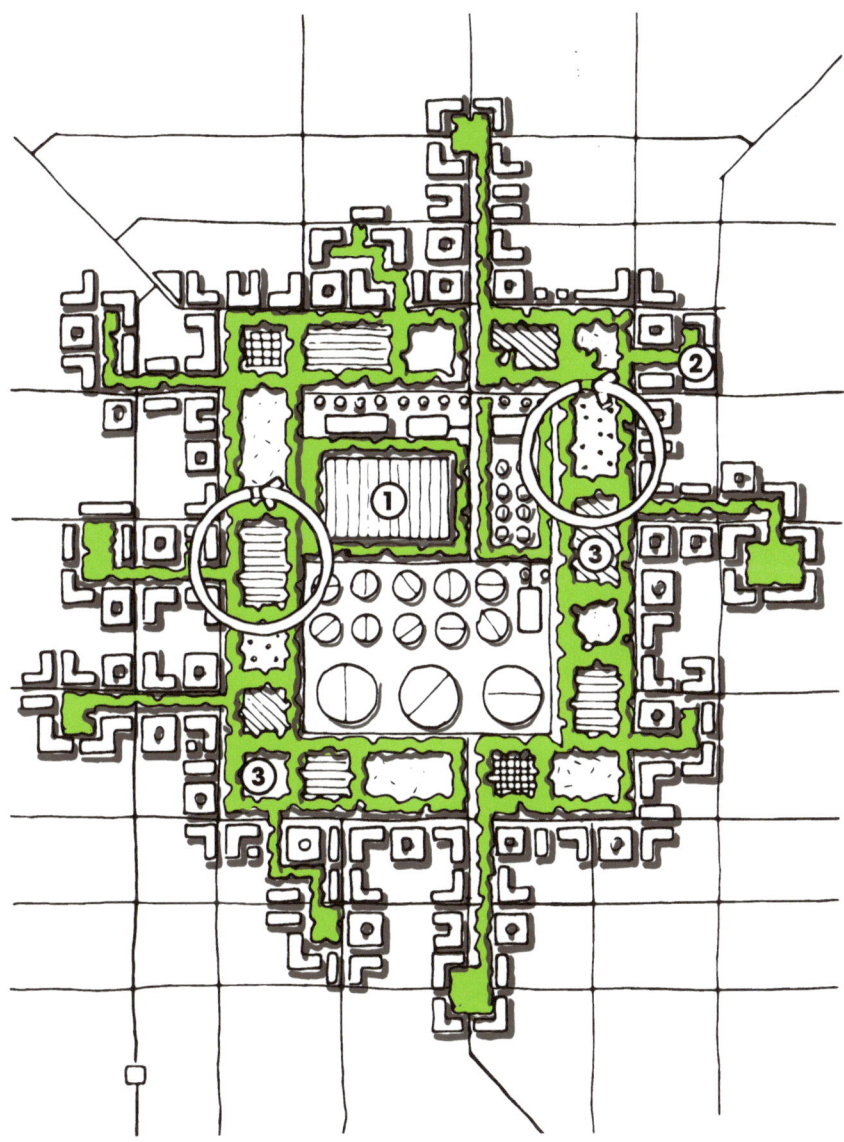

BAUn: Effluent Urbanism

Legend:
1. Sewage treatment plant
2. Medium-density housing
3. Productive open space irrigated with wastewater

Enlightenment Urbanism

> *Our schools are, in a sense, factories in which the raw products (children) are to be shaped and fashioned into products to meet the various demands of life.*[181]
> **Ellwood Cubberley**

There are 7.5 million families in Australia, and 1.1 million are single-parent families, with 80 per cent of these families headed up by single mums[182] (although single dad families are growing rapidly).[183] The prevalence of lone-parent families, due to surging rates of divorce and nonmarital childbearing, has major implications for Australian society. Single parents are almost twice as likely to experience loneliness compared with couples.[184] Moreover, American political scientist Robert Putman attributes the collapse of the traditional family structure (of mum, dad and the kids) to a wider withdrawal from joining and trusting in the broader community.[185] Pragmatic factors can partly explain this. The average frazzled parent spends six hours and forty-three minutes each week driving children to school and other events,[186] leaving precious little time for 'civic engagement', particularly if a lone parent is also running a household and holding down a job. Worryingly, research reveals that children in single-parent households also often score below children in two-parent households on measures of educational achievement.[187] Some commentators have even claimed (perhaps unfairly) that the growth of single-parent families is the dominant cause of school failure and interrelated issues of delinquency, drug use, teenage pregnancies, poverty and welfare dependency.[188]

Concomitantly, as Australian cities densify, cost-of-living pressures are forcing many single-parent families (or otherwise) into apartment living.[189] However, architects have designed these apartments for twenty- to thirty-something professionals or empty nesters, ignoring kids' needs.[190] As a result, a comprehensive literature review of sixty-three studies found that children in high-rise apartment towers exhibited more behavioural issues, stress and poor-socioemotional development.[191]

So, how could we proactively plan for the needs of families with children, particularly lone-parent families? What if we considered our schools 24-7 educational campuses for children *and adults*, surrounded by affordable, family-friendly, medium-rise apartments that have access to the building facilities (e.g., gyms or auditoriums) and open space amenity (e.g., ovals) offered by schools? Time saved doing the school run[192] could appeal to some time-poor families, particularly single-parent families. Local governments could direct increased rates and taxes from apartment development towards upgrading school buildings and turning school grounds (Figure 19) into multifunctional, interactive, biodiverse and productive landscapes (Figure 20).

Schools are a key part of the structure of our societies,[193] and planning for urban density should recognise the need for housing to be co-located with the amenities and educational opportunities they present, a new Age of Enlightenment in our suburbs.

Figure 19: Low-density suburbia surrounds a primary school despite the facilities, amenity and convenience the school potentially offers.

Commentary

Pippa
This applies to all families, not just the stay-at-home or single parent. The daytime school play space becomes the after-school sport and play/recreation space and would increase playtime and decrease driving time (and the need for two cars in many families).

Rob
A boarding school for parents? Interesting idea...

Danicia
Imagine the shared care opportunities, reduced isolation, social and physical benefits for our kids, greener shared spaces and better used and looked after public recreational areas. A concept that builds on the community that schools naturally develop around them.

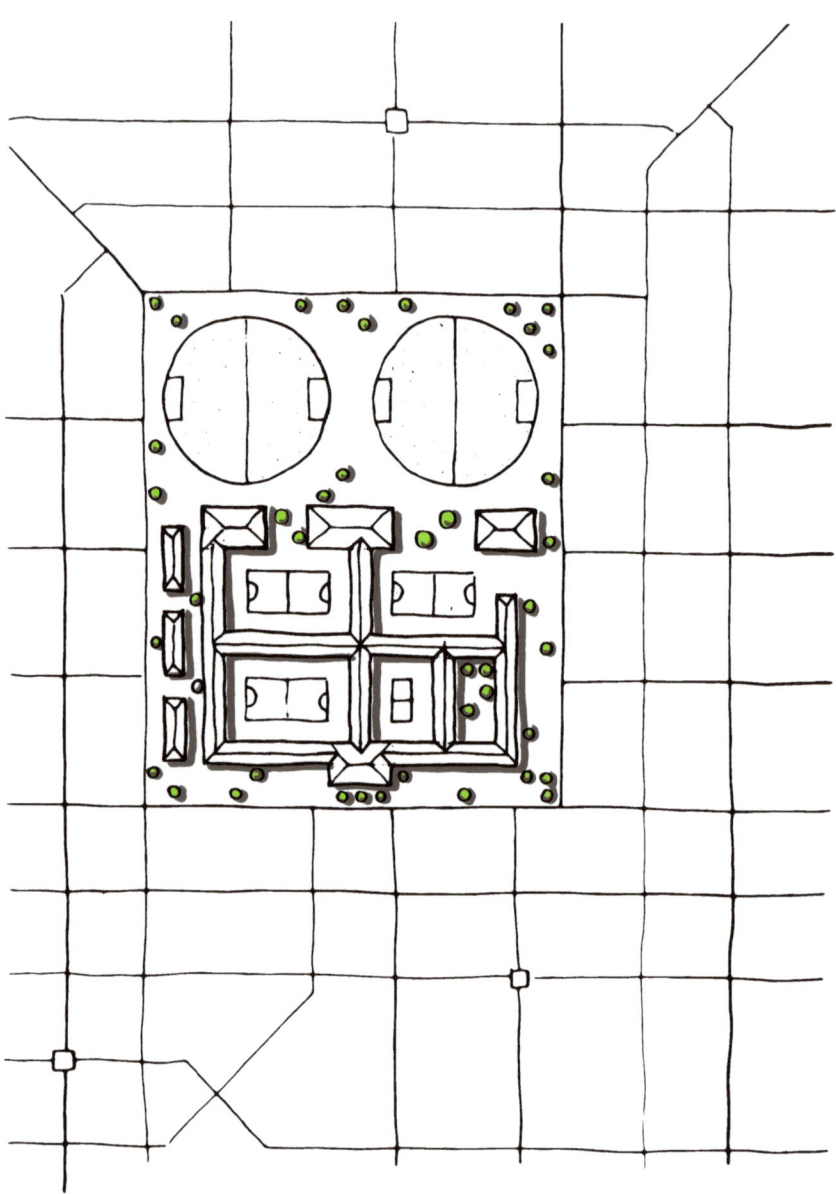

BAU: Urbanism

Figure 20: Enlightenment Urbanism
Site: Existing suburbs
Scale: Neighbourhood
Method: Recombinant innovation (school + urban densification)
Relates to: Fair-Go Urbanism

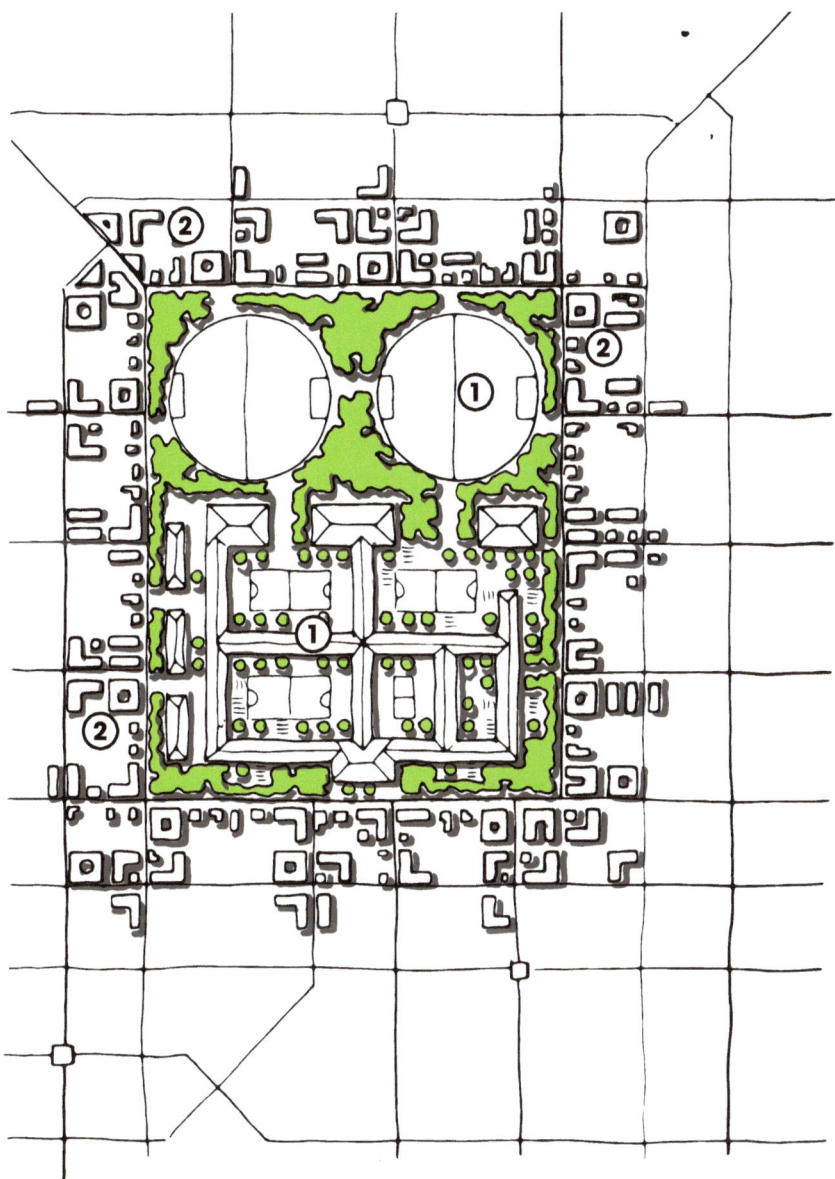

BAUn: Enlightenment Urbanism

Legend:
1. Upgraded, multifunctional school buildings and grounds
2. Family-friendly medium-density housing

Eternal Urbanism

 All created things arise and pass away: joys, sorrows, people, buildings, nations, even whole civilisations. Yet, we expend enormous energy denying our insecurity, fighting pain, death, and loss, and hiding from the basic truths of the natural world and of our own nature.[194]
Jack Kornfield

Historically, the dead have coexisted with the living in urban centres, interred in town squares or churchyards near homes. Such burial grounds were well-visited, multifunctional and often served as spaces for people to socialise or for livestock to graze.[195] In Western cultures, few families were untouched by death, mainly because of the soaring mortality rate of women and children in childbirth. Moreover, health professionals didn't hide the dying in a curtained and sanitised hospital ward; instead, people generally died at home, surrounded by family.[196]

However, by the early 1800s, disease outbreaks and escalating real estate prices began to shunt the dead out of cities, which resulted in graves on far-flung plots distant from population centres.[197] Along with this separation, an intensified consciousness of the desirability of life or at least the allure of prolonging it and evading death arose. As historian Lewis Mumford explains, 'Urban man sought to control natural events his more primitive forerunners once accepted with dumb grace'.[198]

Fast-forward to today, and we expend enormous energy denying our mortality and ducking from the 'fundamental truths of the natural world and our own nature'.[199] We project ourselves into the future through our children, compulsively buy real estate as a form of 'security' and embrace an impregnable and possibly irrational faith in an ultimate rescuer.[200] Zen teacher Jack Kornfield explains that to insulate ourselves from the spectre of ageing and death, 'we promote a myth of youth, which produces a culture of eternal adolescence as our model of reality'.[201] Death, however, is always with us, faintly itching, just under the 'membrane of consciousness'.[202] Concealed and repressed, leaking out in various symptoms, it is the source of many worries.

Although a dread of death can paralyse some people, it can also be an awakening to a richer life.[203] Indeed, as American Psychiatrist Irving Yalom explains, when we finally accept that we are all shuffling towards death (and all other beings with us), a strong sense arises of the 'fragility and preciousness of each moment and each sentient being, and from this can well a deep compassion for all beings'.[204] More pragmatically, we can experience growing freedom from the fears of others, a greater propensity to take risks and fewer worries about rejection.[205]

On the other hand, death can also awaken the sacred in the world.[206] As philosopher and ecologist David Abram explains, for many oral cultures, 'the enveloping and sensuous earth remains the dwelling place of both the living and the dead'.[207] The body is 'not yet a mechanical object in such cultures but is a magical entity, and at death, the body's decomposition into soil, worms, and dust can only signify the gradual reintegration of one's ancestors and elders into the living landscape, from which all to are born'.[208]

In this way, the sacredness of the land can once again be rekindled. Leonie Sandercock notes that an essential ingredient of planning beyond the current pragmatic paradigm is a reinstatement of the sacred as vital dimensions of our cities.[209] A reconceptualisation of death and reintegration into a living landscape is crucial for this reinstatement.

Given its potency, what does contemporary planning have to say about death? A cursory review of all the metropolitan planning documents for Australian cities reveals scant acknowledgement of death and dying, let alone any reflection on how we, as a society, might conceptualise death and integrate it into our cities in an enriching and meaningful manner (Figure 21). Unfortunately, this societal denial of our impending ends can stymie a deeper appreciation of our lives and compound an underlying and unacknowledged terror of death. In response, this proposal asks, what if we integrated multifunctional cemeteries into our daily lives rather than ostracising ourselves from distant cemeteries outside our everyday orbit (Figure 22)? Could our cemeteries also be places for outdoor movies, nature walks, dog exercise and connecting with lost loved ones? Could fringing medium-density housing benefit from proximity to such amenity? Could cemeteries be where the living and dead swirl around each other?

Commentary

Robert
Try cremation instead.

Figure 21: As a society, we lack planning for how we might conceptualise death and integrate it into our cities in an enriching and meaningful manner.

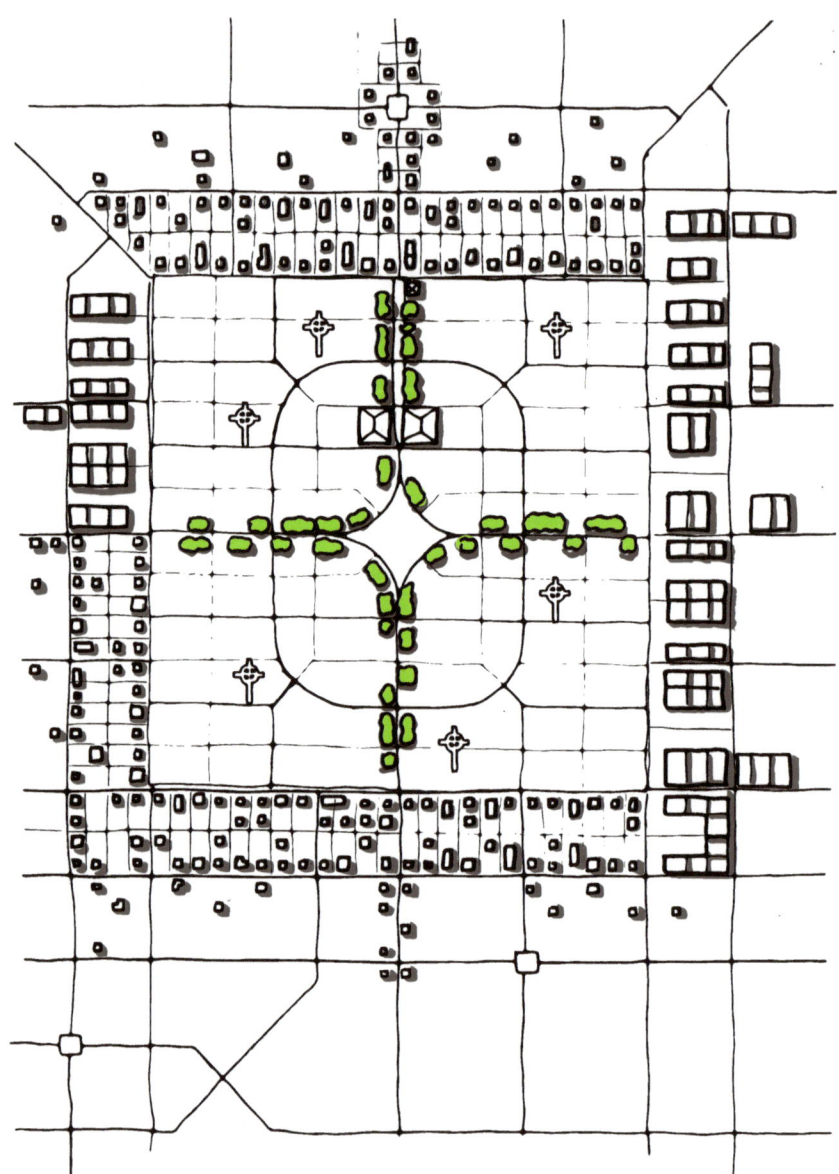

BAU: Urbanism

Figure 22: Eternal Urbanism
Site: Existing suburbs
Scale: Neighbourhood
Method: Recombinant innovation (cemetery + fringing urban densification)
Relates to: Enlightenment Urbanism

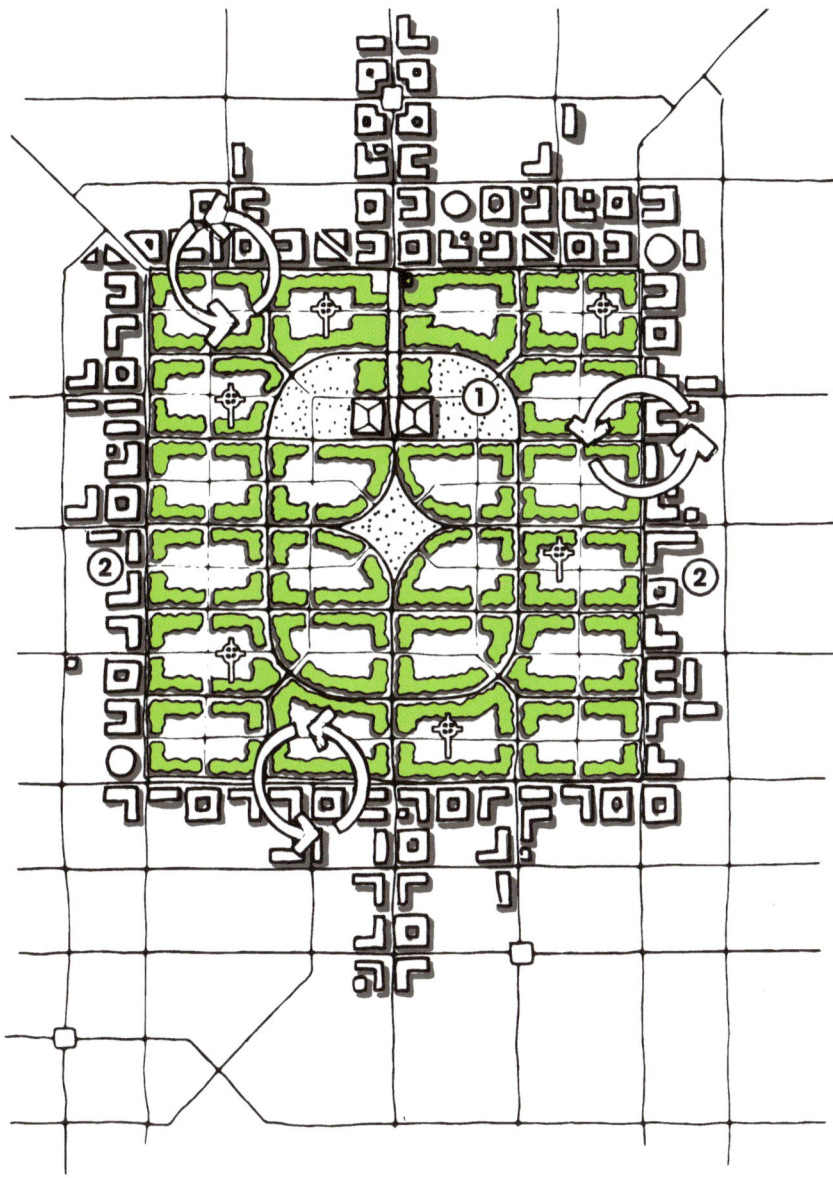

BAUn: Eternal Urbanism

Legend:
1. Upgraded, multifunctional cemetery
2. Medium-density housing

Fair-Go Urbanism

Historically, home ownership in Australia has been within reach of most segments of society. Indeed, working-class families have bought the roof over their heads, seen their assets grow and accumulated an inheritance to hand on to their children. But, over the last generation, rapidly escalating house prices are locking many young (and some not-so-young) Australians out of the market.[210] A massive underlying housing shortfall[211] is partly to blame; currently, over 163,000 people languish on public housing waitlists nationwide. Not surprisingly, the housing affordability problem now dominates the national consciousness (and conversations around the BBQ), cleaving Australia into the 'landed gentry' who own property and the 'peasants' who don't.[212] This schism is responsible for Australia ranking in a low twenty-first position for equality – behind Canada, Korea, Ireland, Poland, France, Luxembourg and fourteen other OECD[213] countries.[214]

There is no one answer to this housing shortage and its divisive effects on our once generally egalitarian society. A possible solution is for state governments to get back into the business of housing provision; currently, generally only developers build houses and apartments and will only build them if they can make a profit.[215] Moreover, reviewing negative gearing and capital gains policies favouring existing homeowners is urgent. However, such a review is currently a long shot, given that two-thirds of the population own property and are unlikely to support policies that work against their interests.[216]

The problem of housing affordability is also spatial. Indeed, if we could get organised to stimulate new apartment buildings for those currently locked out of the housing party, where could we build them? There is a 'public sullenness' towards infill development in existing suburbs, and more outer suburban development will only stretch our sprawled cities further.[217] Sensibly enough, state governments propose that developers deliver dwellings around train stations. However, surrounding neighbourhoods often have heritage building stock, road and rail infrastructure tangles, and fragmented land ownership patterns.[218] Compounding this is an ever-present demand for extensive car parks encircling public transport so commuters can 'park and ride'.[219]

One possible alternative could be the redevelopment of golf courses. Golf courses are land and water hungry, with the average 18-hole course guzzling 124 million litres of water per year, according to the Australian Golf Industry Council.[220] No other urban land use requires so much land and water for so few people (Figure 23). For example, take one unnamed private golf club in Perth: if its playing members were all on the course at one time (an unlikely event), they would have a massive 900 m^2 of land each.[221] Moreover, many private golf clubs are haemorrhaging members as the cost of living and work pressures impact people's free time.

In response, this proposal poses the question, what if governments developed the fairways (not bushland) of centrally located golf courses for affordable housing and publicly accessible open space (Figure 24)? What if others could be rationalised down to nine-hole 'executive' golf courses, with full-size golf courses shunted to the urban fringe? While not to denigrate the delights of golf, surely the self-indulgence of dedicating so much inner-city land to so few people needs reconsideration given the thousands of people languishing on public housing waitlists.

Commentary

John
The last time I checked, Australia had plenty of land that isn't currently used to its full potential. Do we really want to all live on top of each other in concrete jungles?

Stephanus:
Another 'what if' scenario - what if the government built the social housing they have been promising since Noah left the Ark?

Figure 23: An extensive private golf course in a central location. No other urban land use requires so much land and water for so few people.

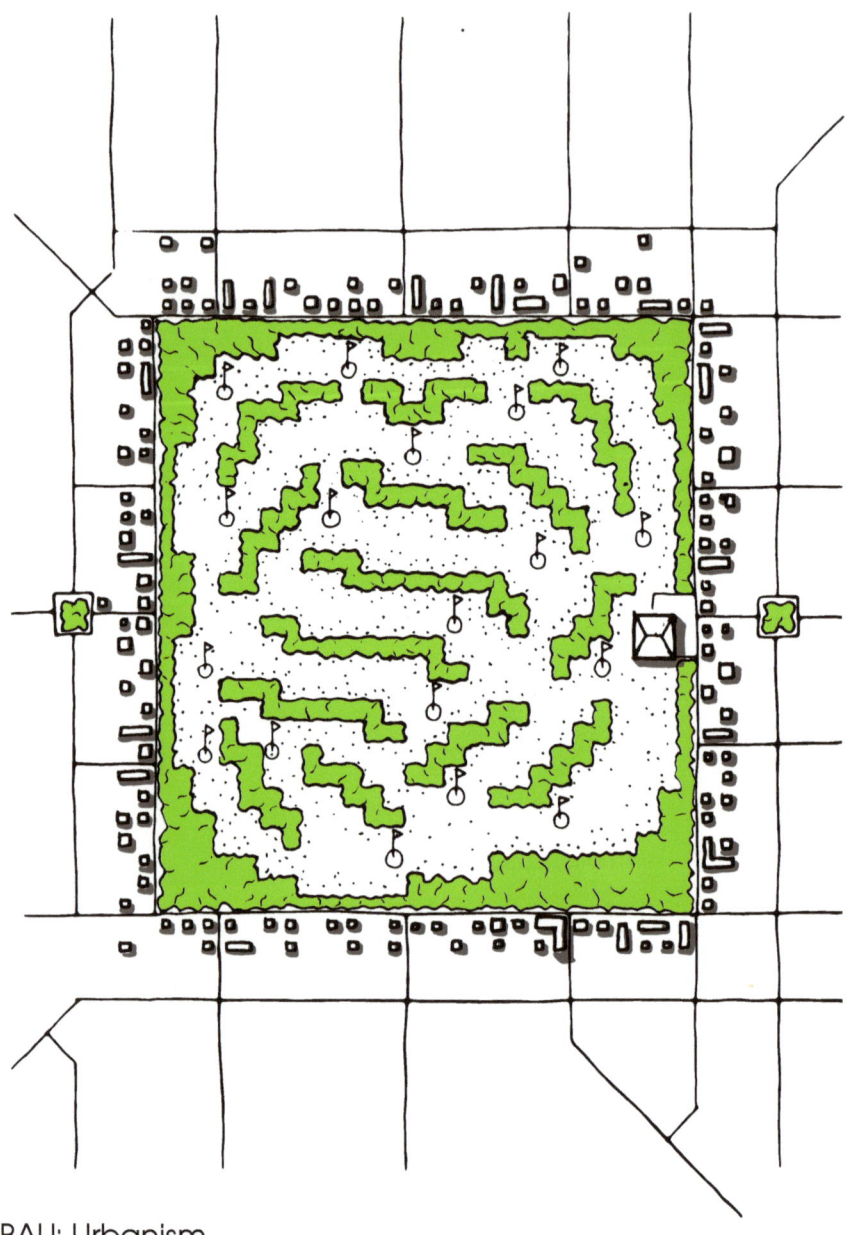

BAU: Urbanism

Figure 24: *Fair-Go Urbanism*
Site: *Existing suburbs*
Scale: *Neighbourhood*
Method: *Recombinant innovation (golf course + urban densification)*
Relates to: *Modern Urbanism 2.0*

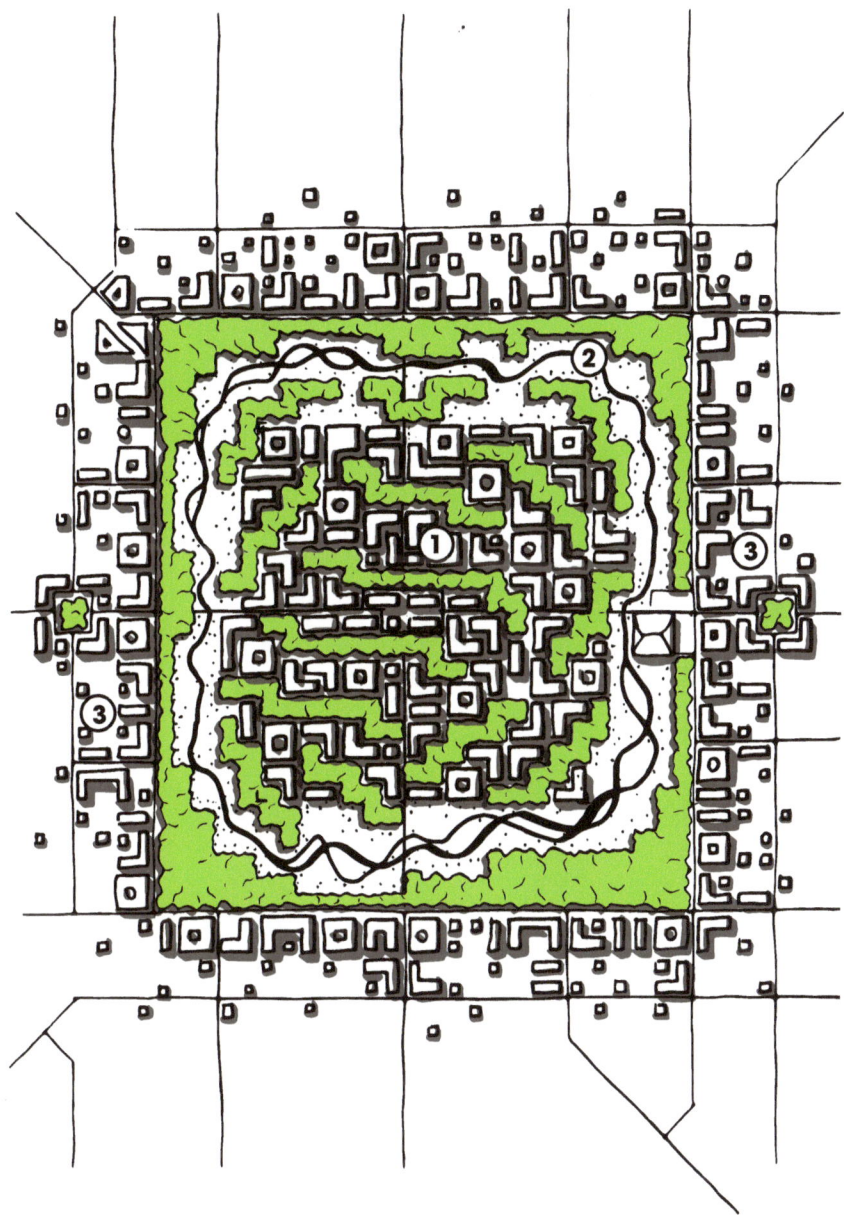

BAUn: Fair-go Urbanism

Legend:
1. Fairways redeveloped for affordable medium-density housing
2. Public open space
3. Fringing medium-density housing

Hamlet Urbanism

> *The overgrown urban complex must be selectively dismantled and dispersed if we are to cure the ills of the megalopolis.*[222]
> **Athelstan Spilhaus**

Since early colonial times, observers expressed disquiet about the unexpected growth of Australia's capital cities, which they saw as an unnatural departure from the English ideal of villages and small proprietorship.[223] As social philosopher Henry George intoned: 'Squalor and misery, and the vices and crimes that spring from them, everywhere increase as the village grows to the city.'[224] Commentators like biologist Paul Ehrlich also assert that 'urbanisation took us on a downward journey in which we began to lose contact with the earth, to pollute and degrade it, and to create bigger and bigger cities where people became more and more alienated'.[225] Building on such concerns, contemporary dystopias are also routinely associated with overcrowded, technologically engineered urban habitats where lives are estranged from experiences of nature.[226] Selective research also confirms that, in the Western world, people in small towns are generally happier than in big cities.[227]

So, if our burgeoning capital cities are too large, with the attendant issues of social and environmental alienation, what is the ideal community size? Dunbar's number provides one guide. British anthropologist Robin Dunbar discovered that about 150 people form a stable and workable community.[228] Why? As we evolved, groups of around 150 people provided enough person power to hunt, raise children, share and even thrive; however, according to the theory, things tend to get weird when communities exceed this population threshold. Managing more than 150 faces, names and social narratives is challenging. As a result, larger societies can be bewildering, complicated and time-consuming, thus requiring labyrinthine systems of rules and enforced norms to sustain a stable, cohesive group.[229] Moreover, violence and exploitation of unknown others increases, and a person cannot depend on others coming to their aid in a time of need.[230]

There is a rich utopian tradition of relatively small cooperative communities living harmoniously with the natural world and embedded in a decentralized society.[231] In England's eighteenth and nineteenth centuries, the landed gentry developed 'model villages' on their country estates. Subsequently, 'utopian socialists', including Robert Owen at New Lanark, Titus Salt at Saltaire, William Lever at Port Sunlight and George Cadbury at Bournville, built model villages to house industrial workers.[232] These social reformers believed these model communities could act as an antidote to the pathologies of the cities of the industrial revolution.

While Ebenezer Howard and his English Garden City movement were influenced by this lineage of communitarian thinking,[233] in its Australian application, the movement predictably charted a more conservative course, mainly due to the rejection of leasehold and co-ownership models in favour of private ownership.[234] Nevertheless, Australia has had its fair share of eccentric, utopian groups experimenting with small cooperative agricultural communities; one example being the Reverend Horace Tucker's communities in Victoria.[235]

So, what is the contemporary relevance of such quirky, communitarian, back-to-the-land experiments? Cultural ecologist David Abram believes 'technological civilization must accept the invitation of gravity and settle back into the land, its political and economic structures diversifying into the varied contours and rhythms of a more-than-human earth'.[236] And why not? Research estimates that artificial intelligence will threaten at least 47 per cent of jobs in the US and 54 per cent in Europe, not in a hundred years, but in the next twenty.[237] So, what else will we do? Could we reorganise life around the 'principles of sufficiency' whereby 'people would work as much as they need' and no more?[238] Could communitarian living in small hamlets orbiting existing cities and towns, surrounded by nature and productive land and served by transformative transportation systems (e.g., trackless trams[239]), be an Australian dream for the twenty-first century (Figure 25)?

Commentary

Steve
The words 'hamlet' and 'urbanism' don't really belong together. Towns and cities are far more complex than this claustrophobic vision of urbanism. Nice and romantic, though it all sounds.

Jim
Cities are unsustainable monstrosities, and I hate even going to them.

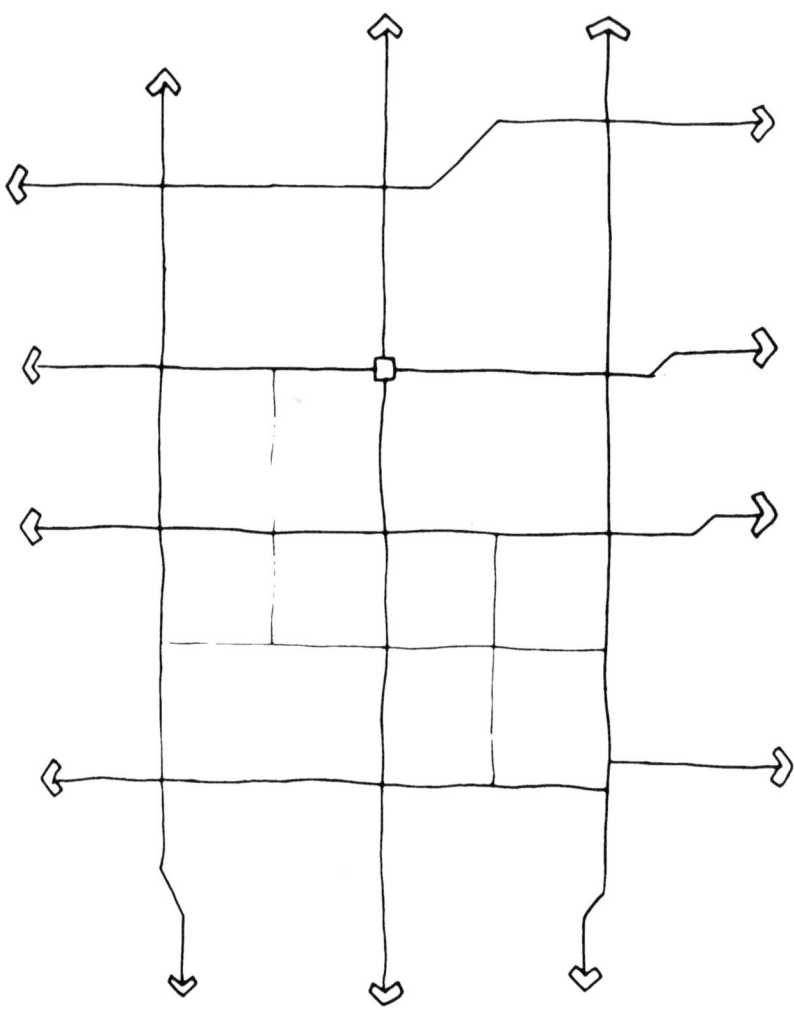

BAU: Urbanism

Figure 25: Hamlet Urbanism
Site: New suburbs
Scale: District
Method: Recombinant innovation (city + hamlet)
Relates to: National Park Urbanism, Edible Urbanism

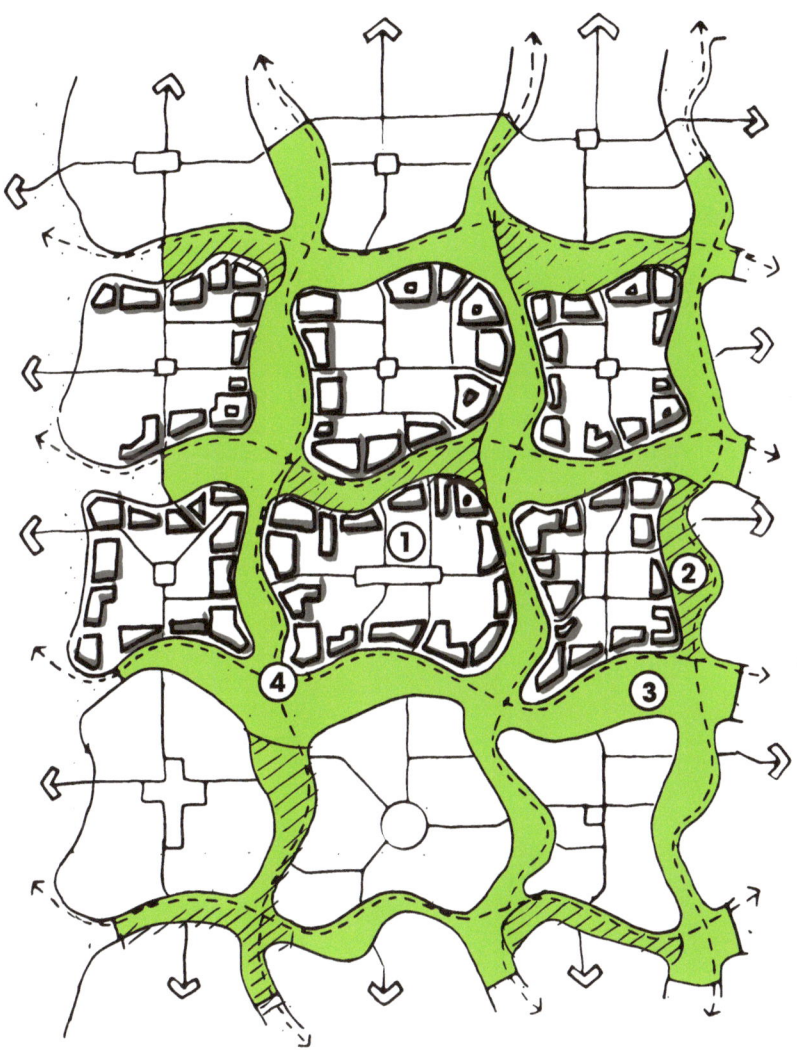

BAUn: Hamlet Urbanism

Legend:
1. Hamlets
2. Productive land
3. Natural land
4. Trackless tram corridors

Incentive Urbanism

Community angst towards urban infill projects is entrenched across Australian cities.[240] Indeed, resistance to densification is such an endemic experience that planners have acronyms to sum up (and in some respects dismiss) the views of the recalcitrant residents, including NIMBY (not in my backyard) or even BANANA (build absolutely nothing anywhere near anything).[241]

Why are so many suburban residents resistant? Sometimes, people feel 'the government' is imposing change on them without having any say in it, and the only response is to resist, resulting in 'public sullenness'.[242] Indeed, many people don't want their neighbourhood to change for valid reasons. Research shows that neighbourhoods with cohesive communities provide residents with a feeling of 'rootedness' instrumental in consolidating a sense of identity and purpose. In contrast, the degradation of a neighbourhood's cohesiveness and character can cause residents to genuinely grieve for losing something other than a loved one.[243] This finding reflects behavioural science, which has revealed that people's urge to clutch on to what they already have is more persistent than the desire to gain something new, an aspect of human behaviour called 'loss aversion'.[244]

Perhaps where policymakers have (sometimes) got it wrong is in justifying densification to existing communities in terms of broader concerns about urban sprawl. The British sociologist Peter Marris wrote in the 1970s: 'People cannot reconcile themselves to the loss of familiar attachments in terms of some impersonal utilitarian calculation of the common good. They have to find their own meaning in these changes before they can live with them.'[245] Moreover, the brutal reality is that people are driven not just by moral considerations of the common good but also by personal self-interest.[246]

If we accept this somewhat transactional facet of human nature, how could we integrate this into our planning for densification? Research shows that communities are not necessarily hostile to higher-density housing if it 'gives something back' to the neighbourhood, e.g., improvements to public amenities.[247] Social bonus zoning in Vancouver is instructive. This form of zoning allows higher-density development in exchange for public parks, schools and affordable housing. This situation means the more households a neighbourhood has, the higher the tax revenue and the bigger the stash for spending on public amenities.[248]

So, what sweetener should we offer Australian communities who are resisting densification? Regardless of how Australian cities grow, population growth on the scale projected will see access to private and public green space diminish. Therefore, the primary focus should be improving the city's public realm by upgrading typically banal suburban Recreation Movement–inspired parks into more multifunctional and biodiverse spaces (Figure 26).[249] This offering is a deal sweetener from several perspectives. On a pragmatic level, upgrading parks increases property values for the surrounding areas, delivering higher property tax revenues and stimulating higher-density redevelopment as land values increase in relation to house values.[250] Residents of neighbourhoods with higher quality parks are also more likely to have better mental health than residents living in neighbourhoods with low-quality parks.[251] Moreover, for many people, having time in nature also has a metaphysical or spiritual dimension, even if only subconsciously; therefore, upgrading banal turfed parks to provide a rich natural experience is a consequential compensation for supporting urban densification (Figure 27).[252] Given these potentials, this proposal poses the question: Would we have more success with urban densification if we were more realistic about the transactional nature of our human subjects – and didn't ask for something for nothing?

Commentary

Aaron
Yasssss! The need for expanses of grass is understood for playing fields – but it doesn't need to be an outdoor carpet for everywhere you might possibly walk. Love this idea.

Jordan
Do we need more development? The proposed solutions cost resources and energy, and the benefits won't be realised for 20 to 50 years. Change the focus of your work! Think outside the box, please!

Anna
Densification of everything though, not just buildings. We need more green space to accommodate the increasing density of people.

Rob
This hardly feels like a rebel idea when it is about incentivising the status quo.

John
Such development destroys the idea of a park being a peaceful space away from buildings, bustle and people. Increased density means they will become hangouts or gang territories with anti-social behaviour and crime.

Jim
Never thought Australian researchers would consider density around parks. You seem obsessed with train stations.

Figure 26: Recreation Movement–inspired open space surrounded by low-density suburbia.

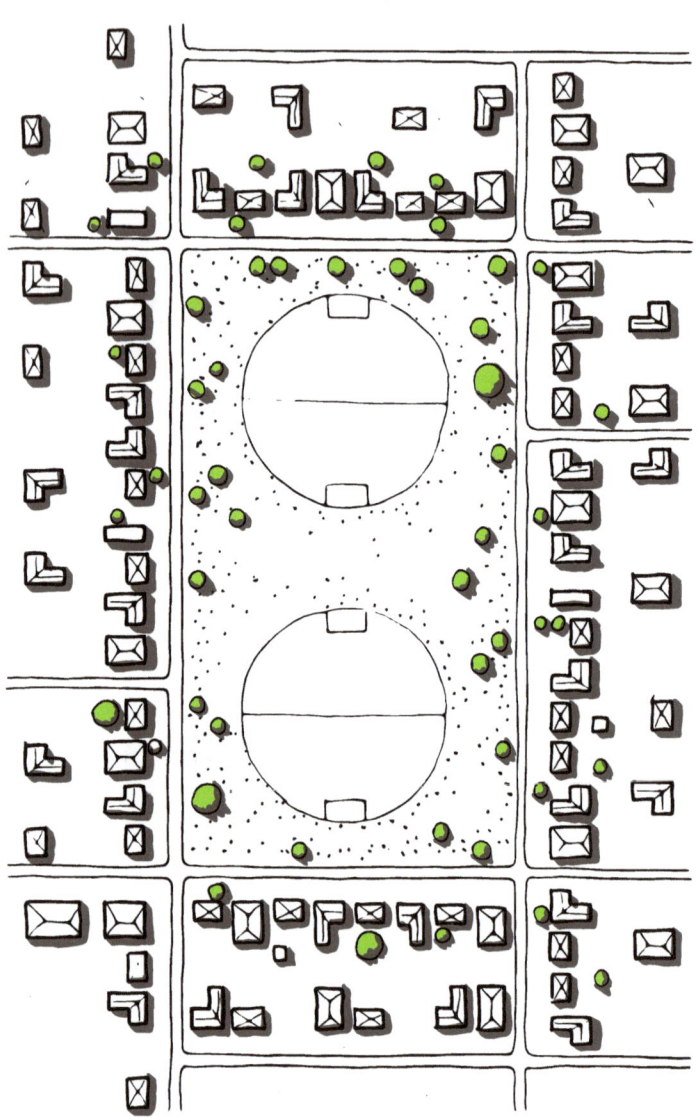

BAU: Urbanism

Figure 27: *Incentivised Urbanism*
Site: *Existing suburbs*
Scale: *Neighbourhood*
Method: *Assumption reversal (Assumption reversed: 'Residents make decisions based on a perception of the common good')*

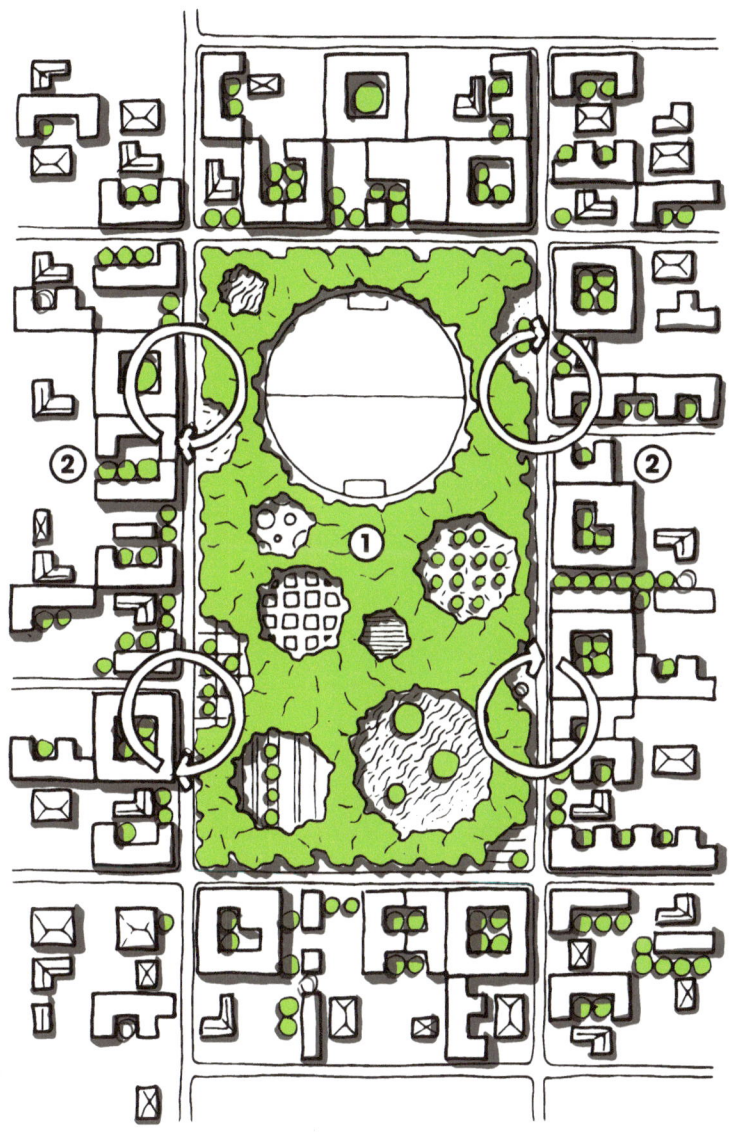

BAUn: Incentive Urbanism

Legend:
1. Upgraded multifunctional open space
2. Medium density housing

Inside Out Urbanism

Some people perceive the multicultural city as more of a threat than an opportunity. As planning academic Leonie Sandercock explains, the danger is many-faceted. It can be perceived as economic, cultural, religious and psychological. It is a complex experience of fear of the 'other': losing your job, a whole way of life being ground out of existence and an all-encompassing fear of change.[253] In European cities, a wave of Muslim immigrants fleeing war in Syria and elsewhere precipitated public outrage over governments' powerlessness to proactively respond to the perceived 'invasion' of local cultures and neighbourhoods.[254] While Australia is by most measures a multicultural success story, tensions are evident in hysteria about 'boat people' and conflicts over proposals for places of worship – and schools – for minority religious groups. Residents (and outside agitators) often fiercely contest proposals for mosques, in particular (Figure 28).[255]

Unfortunately, the heated rhetoric swirling around proposals for mosques has averted a more profound and wide-ranging consideration of what Arabic Islamic urbanism (for instance) could offer the Western canon of planning theory. Characteristics of Arabic Islamic urbanism include the self-contained neighbourhood, the introspective courtyard dwelling with unconnected rooms wrapped around a lush paradise garden,[256] the partially hidden entranceway to individual dwellings, and the roof terrace as an occupiable space for taking in the evening air.[257] Adopting this model flips BAU suburban layouts. Rather than encircling the house with a garden (which is becoming progressively narrow and mean),[258] the house wraps around the garden to make a central, protected and comfortable garden space. Moreover, this model turns the house upside down, with the bedrooms on the lower floors and the living areas on the upper levels and roof.[259] This former shift is timely as the climate in Australia's southern cities increasingly resembles the parched, furnace of the Arabian Gulf region – the central garden space losing much less water to evaporation courtesy of the protection from the surrounding dwelling.[260] More broadly, we should engage with the complex cultural diversity that now characterises our bustling, multicultural cities and reposition urban design and planning to be enriched by the new understandings that ensue.[261]

Accordingly, this proposal poses the question: What could our suburbs become if we turned our houses upside down and inside out (Figure 29)? Could this be a denser yet delightful, climate-adapted model for future Australian suburbs that leans into cultural diversity?

Commentary

Justin
Looks like a street block from Tangier. I think you'll be waiting a while!

Aaron
I'd love to see a model that accommodates a proper Mediterranean climate, with Roman-style central courtyard homes with no setbacks.

Rawal
Yes... If the glass can be seen as a universally identical Expression, why can't mud? We need to learn more from our past and integrate technology to live in future.

Figure 28: While Australia is by most measures a multicultural success story, tensions can be evident in conflicts over proposals for places of worship – and schools – for minority religious groups.

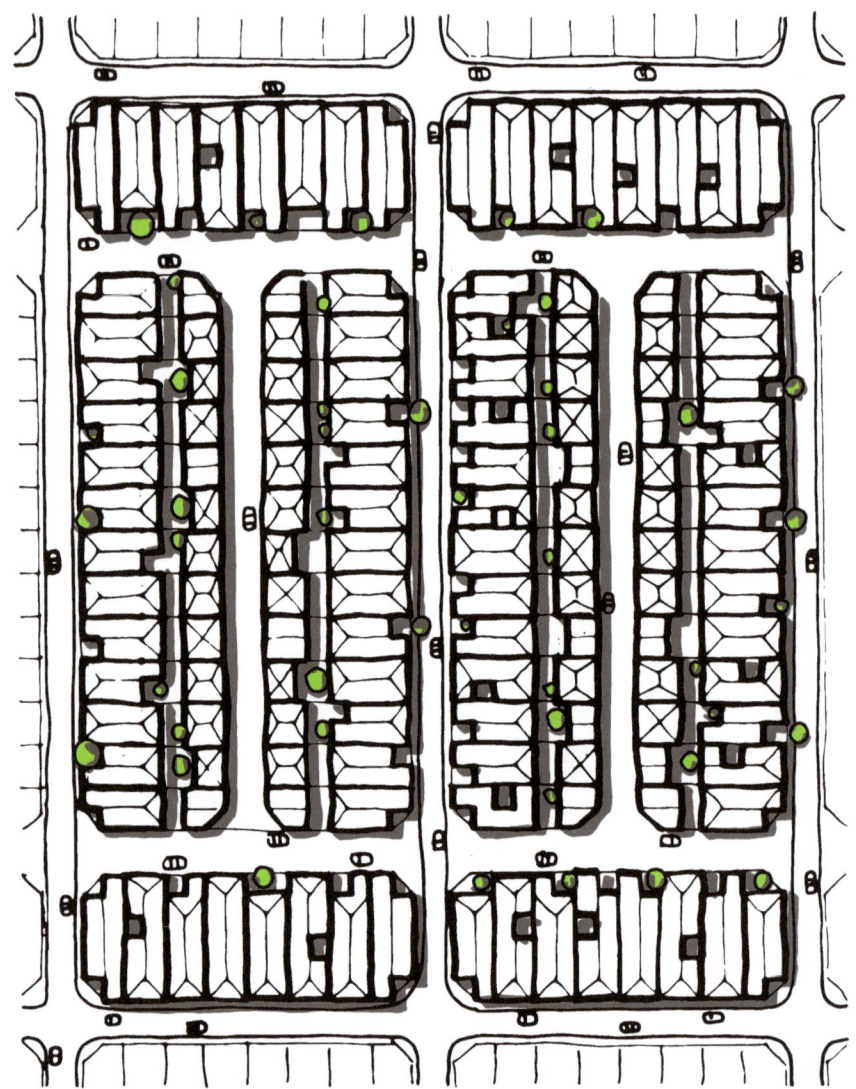

BAU: Urbanism

Figure 29: Inside Out Urbanism
Site: New suburbs
Scale: Street block
Method: Recombinant innovation (Arabic Islamic Urbanism + Australian suburbs)
Relates to: Island Urbanism

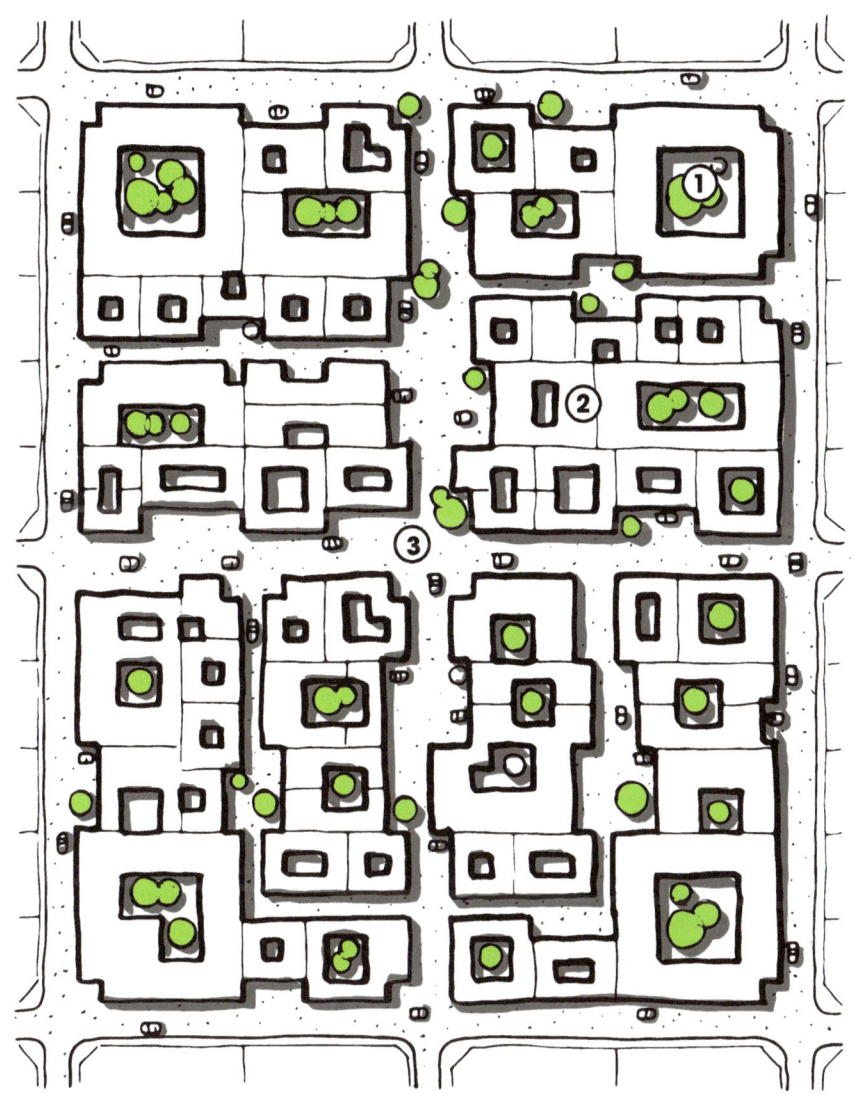

BAUn: Inside Out Urbanism

Legend:
1. *Courtyard garden*
2. *Courtyard dwelling with living areas on roof*
3. *Laneway*

Island Urbanism

 A city should consist of many cities, villages, and worlds – from the smallest scrap of site to the largest.[262]
Shumon Basar

Urbanists persistently believe diversity is a 'positive force in a society, a mode of existence that enhances human experience'.[263] Reflecting this, major immigrant-receiving countries like Australia have embraced a multicultural model where governments officially accept and celebrate differences.[264] Until the mid-1960s, official attitudes toward accommodating immigrant flows were concerned with 'assimilation', which required conformity to the dominant Anglo culture. During the 1980s and 90s, official attitudes changed to 'integration', expecting immigrants to be part of the host society without necessarily relinquishing their distinct identity. The policy then shifted again from integration to multiculturalism, aiming to create 'difference blindness'.[265]

While the multicultural 'melting pot' is the contemporary standard, this can translate to a melting pot of conformance to Western values.[266] Indeed, despite its apparent focus on an 'implicitly plural society', some commentators note that the Australian multiculturalism model can comprise 'assimilation in slow motion'.[267] In this way, the core hegemony of Anglo culture remains firmly asserted[268] and causes immigrants to rescind their cultural identities over the longer term.[269]

Urban planning has long championed social integration as a guiding value, aiming to promote communities of mixed cultures and classes.[270] However, urban settlements often organically segregate into homogenous areas, and ethnic segregation may, in some cases, be a 'naturally' occurring phenomenon.[271] People within minority cultural groups sometimes maintain their own cultures and refuse to adopt the host culture, creating ethnic enclaves (e.g., some Chinatowns).[272] This 'ethnic federalism' is understandable because it nourishes group identity, heritage and the support systems accompanying cultural connection.[273] Indeed, as suburbanisation surged through the twentieth century, 'suburbs themselves often fragmented into a sociological mosaic – collectively heterogeneous but individually homogeneous, as people sorted themselves into more and more finely distinguished lifestyle enclaves, segregated by race, class, education, life stage, and so on'.[274]

Despite urban planning's long history of attempting to deliver social integration,[275] the concentration of a specific culture may not require planning intervention if it constitutes a voluntary rather than enforced enclave. Indeed, Professor of Urbanism Emily Talen notes that the 'voluntary enclave' can be a 'legitimate act of empowerment'.[276] Some acceptance of such enclaves could underwrite more stimulating and enriching cities for all citizens. As design theorist Christopher Alexander explained, in the heterogeneous (integrated melting pot) city, 'people are mixed together, irrespective of their lifestyle or culture. This dampens all significant variety, arrests most possibilities for differentiation, and encourages conformity. What appears heterogeneous turns out to be homogeneous and dull. Conversely, in a city of many subcultures, relatively small in size, occupying an identifiable place, new ways of life can develop.'[277] Critical to the success of such a model are collective spaces that promote exchange between subcultures. This exchange is crucial in countering peoples' distrust of others unlike themselves. Indeed, collective spaces promote interaction, providing an opportunity for 'reconciling and overcoming ethnic and cultural differences'.[278]

In response, this proposal poses the question, what if our homogenous, 'melting pot' planning methods – which assume cultural and societal assimilation and encourage conformity in the long term – produce dull cities? What about islands of difference rather than a sea of suburban sameness? With the cultural model of the 'melting pot' under assault in many world cities, Island Urbanism offers the 'salad bowl' model in which ingredients realise the overall effect by retaining their original flavour or, in urban terms, a city can develop islands of cultural specificity yet an overall cultural richness (Figure 30).

Commentary

Ian
Cities are sub-culture generating machines, it's intrinsic to what urbanism is as a process. Even extremely authoritarian planning cannot override the processes of encounter, connection and aggregation that iterate continuously to create, change, and re-formulate subcultures. Physical determinists may not like this, but there's little they can do to stop it. Even gaols have subcultures.

Rob
This approach ignores class divides in the capacity to develop cities.

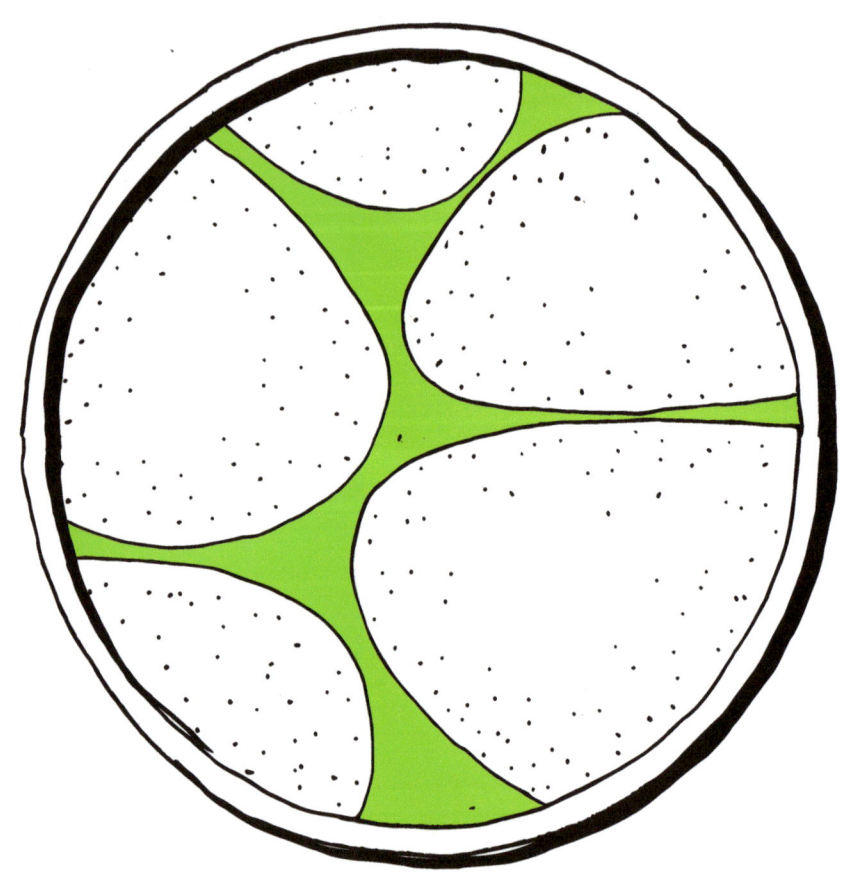

BAU: Urbanism

Figure 30: *Island Urbanism*
Site: *Existing suburbs/new suburbs*
Scale: *Metropolitan*
Method: *Assumption reversal (Assumption reversed: 'Planning should aspire to full cultural and social assimilation.')*
Relates to: *Inside Out Urbanism*

BAUn: Island Urbanism

Legend:
1. Subcultures
2. Public space

Kibbutz Urbanism

> *The accumulation of wealth and goods is endless and unsatisfying; the more we possess, the more our claims multiply. Wealth is like seawater: the more we drink, the thirstier we become. In the end, we don't have our goods – they have us.*[279]
> **Irvin Yalom**

Early suburbia was a form of built socialism, and each house was individually and – with its public parks, schools and pools – community-spirited.[280] Indeed, as political scientist Robert Putnam explains, for the early to mid-twentieth century, 'a powerful tide bore us into ever deeper engagement in the life of our communities'.[281] This spirit faltered with the mass shift to suburban living in the latter twentieth century, 'silently, without warning, that tide reversed, and a treacherous rip current overtook us, and we have drifted apart from one another and our communities'.[282] Architectural critic Elizabeth Farrelly notes that increasing privatisation was important; wealthier residents had private gardens, so they no longer went to parks and they installed swimming pools so they could avoid public pools. They built home gyms to avoid sweating it out at the local gym and cinema rooms as an alternative to going out to the movies. Under this logic, having your own amenities was always better than sharing.[283]

As community spaces eroded in the face of private alternatives, only those who could afford to buy their own amenities could access the benefits. Increasing privatisation diminished the public sphere, along with communities and social bonds.[284] Indeed, the whole point of the suburban project became to stop you from having to live in public.[285] Urbanist Lewis Mumford presciently observed in the 1940s that 'suburbia is a collective effort to lead a private life'.[286] However, despite the apparent 'success' of the privatisation of suburban life, it has left a lonely ache.[287]

Traditional sociocultural sharing has largely broken down in our cities, nonetheless, humans are natural sharers.[288] Community networks foster reciprocity: I'll do this for you now if you return the favour down the track.[289] There is conclusive evidence from the study of primates, early human cultures and contemporary societies that our need to belong is enduring: We have always lived in social groups with deep and reciprocal relationships among people.[290] The most significant level of human happiness is found in working and playing cooperatively with others. As oxytocin studies illustrate, our brains reward us for working well together.[291] People feel their lives are meaningful when they express compassion, cooperation, community and human connection. As anthropologist Jason Hickel notes, we flourish in settings that allow us to express such instincts and suffer in those that suppress them.[292]

We need suburban environments that support our innate desire to share and engage in more communal modes of living. While the communal kibbutz[293] is on the wane in Israel, it could offer a model for living a more communal, considered and connected lifestyle.[294] What could this look like? As urban theorist Leon Krier famously evoked, 'Forward, comrades, we must go back!' The early twentieth-century internal 'communal' reserve was a Garden City planning response to various opportunities: a haven for children's playgrounds, a space for communal gatherings and enabled the cultivation of small agricultural plots (Figure 31).[295] Spinning off this precedent, this proposal poses the question: What about medium-density housing wrapped around an internal communal open space (which could be socialised land[296]) where residents can share cars, bikes, tools, toys, vegetables, cooking, capabilities, experiences and lives (Figure 32)? Could this simultaneously address our overconsumption and epidemic of suburban loneliness by creating inclusionary spaces to 'mitigate social isolation'?[297] Ultimately, a city should be a shared project where we can forge a common good that we cannot construct alone. This sense of a shared future is more important now than ever before.[298]

Commentary

Jennifer
My dream, was to knock down the back fence and share my garden with the neighbours. It would never have been approved in the inner-city area. So, I sold up and bought land in the country to do it. Now, I share my produce with friends and family, which tastes much better and feels great!

Mario
The best thing is to experience wealth and comfort before you start commenting on it. That is a true experience.

Malc
To quote Margaret Thatcher, 'You would rather the poor were poorer as long as the rich were less rich.'

Figure 31:
The early twentieth-century internal 'communal' reserve was a haven for children's playgrounds, and a space for communal gatherings.

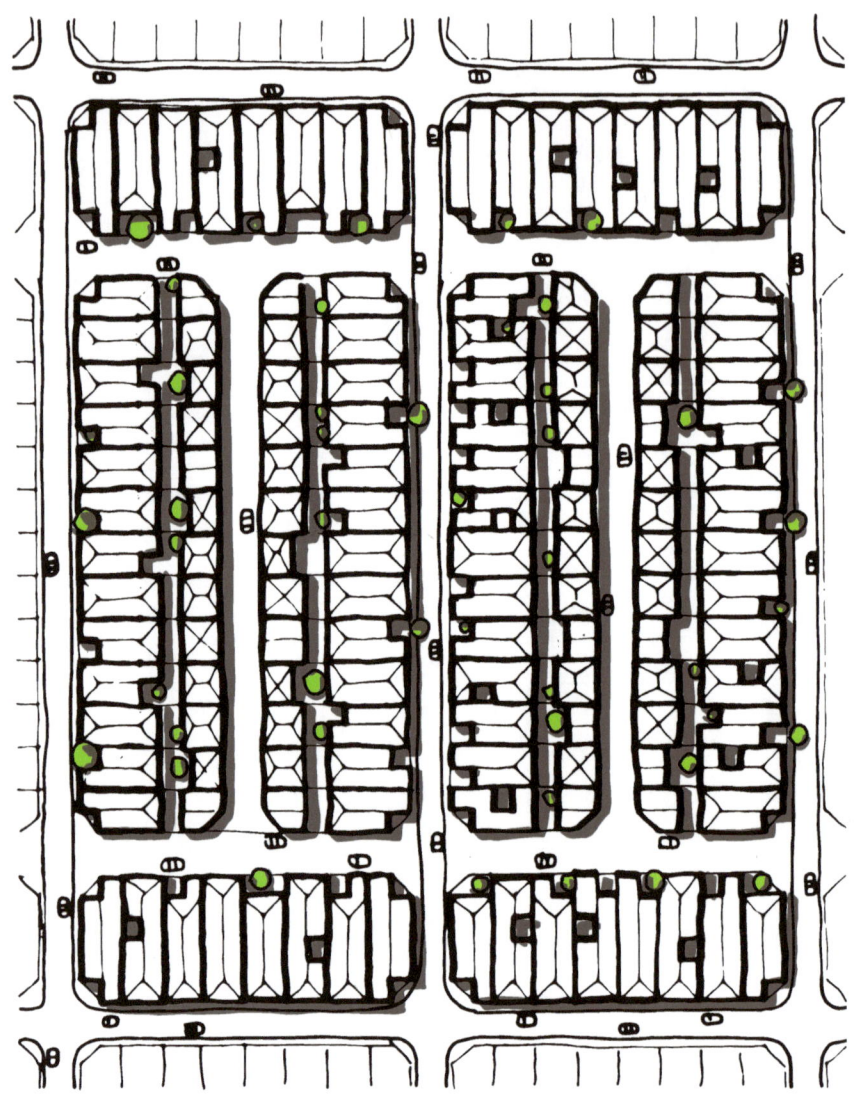

BAU: Urbanism

Figure 32: *Kibbutz Urbanism*
Site: *New suburbs*
Scale: *Street block*
Method: *Recombinant innovation (Suburb + collaborative consumption)*
Relates to: *Bunnings-Lite Urbanism, Woollies-Lite Urbanism*

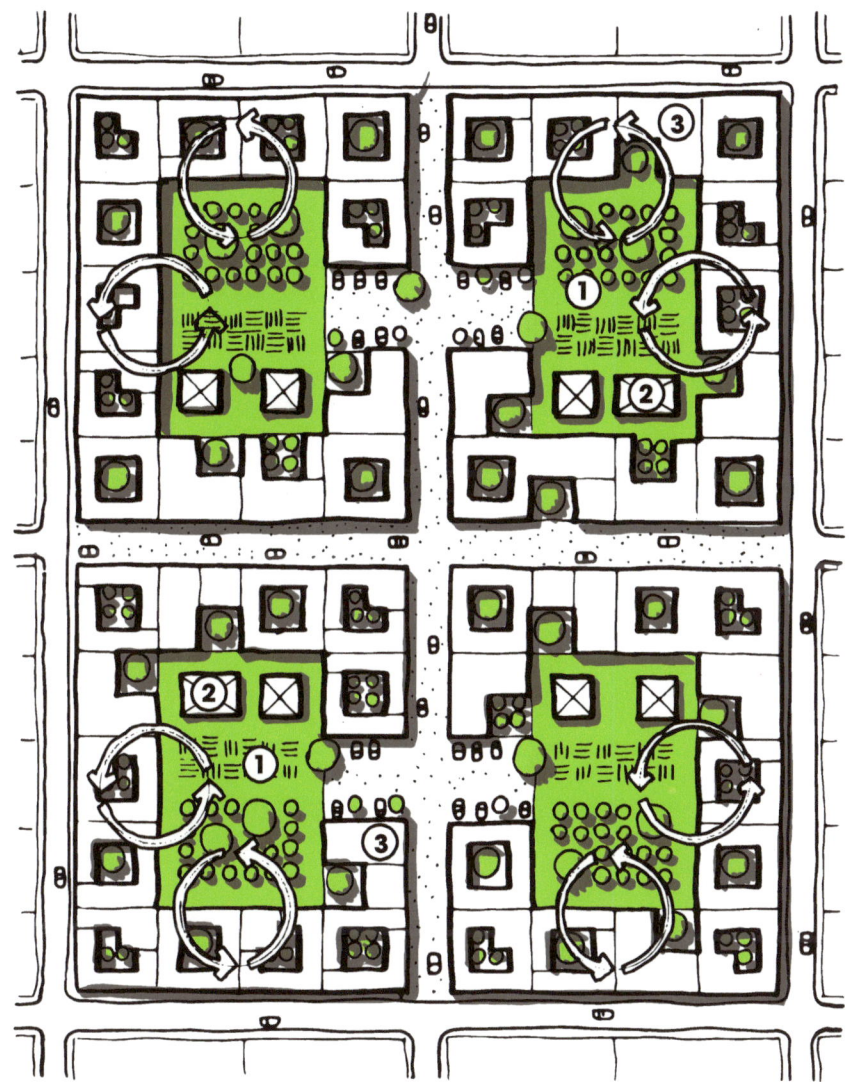

BAUn: Kibbutz Urbanism

Legend:
1. *Communal reserve*
2. *Communal facilities*
3. *Medium density housing*

Lifeboat Urbanism

 It's not a house. It's a home.[299]
Darryl Kerrigan

Heavily stage-managed community 'consultation' sessions are now de rigueur for all major urban developments, and an entire industry devoted to community consultation has arisen. However, with all the groups consulted about the planning of our cities, we often forget the most critical group, 'We don't know who they are or what they want as individuals, and we can only make judgements or suppositions about them. These people will be living in our new suburbs or developments in the future, possibly for hundreds of years into the future.'[300]

However, in Australia, existing property owners hold the whip hand concerning how their neighbourhood changes (or, more to the point, doesn't change), and they often trample on prospective 'future' citizens' rights to live in accessible and amenable areas. Not uncommonly, community resistance to urban infill is fed by an unspoken societal dimension, including efforts to defend class status, exclude poorer households and safeguard house values.[301] Moreover, where infill projects include affordable housing, those resisting densification sometimes 'frame prospective tenants as freeloaders, anti-social, and even potentially criminal'.[302] But given the current housing crisis, shouldn't the right of 'future' residents to a place to live trump concerns by existing communities about diminishing status or house prices?

Australian planning academic Brendan Gleeson suggests that cities must be reconceptualised as 'lifeboats' to carry us through the ensuing storms of societal unravelling and out-of-control climate change. As he explains, the ethics of this 'lifeboat world' must be 'wholly different from those of the cosy self-indulgence of the latter part of the twentieth century'; rather, the basics will be finite and appointed captains must ration them amongst passengers. Passengers must also share tasks, and 'everyone will need to surrender much personal space and all preciousness in what will feel like an ever more cramped situation'.[303]

Accordingly, this alternative urbanism poses the question: what if policymakers afforded prospective future residents equal rights to existing residents when considering how they plan our suburban 'lifeboats'? If so, suburban corner lots (Figure 33) should be sites for targeted medium-to high-density housing alongside a concerted program to increase ecosystem services (e.g., mental health benefits or urban cooling) in adjacent streets. Why corner lots? These lots are straightforward to develop, have the longest street frontage and have the highest potential to support small shops or cafes on the ground floor. In the spirit of 'lifeboat ethics', which reflect social values, restraint and sacrifice solidarity,[304] the government could consider compulsory acquisition of these strategic suburban corner lots, where owners can't be incentivised to sell up.

Figure 33: Suburban corner lots are the most straightforward to develop for medium-to high-density housing.

While this may sound drastic, governments regularly forcibly acquire land for public works, such as road widening or freeway building all the time – as the heroic planner and public official Robert Moses explained about carving freeways through Manhattan, 'sometimes you have to hack your way through the city with a meat axe'.[305] While Moses' approach was taking things a step too far, what better reason to acquire land compulsorily than to provide medium-to-high density housing for the legions currently enduring a storm of housing insecurity (Figure 34)

Commentary

Aaron
I think Perth's general allergy to height is more common than a reaction to pollen on the morning Easterly.

Tania
There are many large properties that could be compulsorily acquired and subdivided. It's time to stop indulging the rich in this regard. The era of 2000m2 properties for two-to-three people should be brought to a close.

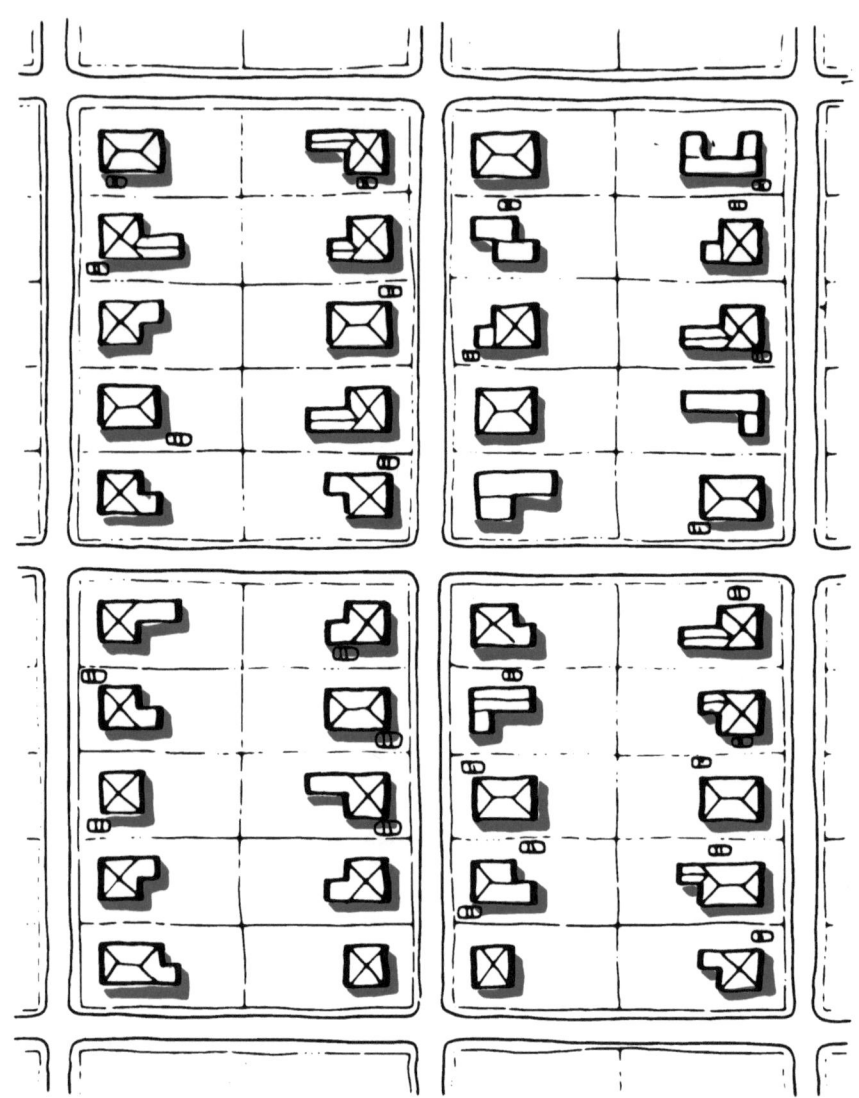

BAU: Urbanism

Figure 34: Lifeboat Urbanism
Site: Existing suburbs
Scale: Street block
Method: Assumption reversal (Assumption reversed: 'Existing residents should have the unalienable right to obstruct housing proposals')
Relates to: Tax-break Urbanism

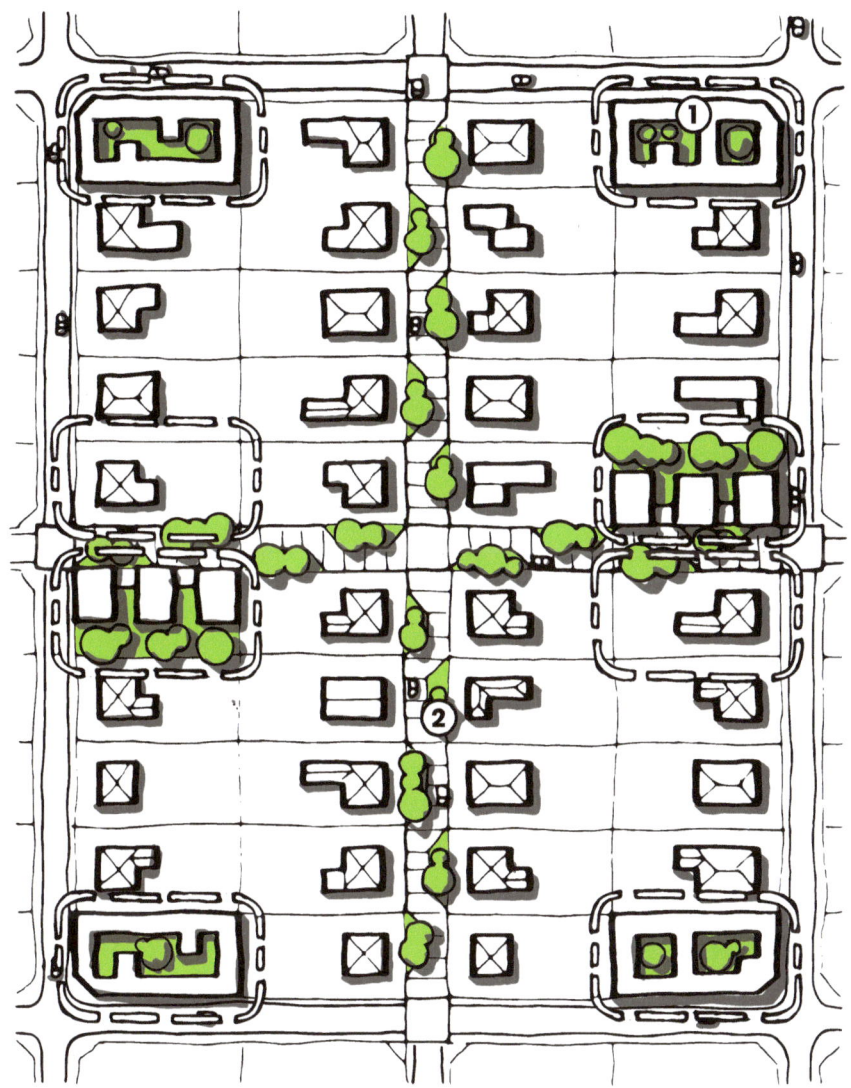

BAUn: Lifeboat Urbanism

Legend:
1. Medium-to-high-density housing on corner lots
2. Increased ecosystems services in adjacent streets

Laneway Urbanism

While the forging of Australian cities has been a holocaust for biodiversity through habitat destruction and truncating ecological flows,[306] the urban areas of our cities remain remarkably biodiverse. Indeed, research by the Nature Conservation Council shows that one-quarter of all threatened plants and just under half of threatened animals exist in Australia's 100 (or thereabouts) largest urban centres. They also identified that such urban centres contain three times as many threatened species per hectare as country areas.[307] We can't just shunt biodiversity conservation to city edges for this simple reason.[308] As landscape architect and academic Richard Weller explains, 'It is unhelpful and even dangerous to continue to see the city set against nature's backdrop or as something that can be reductively categorized into exclusive types along a New Urbanist transect that fixes "nature" at one end and "culture" at the other.'[309]

So, how should we better interweave natural systems into our cities? Locking in large swathes of remnant natural habitat is an essential first step. Subsequently, these 'islands' need to be woven together using greenways.[310] In the 1980s, the White House endorsed greenways when The President's Commission on Americans Outdoors declared that they should weave 'through cities and countryside like a giant circulation system' and 'give every American easy access to the natural world'.[311] Given the ability of greenways to connect people with nature and inspire interest in conservation,[312] how could they be deployed in new suburban areas?

Historic suburban layouts provide a clue. Planners interwove Federation suburbs with a grid of laneways (Figure 35), which started life as private service ways, allowing 'nightsoil' collectors to haul away human waste, servants to enter households and horse-drawn carts to haul goods. In urban areas, laneways were home to stables, brothels, laundries, opium dens and boarding houses.[313] Nonetheless, by the late twentieth century, many laneways, particularly in the suburbs, had become messy, overgrown and wild habitats for children and biodiversity.

Meanwhile, inner-city areas like Melbourne's CBD made a roaring trade in invigorating dilapidated, garbage-strewn urban laneways with lighting, artworks, cafes and small bars.[314] However, the potential of the laneway for creatures other than hipsters has had scant consideration. Accordingly, this proposal poses the question: What if we reimagined the Federation-era rear laneway into an interconnected green network funnelling biodiversity through new compact suburbs (Figure 36)? We urgently need compact urban models interwoven with biodiversity as we lurch through this era of mass species extinction – long live the leafy lane.

Figure 35: Planners interwove Federation suburbs with a grid of laneways, allowing 'nightsoil' collectors to haul away human waste, servants to enter households and horse-drawn carts to haul goods.

Commentary

Phil
I've experimented with some of this in the UK, retaining hedgerows to form some of the framework for housing and strips of unmown verges to these to act as 'meadow highways'. Twelve years later, these have been mowed, but what is still there are the systems that form similar links. We have the opportunity to do the same in Australia.

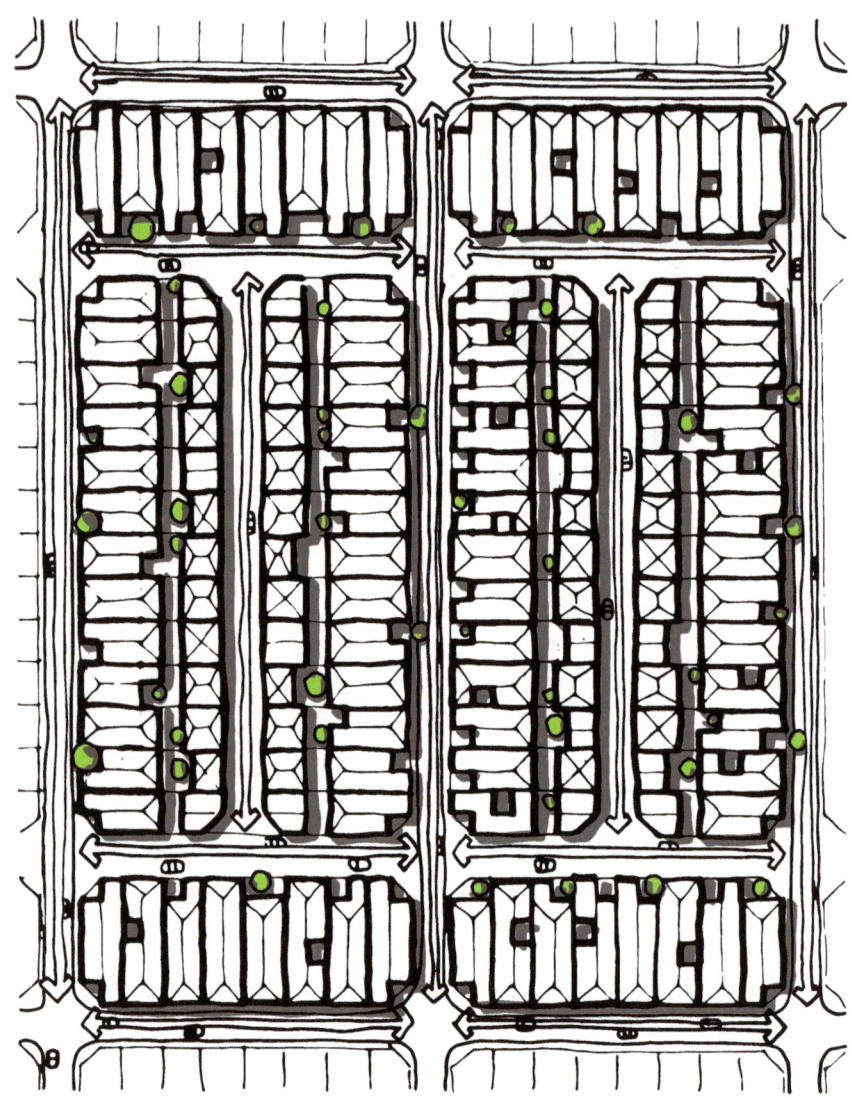

BAU: Urbanism

Figure 36: Laneway Urbanism
Site: New suburbs
Scale: Street block
Method: Recombinant innovation (Suburb + greenway)
Relates to: Nature-Play Urbanism

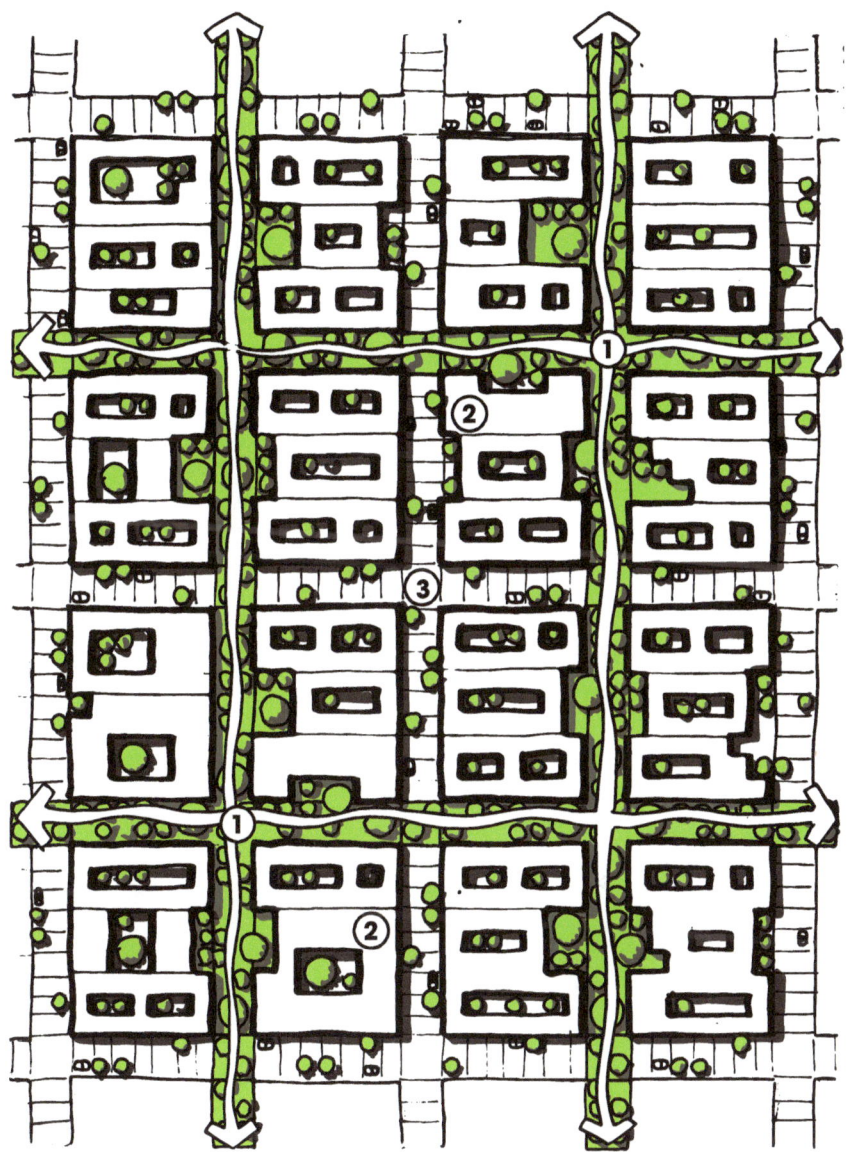

BAUn: Laneway Urbanism

Legend:
1. Interconnected green network
2. Medium density housing
3. Street network

Modern Urbanism 2.0

> *Civilised human beings need houses here and now. They can be fobbed off with investigations, plans, decisions and conferences – for a time – but when enough people want their rights urgently enough, things begin to happen.*[315]
> **Clayton Burns**

Net migration, averaging about 200,000 people a year for the past two decades, has seen Australia's population surge by 7.2 million, while the total number of dwellings has increased by only 3 million. As a result, financial journalist Alan Kohler has calculated Australia has a shortfall of 1.2 million houses.[316] To put this in perspective, Greater Brisbane only has just over 1 million dwellings. It is an understatement to say construction has not been keeping up with demand.[317]

The decline in public housing after the mid-1960s compounds this crushing shortage. Fewer than 4 per cent of households now live in public housing in Australia, a proportion steadily dropping over time.[318] What explains this situation? In the early 1970s, much of the Western world underwent significant economic and political realignment, known as the 'neoliberal turn'. The state's function shifted from modest welfare provision to gross deregulation,[319] heralding a new era of persistent underinvestment in public housing.[320] In Australia, the election of conservative prime minister Malcolm Fraser at the end of 1975 ended the idea that public housing was a right for all. Subsequently, it has become nothing more than welfare for the neediest.[321] Moreover, governments generally no longer build social or designated affordable housing. Instead, courtesy of the neoliberal turn, developers deliver social housing, however, only if they can make a profit.[322] This situation means that where governments wish to increase social housing, they must do so principally by influencing the decisions made by private developers.[323]

The intractable problem of housing affordability now dominates the national consciousness.[324] The flow-on effects of housing insecurity for residents and broader society are severe. American behavioural scientist Elda Shafir explains that 'scarcity' constrains your focus on your immediate predicament. The longer-term perspective necessarily goes out the window. 'Scarcity consumes you; you're less able to focus on other things that are also important to you.'[325] Similarly, George Orwell noted that the crux of poverty is that it 'annihilates the future; all that remains is surviving here and now'.[326] Dutch historian Rutger Bregman noted that this leads to people in poverty tending to borrow more money, smoke more cigarettes, drink more alcohol and eat more fast food while, conversely, saving less money and exercising less.[327]

As it turns out, providing free public housing is a boon for government budgets despite perceptions otherwise. In a trial program in Utah in the US, economists calculated that a homeless person living on the street costs the government $25,270 yearly (reflecting costs for social services, police, court time, etc.). An apartment, by contrast, costs a modest $16,675.[328] Moreover, US kids who grow up poor and likely in insecure housing, on average, end up with two years' less educational attainment, work 450 fewer hours annually, and run three times the risk of health issues than those raised in comfortably well-off families – all of which have major implications for government budgets.[329]

Housing security for all is good for society, and a secure dwelling 'is not only the need but the right of every citizen'.[330] Therefore, public housing should not be a dream but a reality that governments deliver, improve and expand.[331] But what about modernist public housing disasters ('filing cabinets for people') like St Louis' Pruitt Igoe, which city officials dynamited in 1972, just two decades after its construction?[332] It is vital to make clear that such housing programs did not fail based on some inherent deficiency in the policy of providing social housing; they faltered because they were starved of government resources and funding.[333] A counter-example of successful public housing provision is state-capitalist Singapore, where over 80 per cent of residents from all classes live in public housing and where government investment is commensurate with the importance of secure housing for broader society.[334]

Given the clear benefits of secure housing provision for all, this proposal asks what form the 1.2 million new dwellings needed to address Australia's housing shortage should take. Given the scale of housing required, there is reason to think that modernism (in central locations) remains the weapon of choice (Figure 37), much like that of Singapore. Indeed, governments will need the modernist emphasis on machine-age efficiency, large scale, density and speed[335] to deliver the required millions of dwellings (Figure 38). While critics may bemoan the 'mild boredom of order'[336] and lack of heart and soul that results,[337] residents would likely be glad of a roof over their heads – something the critics have learned to take for granted.

Commentary

Rob
Meeting the demands of population growth won't solve the underlying economic, cultural, and ideological problems. Investing a national surplus into social housing will stimulate further growth—Jevon's paradox.

Tim
Nothing ages so badly than yesterday's future.

Figure 37: Governments will require the modernist emphasis on machine-age efficiency, large scale, density and speed to deliver the required 1.2 million dwellings urgently.

BAU: Urbanism

Figure 38: *Modernist Urbanism 2.0*
Site: *Existing suburbs/new suburbs*
Scale: *Street block*
Method: *Assumption reversal (Assumption reversed: 'Modernism is dead and buried, or at least should be')*
Relates to: *Fair-Go Urbanism*

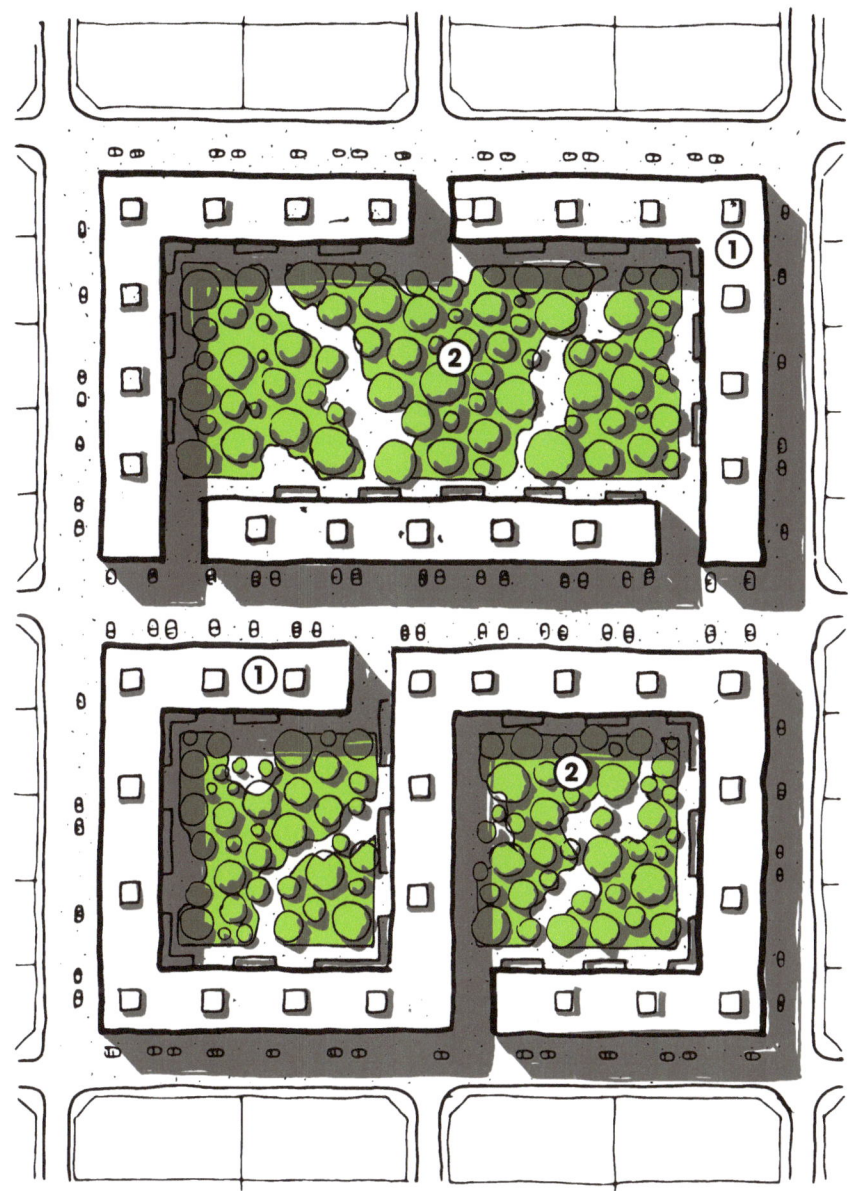

BAUn: Modernist Urbanism 2.0

Legend:
1. Modernist, high density perimeter block housing
2. Forested courtyards

National Park Urbanism

 London was formally declared a National Park City in 2019,[338] and a charter was produced to support other cities in doing the same. Why not, indeed? And what if? It is a powerful example of how to rekindle the collective imagination.[339]
Rob Hopkins

Research has identified a set of 35 global biodiversity hotspots, which collectively contain 60 per cent of all threatened mammals, 63 per cent of threatened birds and 79 per cent of threatened amphibians. This irreplaceable biodiversity is concentrated in the precious remaining habitat, which comprises just over 2 per cent of the global land area.[340] The hotspots also house a disproportionate share of people, equalling one-third of the world's population. Even more alarming, human populations in the hotspots are surging faster than elsewhere, posing an epic challenge for policymakers in managing biodiversity conservation and housing provision. Despite the scale of the challenge, we cannot falter in our conservation efforts. Indeed, research tells us, 'If we fail in the hotspots, we will lose nearly half of all terrestrial species regardless of how successful we are everywhere else.'[341]

Over the last two centuries, we have hacked several of Australia's most extensive and fastest-growing urban areas – Brisbane, Perth and Sydney – from two globally significant biodiversity hotspots (Figure 39).[342] So, what strategies exist to protect the hotspots from ongoing urbanisation? According to the compact city agenda, Brisbane, Perth and Sydney have planned for substantial urban densification to reduce peri-urban land clearing; Perth has a modest 47:53 ratio infill to sprawl, South-East Queensland (including Brisbane) 60:40 and Sydney 70:30.[343] However, sprawl in Perth and Brisbane continues apace.

Surprisingly, research by renowned urban ecologist Richard T Forman into reconciling urbanisation and biodiversity advocates for urban growth in satellite cities (within a larger multi-city region) to protect biodiversity-rich land near an existing city.[344] This strategy differs from BAU urban sprawl, which tends to comprise strip development along major radial transportation corridors spreading out from the city, progressively subdividing the landscape.[345] The resulting urban morphology leaves only hapless remnants of habitats, severs ecological connectivity and obliterates much of the heterogeneity characteristic of species-rich communities.[346]

Figure 39: Housing nibbles away at the Southwest Australia Biodiversity Hotspot.

So, what to do? This proposal suggests formally declaring Brisbane, Perth and Sydney National Park cities based on the Universal Charter.[347] Such a declaration would be potent in rekindling our collective thinking about our interconnection with the natural world. How? The (albeit dangerous) point is not to regard cities as anti-ecological. As Professor of Anthropology and Geography David Harvey notes, from a particular perspective, 'cities are fundamental ecological features in themselves', and the processes that build cities are, from a specific perspective, 'ecological processes'.[348] If we accept ecological and urban worlds as part and parcel of each other, we should interlink them more deeply,[349] and the declaration of National Park Cities could formalise this reconceptualization. Under the National Park City rubric, we should develop regional-scale plans for our hotspot cities in which natural systems provide a template guiding patterns of future urbanism (Figure 40). Rather than vainly attempting to lockdown compact cities, appropriate urban development could leap over precious remaining habitats to create a polycentric network comprising a core city and orbiting satellite cities interwoven with biodiversity.

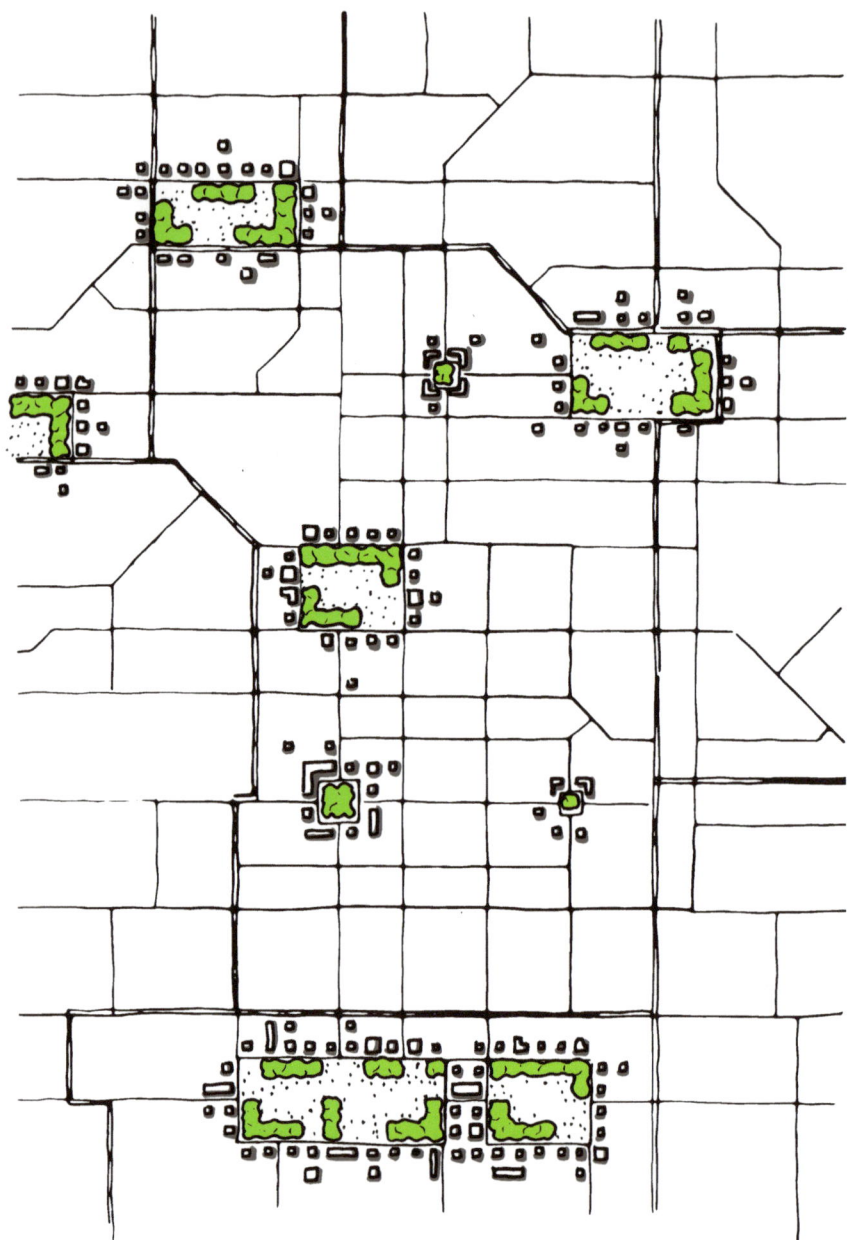

BAU: Urbanism

Figure 40: National Park Urbanism
Site: New suburbs
Scale: Metropolitan
Method: Recombinant innovation (National Park + city)
Relates to: Laneway Urbanism, Nature-Play Urbanism

BAUn: National Park Urbanism

Legend:
1. Polycentric network of satellite cities
2. Biodiversity

Nature-Play Urbanism

The World Health Organization recently concluded that depression is the most significant health problem among teens.[350] Indeed, anxiety disorders have multiplied twentyfold in the past three decades,[351] and young people are faring particularly poorly.[352] Indeed, many children and teenagers have minimal contact with the natural world and engage almost exclusively with other humans and human-made technologies.[353] Accordingly, visitation to urban parks has dropped over time in developed countries, and researchers have attributed this to preferences for online games and social media over real-world experiences.[354] Indeed, research has found that Australian children spend an alarming amount of their lives glued to screens at home. Infants and toddlers averaged 14 hours per week, the two-to five-year-olds 26 hours, and the six-to twelve-year-olds a whopping 32 hours per week. Teenagers used a staggering 44 hours per week – more than a full-time job.[355] For screen-addicted children, digital tech has overrun the experiential world.[356]

This retreat of young people from the natural world (as the natural world retreats from us) means young people lose valuable resources that could support their mental health. As cultural ecologist David Abram explains, given our age-old reciprocity with the natural world, 'we still need that other than ourselves and our creations'.[357] Moreover, the psychiatrist Carl Jung wrote that 'the concept of nature was an essential psychological construct.' He noted that 'belonging to one's natural surroundings is vital for healthy mental functioning and that fostering this relationship promotes well-being, creative introspection, and personal transformation.'[358] Indeed, research shows that even a brief period in natural settings reduces young people's stress levels. There is also evidence that time spent in nature relieves the children's symptoms of ADHD. These mental health benefits are on top of the myriad of physical health benefits, such as combatting obesity; indeed, kids with better access to parks (the main stand-in for nature in cities) typically have consistently lower levels of obesity than those without.[359]

Given the manifest health benefits of nature to young people, nature-play areas are proliferating across Australia, and rightly so (Figure 41). However, they are typically human-cultivated specks of 'nature' within the expanse of our cities. Therefore, they usually need cars and parents to access them (how boring). Accordingly, this proposal poses the question: What if we extended the principles of nature playgrounds to our suburbs and houses were set within a forested landscape, allowing free reign for children (Figure 42)? Shouldn't nature be something kids don't need to get in a car to enjoy? Of course, critics will recognise buildings floating in 'landscape' as a characteristic of the much-maligned Modernist movement. But surely there is a place for contemporary experiments where built form is subservient to landscape? As biologist Tim Lowe describes: 'To experience wildness so close to home is to live more fully and to understand more deeply. The wilderness, after all, begins here.'[360]

Commentary

Russell
I love the idea. But unless existing neighbourhoods can transition towards it (and densify), we have to carve out more native habitat on the city fringe to try another new urbanism...not unlike the other suburban experiments. If only city design started with a blank sheet!

Hootan
I am always wondering if what you are presenting here is simply a question of policy and/or economics. The policy has been that suburbs are private industry commercial ventures. For this reason, and as much as possible, the intention will be to generate the image on the left. Engagement with land developers will bring that ethos right out. And they want to sell land. It's the easiest and cheapest product, so the outcomes to the right will happen rarely and by extreme force or where it is a small part of an overall estate.

Rob
This scheme fiddles around the edges and uses urban design to react to symptoms of unchecked growth rather than address the root problem. To amend the existing urban fabric in these ways would push us over climate thresholds like green capitalism does.

Lara
Yes to this!

Figure 41: Given the manifest health benefits of nature to young people, nature-play areas are proliferating across Australia.

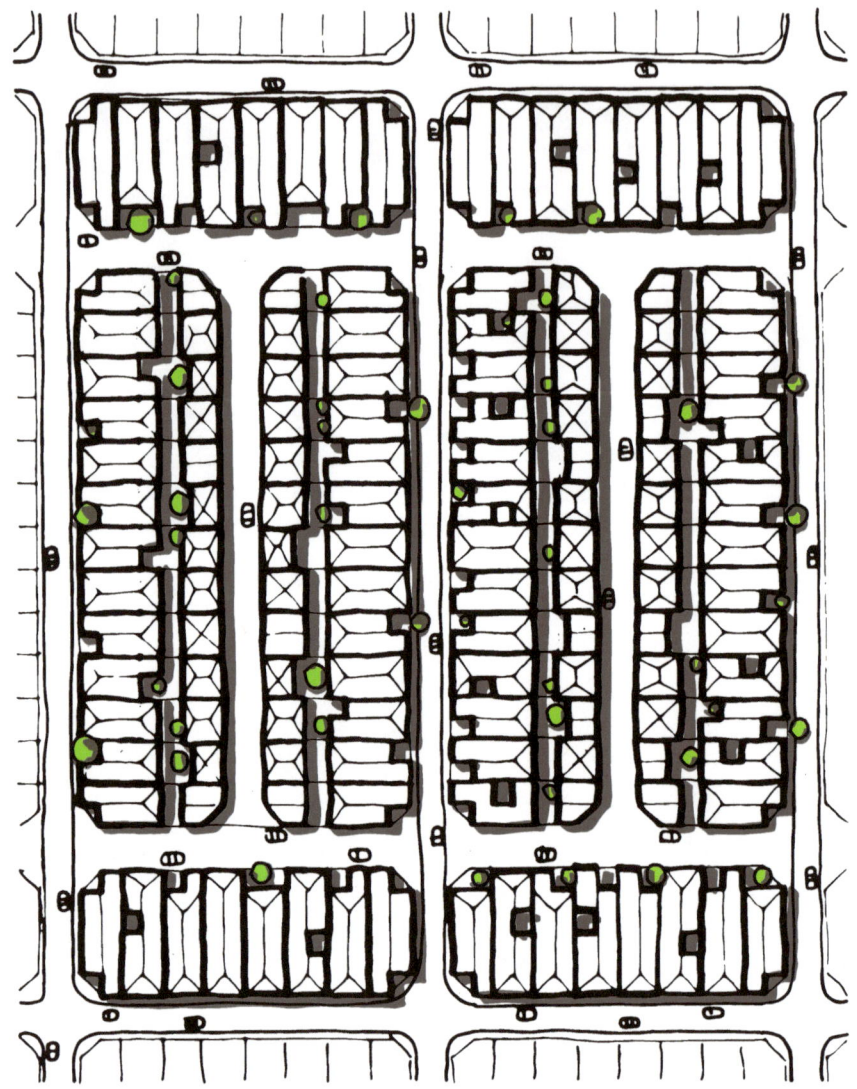

BAU: Urbanism

Figure 42: *Nature-Play Urbanism*
Site: *New suburbs*
Scale: *Street block*
Method: *Recombinant innovation (Suburb + nature-play)*
Relates to: *National Park Urbanism, Radburn Urbanism 2.0*

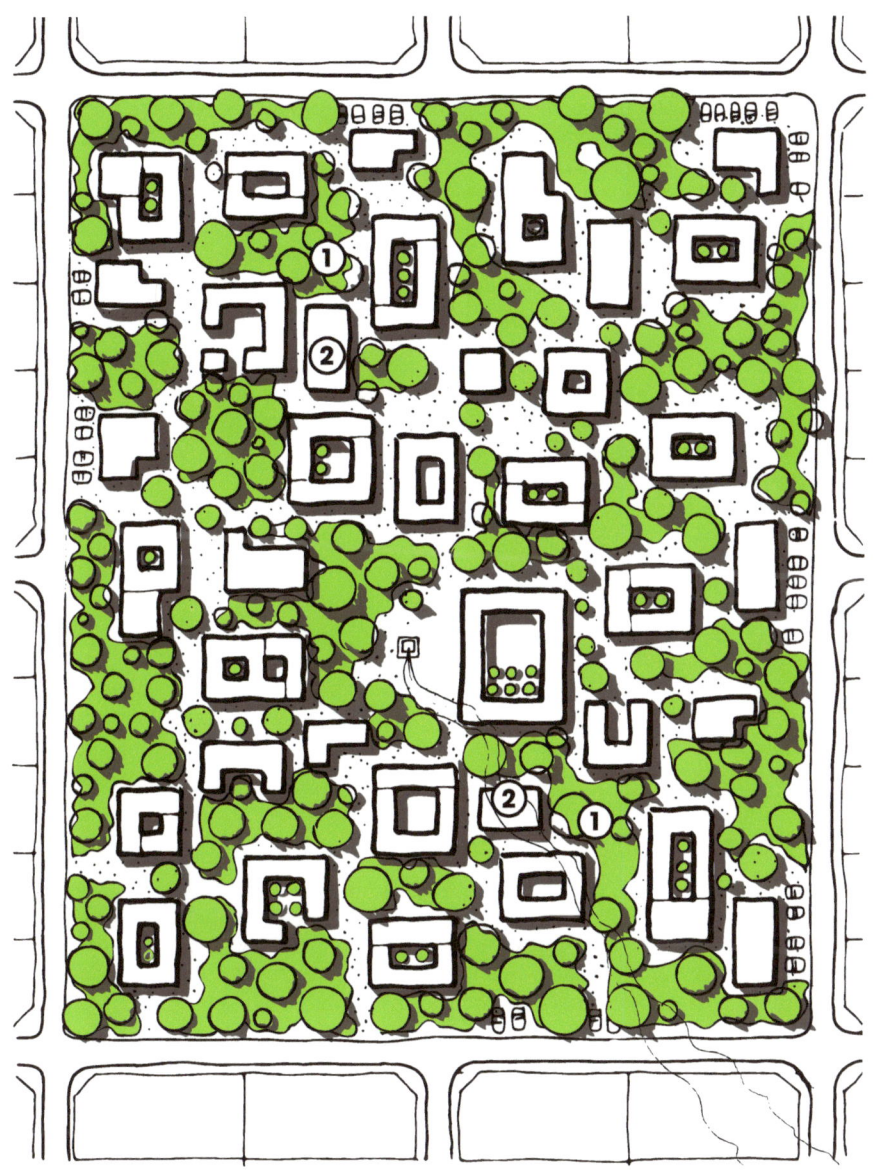

BAUn: Nature-Play Urbanism

Legend:
1. *Nature-play*
2. *Medium density housing*

Radburn Urbanism 2.0

The suburb of Radburn (founded in 1929) in New Jersey, USA, and its planning principles have proved transferable yet problematic. At Radburn, architects Clarence Stein and Henry Wright neatly separated vehicles and pedestrians by introducing internal open space spines that functioned as parks and pathways linking housing to central community cores. Meanwhile, they used cul-de-sacs to discourage traffic from flowing through residential streets.[361] What came to be known as the Radburn plan got quite a workout in Australia in the 1970s and 80s (Figure 43), with the design approach washing up in Canberra, Macquarie Fields (in Sydney), Kwinana, Crestwood (in Perth), South Hedland, Paraburdoo, Kambalda, Leinster (all in WA's Pilbara region) and Moranbah (in Queensland).[362]

Despite the Radburn plan's proliferation, it fell from grace in the 1990s. Its 'intrinsic shortcomings' related to its inward focus,[363] where suburban houses tried in vain to front both streets and internal open space spines – and, ultimately, got in a muddle and failed to do either. Justly or otherwise, Radburn plans also became deeply unfashionable due to their association with public housing developments (for example, Macquarie Fields in Sydney) and a belief that they beget bad behaviour. This assumption is, to some degree, unfair; neighbourhoods with high concentrations of public housing and a shortage of meaningful jobs or transit connectivity were likely to face social challenges no matter how planners arranged ensembles of open space and housing. Nonetheless, the charismatic leader of New Urbanism, Andrés Duany, has been particularly critical of Radburn's open space spines as zones of conveyance and, as such, transitory content that are poorly surveilled and likely dangerous.[364] Accordingly, he depicts them as 'an extended venue for crime' and as a reoffering of the 'matrix of green as a buffer' which, in his opinion, will perpetuate the problematic dispersive propensities of the modern city.[365]

So, is there a way of achieving the conveyance of people (and biodiversity) typical of the Radburn plan's internal open space spines while ensuring all-important passive surveillance and activation from adjacent housing?[366] Sure. Instead of the Radburn plan's tendency to provide low-density housing with ample gardens and open space, which is therefore hard to animate and surveil, this proposal lines the open space spines with group dwellings that overlook and spill directly into these spaces. Moreover, Radburn Urbanism 2.0 would ensure local people have a stake in internal open space spines. The most successful internal reserves are those where residents have a stake through title covenants, legal associations or active cooperation. 'Ownership' in a metaphorical sense, as much as a legal one, creates interest, perception of value and a desire to cooperate with neighbours.[367]

The result could be a Radburn plan for the twenty-first century, which allows walkers and wildlife to move through internal green spaces while avoiding the menace of cars.[368] Research shows that people who spend two hours a week walking in green spaces enjoy more significant physical and psychological well-being (with less tension, anxiety, hostility, depression and tiredness) than those who don't.[369] So, how do we build our cities so that residents exceed the target of two hours a week in nature? How about wrapping urban density around a five-minute (400 metre) Radburn-esque walking loop ensconced in nature (Figure 44)? Your prescription for health and well-being is 24 laps per week.

Commentary

Jonathan
I agree with the sentiment here. But the graphic shoots the argument in the foot, in my opinion. If we create low-density 'green' places, the city/settlement will expand and use more carbon and green belts. Greenwash is a clear and present danger. And attractive novel graphics don't automatically help the cause. Retrofitting option A and respecting underlying core sustainability might be a better way forward. Rant over!

Soumaya
The moment we start treating the urban realm as human-centred rather than vehicle-oriented, things might change! Looks like the first one cares more about how the car will move than how people will!

Jacques
Where is my car?

Stephen
Julian Bolleter, you seem to be finding diagrams that exemplify gaps in understanding prevalent amongst the urban design community.

Geoffrey
Sorry, but it's a disaster. Simplistically, it has a lot of green. But who owns it? Who dominates it? Is it public or private? This looks an awful lot like Le Corbusier's 'free space' – and how did that turn out?

Rob
Nature is subservient to Capital. Its needs trump all else.

Figure 43: The Radburn plan separates vehicles and pedestrians by introducing internal open space spines that function as parks and pathways linking housing to central community cores. Photo by Maassoumeh Barghchi.

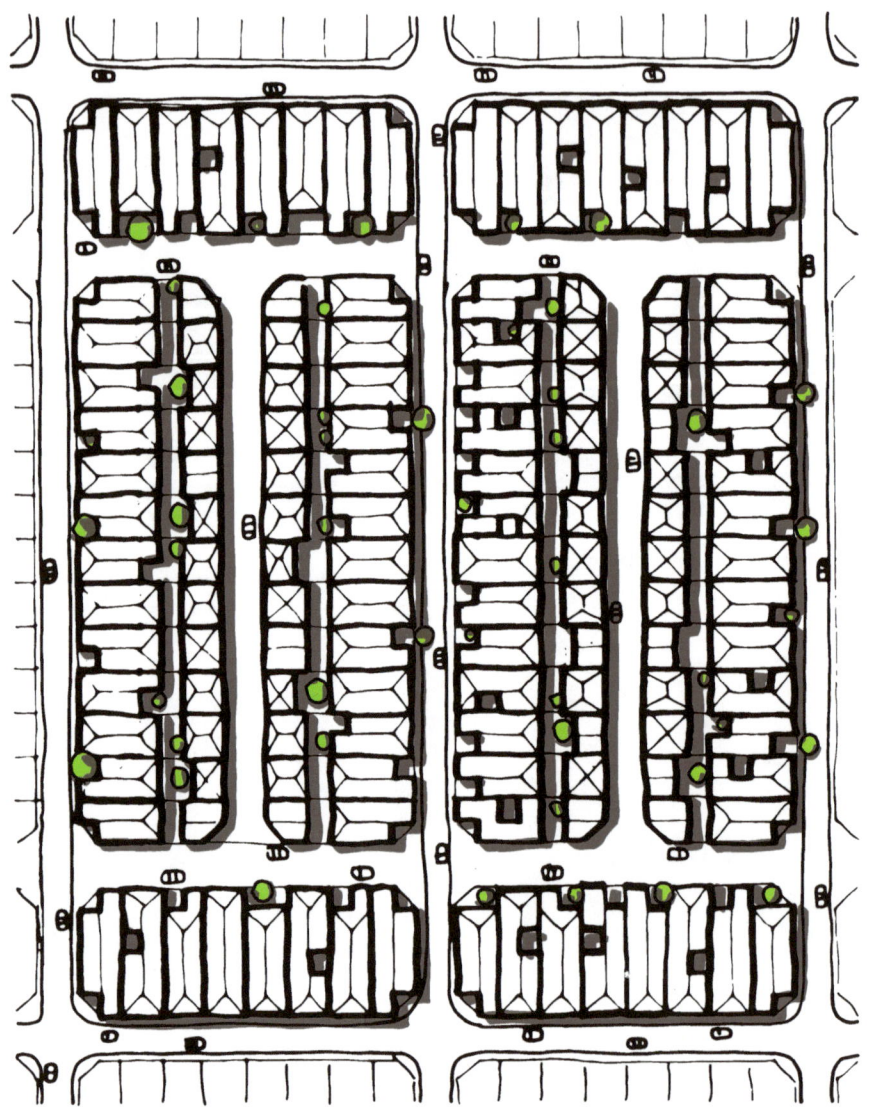

BAU: Urbanism

Figure 44: *Radburn Urbanism 2.0*
Site: *New suburbs*
Scale: *Street block*
Method: *Assumption reversal (Assumption reversed: 'The Radburn plan is dead and buried or at least should be')*
Relates to: *Nature-Play Urbanism*

BAUn: Radburn Urbanism 2.0

Legend:
1. *Radburn-esque walking loop*
2. *Medium density housing overlooking the loop*

Resignation Urbanism

 The only hope of hitting the International Panel on Climate Change's (IPCC) emissions numbers is the radical transformation of almost every aspect of daily life. Which would be, to put it mildly, socially disruptive.[370]
Jonathan Franzen

Despite policymakers' sluggish response to mitigating climate change, Australia has much to lose from a changing climate. The authoritative IPCC warns that 'the region faces an extremely challenging future that will be highly disruptive for many human and natural systems'.[371] Indeed, the worst-case projections of future climate change in southern regions (e.g., Perth and Melbourne) for 2090 include annual temp increases up to 4.2°C.[372] In the eastern regions (e.g., Sydney), annual temp increases up to 5.0°C.[373]

These figures are alarming because Australia is underprepared for even contemporary heatwaves. Indeed, amped-up heat stress during summer causes more than 1000 'extra' annual deaths,[374] which is more than any other natural cause (and even more than those who die on the roads).[375] Cumulatively, heat-stress-related complications have killed as many as 1.7 million people between 2006 and 2017[376] (picture a city of the dead larger than Adelaide).

Accordingly, policymakers responsible for our cities should take the worst-case climate projections seriously and undertake a comprehensive program of adaptation to extreme heat.[377] Indeed, the total emission reductions pledged as per the Paris Agreement, even if miraculously implemented on schedule, will still result in average global surface temps of 3°C (or more) above the pre-industrial period by 2100.[378] Even this more modest temperature increase will have severe implications for Australian cities that require proactive adaptation planning.

Policymakers have attempted climate change mitigation through planning for higher-density, mixed-use development adjacent to public transport hubs or corridors that should, in theory, reduce car dependence.[379] Such is the ascendency of Transit Oriented Development (TOD) thinking, that Australia's major cities have all adopted medium to high-density TOD scenarios.[380] While TOD living should reduce car use (and, as such, emissions), it can expose residents to Urban Heat Island effects. How is this? Public transport corridors and nodes tend to have large expanses of asphalt (for example, in car parks or wide roads) and hard building surfaces associated with increased urban density. High temperatures result from buildings, paving and roads trapping solar energy during summer days and slowly releasing it throughout the evening and night. As temperatures increase, sweltering residents switch on air conditioners, producing more anthropogenic heat, further exacerbating urban heat islands and climate change generally.[381]

While climate change mitigation is crucial, we must proactively consider adapting to future climates. As Jonathan Franzen puts it:

> *All-out war on climate change made sense only as long as it was winnable. Once you accept that we've lost it, other kinds of action take on greater meaning.*[382]

However, as emissions have accumulated in the atmosphere and the climate has deteriorated, Australia has been flying almost blind regarding adaptation.[383] While eminently logical from a reductive public transport perspective, TOD zones can be heat sinks in summer (Figure 45). Rather than densifying sites, which are already some of the hottest in our cities, we should be targeting the coolest areas, namely around parks. The name for the cooling effects of parks is very befitting: Park Cool Islands.[384] How does this cooling effect occur? In parks, vegetation intercepts most of the sun's energy, reflecting some and absorbing some for photosynthesis, reducing the total amount of heat absorbed. Furthermore, evaporation of water from vegetation also lowers the air temperature.[385] As a result of these processes, Park Cool Islands can offer refuge on hot summer days and even extend a marginal cooling effect into immediately adjacent urban areas.[386]

Given that heat stress is a serial killer in Australia, this proposal poses the question: What if we arranged apartments around green spaces that moderate summer temperatures (Figure 46) – through the Park Cool Island effect – and provide a wealth of other health benefits? Whatever we do to mitigate climate change, Australia should be adapting to hotter conditions. The 'adaptation task is vast and almost unquantifiable. But the quicker we confront it, the better we can manage it.'[387] Surely, putting people where they are at least risk from extreme heat, Australia's biggest natural killer, would be a good start.

Commentary

Keith
This is one of the many places where the solutions to climate change are a net gain for humanity.

John
People in apartments must be able to access clean and fresh air and open space – not pollution, noise and fumes, no one should have to live in that hellscape.

Alistair
The possible unintended error is likely to be down in the detail. We talk a lot about the need to re-establish patches of urban 'nature' to moderate summer temperatures and, in turn, buffer humans against episodic heatwave events within a changing climate. The Achilles heel is that 'nature', like humans, is also a living entity and is equally in line to be hammered by either slow, chronic stressors of climate change (E.g. long-term drying) or the intermittent cumulative products of slow change like 2019-20 black summer east coast blazes.

Figure 45: The hard surfaces associated with increased urban density and anthropogenic heat from air conditioners and cars can compound urban heat island effects.

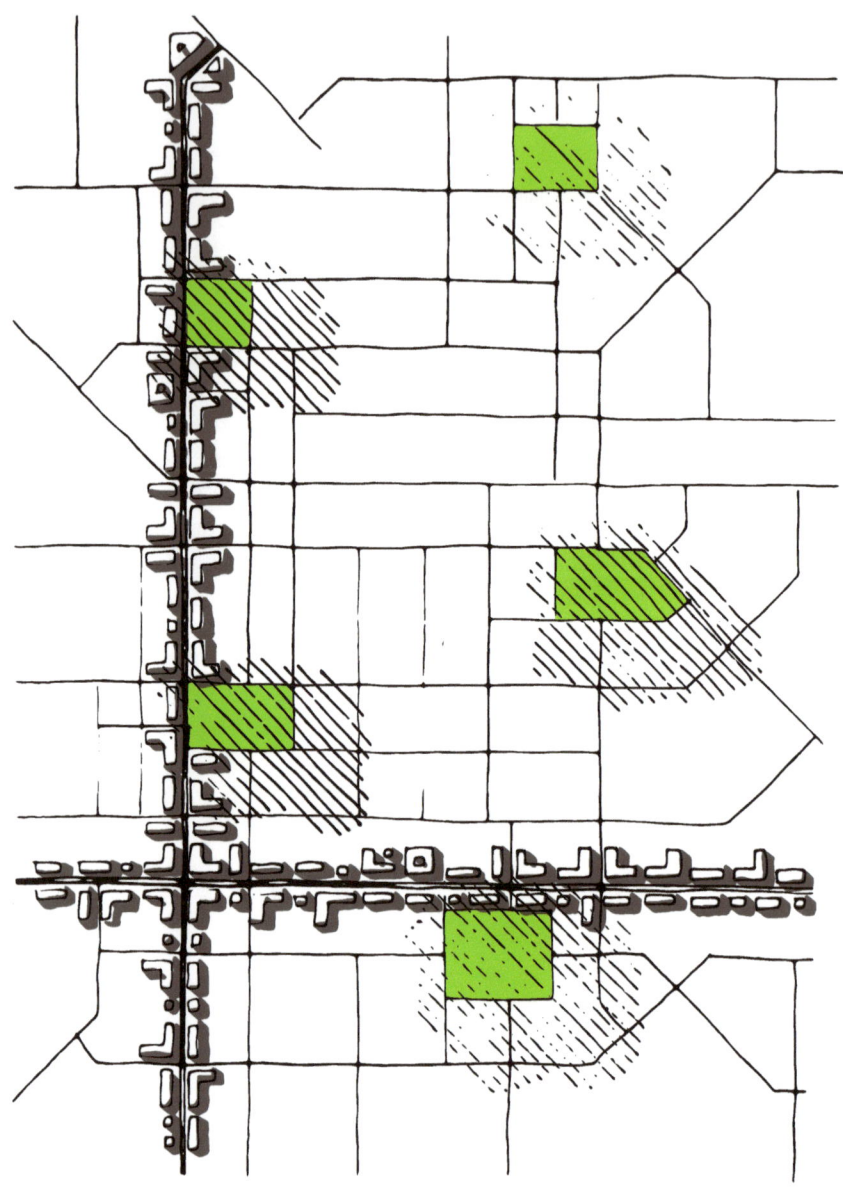

BAU: Urbanism

Figure 46: Resignation Urbanism
Site: Existing suburbs
Scale: District
Method: Assumption reversal (Assumption reversed: 'A focus on adapting our cities to future climate change is conceding defeat')
Relates to: Incentivised Urbanism

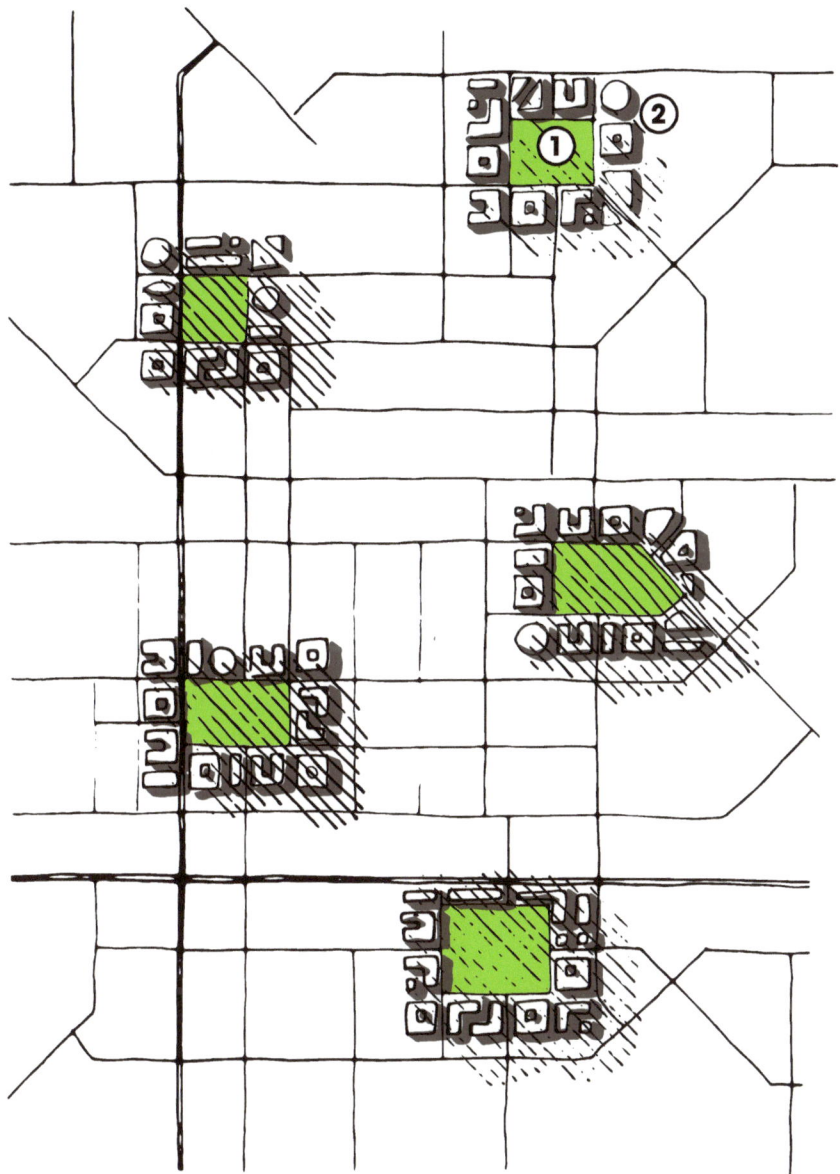

BAUn: Resignation Urbanism

Legend:
1. Park Cool Islands
2. Medium density housing

Shame Urbanism

As environmental activist Rob Hopkins explains, capitalism is a model that thrives by framing us as isolated consumers, encouraging a desire for things we don't need and a feeling of inadequacy if we fail to attain them.[388] Indeed, capitalism inherently relies on sustained economic growth, which requires it to incite new appetites constantly. In response, a fast-growing global middle class has embraced conspicuous consumption, an ideal propagated through advertising and the media.[389] As British writer Shumon Basar notes, shopping has become one of the celebrated contemporary panaceas for market-driven, liberal societies.[390]

The problem is that the profusion of cheap goods relies on global supply chains where meagre wages, brutal working conditions and trashing of the environment are not merely by-products of the production process but are vital to keeping prices low.[391] Our overconsumption collectively draws on natural capital stocks faster than natural systems can replenish them.[392] Moreover, suppose we were to estimate human happiness by pure purchasing power. In that case, the last half century should have been a joyfully happy time for people in wealthy nations such as Australia, the USA and Canada. As urbanist and writer Charles Montgomery explains:

> *Riches were piled upon riches. By the turn of the century, we ate more, bought more and threw away more stuff than ever before. More people than ever got to live the dream of having their own detached home. The stock of cars – and bedrooms and toilets – far surpassed the number of humans who used them.*[393]

Yet, a surge in joy did not accompany the late twentieth-century boom. Various surveys reveal that people's well-being assessment, instead, flatlined.[394] As historian Rutger Bregman neatly surmised, 'we live in an era of wealth and overabundance, but how bleak it is'.[395]

So, given the struggle to educate people about the effects of overconsumption, what more drastic approaches could we consider? The function of shame is to regulate social systems and hierarchies, and local governments could utilise it to curtail consumption. Activists first coined the term 'flygskam' or 'flight shame' in Sweden to evoke the unease about flying felt by environmentally aware travellers.[396] Spread online through Facebook groups such as 'Jag flyger inte – för klimatets skull' (which translates to 'I'm not flying – for the sake of the climate'), the campaign reputedly lowered the number of international flights into Swedish airports by 4 per cent within one year.[397]

But what about shame on the home front? This proposal poses the question, what if utilities shared household electricity and water meter readings on verges – would the shame of being the most significant energy or water user in the street cause us to change our behaviour? What if bins were transparent and communal and located at one end of the street, so you must do a 'walk of shame' down the street with your overflowing garbage bags full of ill-considered Shein and Temu purchases (Figure 47)? Ideally, people would change their consumption patterns because they care about the planet and its people – but if not, perhaps shame could be the key that unlocks stubborn behaviour.

Commentary

> **Tristan**
> Love your work, but this ain't it!

> **Momoh**
> Love this. Shame is a core concept in carceral logic, the structure of the prison system the world over. Very intriguing question for potential projects aimed at the missing middle urban design. This ultimately raises questions about the construction of our society. Shaking the table with this one!

> **Ben**
> Given the prevalence of increasingly large 'monster' trucks cluttering our streets and verges, I fear this would be a source of pride for many in WA!

> **Chloe**
> Shame used to oppress, switch channels, Julian!

> **Aaron**
> Gosh – that's walking a fine line of 'social credit score'?!

> **Edmund**
> I like the Japanese system. Everyone needs to buy the local transparent trash bags for plastics and organics and use those, then sort bottles, cans, metal objects, batteries, clothes, electronics, etc, outside at the local collection point in front of the watchful neighbours on collection days! Equally, they may be motivated by the praise they receive from neighbours, the status of being an organised person, or genuinely ulterior motives of doing good for society.

> **Rob**
> Some people use overconsumptionas a chauvinistic badge of honour (e.g., yank-tanks). Regulation would be much more effective. Tax residents for their waste the same way we measure water or power consumption.

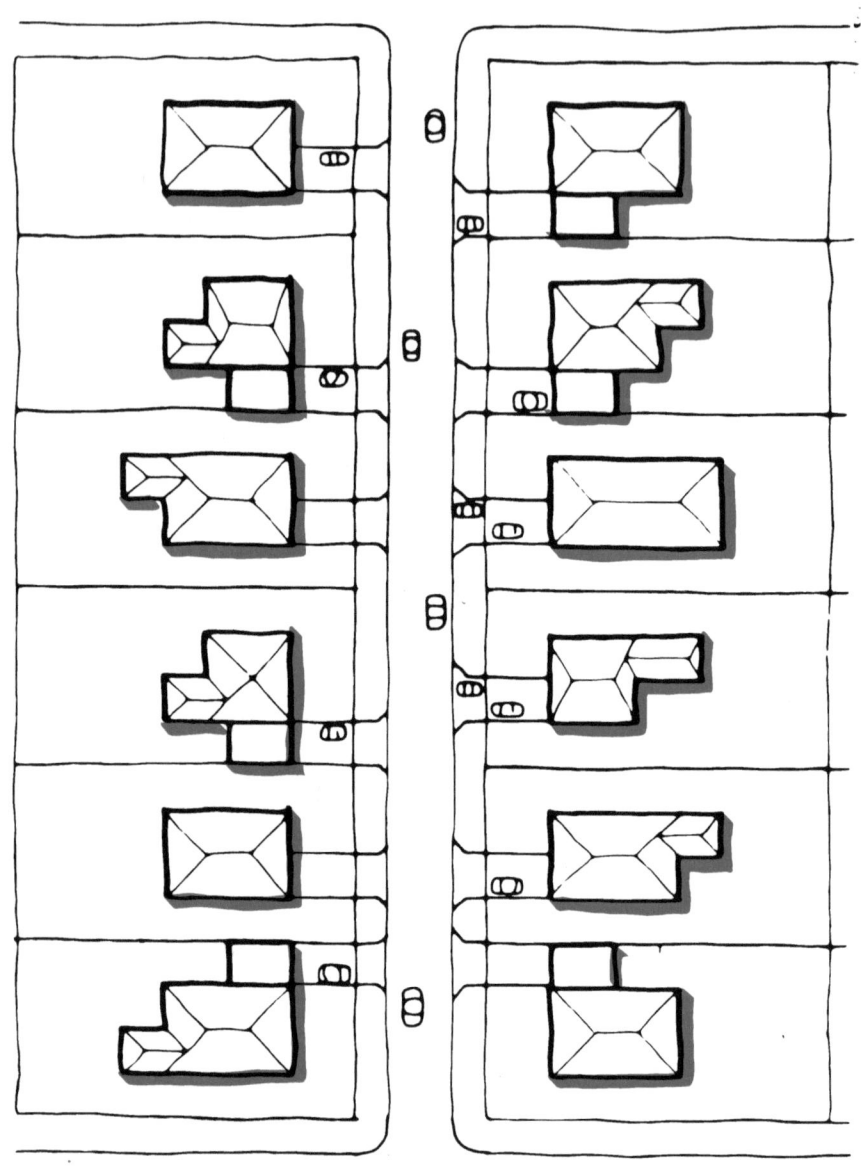

BAU: Urbanism

Figure 47: Shame Urbanism
Site: Existing suburbs/new suburbs
Scale: Street block
Method: Assumption reversal (Assumption reversed: 'Shame isn't an effective tool for affecting human behaviour in urban environments')
Relates to: Kibbutz Urbanism, Bunnings-lite Urbanism

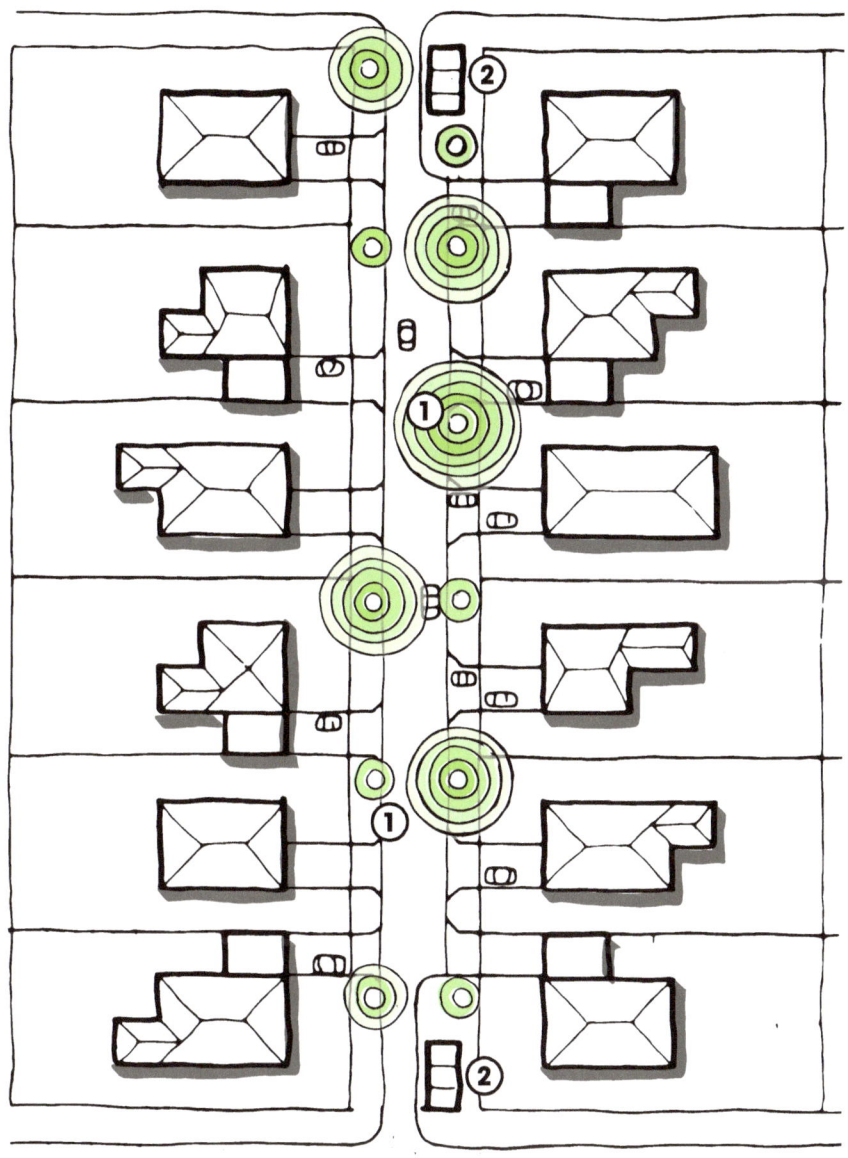

BAUn: Shame Urbanism

Legend:
1. Public electricity and water meter displays
2. Communal bins

Supergraphic Urbanism

 A few years ago, there were two structures in the world that could be seen from space: the Great Wall of China and the Hoover Dam. If we told people in 1977 that we intended to join China and the US and build a structure that could be seen from space, the response might have been, 'Dream on!' But, this unique 'club' of structures has now been joined by Dubai's The Palm Islands, the world's largest residential and tourism man-made islands.[398]
Mohammed bin Rashid Al Maktoum

When we get lost, the sense of anxiety reveals how directly our sense of orientation connects with our feelings of balance and well-being. Indeed, as American planner and author Kevin Lynch explains, the word 'lost' in our language means much more than simple geographical disorientation; 'it carries overtones of utter disaster'.[399] Conversely, a legible urban setting, producing a 'sharp image', facilitates wayfinding and enables us to move about simply and quickly: to find a friend's house, Hungry Jacks or a mobile phone store. However, this sharp image also plays an essential social role in providing the 'raw material for the symbols and collective memories of group communication'.[400] Indeed, a neighbourhood's images, symbols and landmarks can collectively hold a diverse population together, providing a rallying point binding disparate people and places.[401] A sharp urban image also gives its possessor a strong sense of emotional security. Through the image, they can forge a harmonious relationship between themselves and the world.[402] For instance, rivers can create physical boundaries that set limits and define territories.[403] Moreover, a line of rocky outcrops often surrounds traditional Middle Eastern villages, and the resulting sense of enclosure can have a powerful psychological effect on the population's identity and sense of belonging.[404]

Given the benefits of a sharp image of urban areas, it's surprising that more contemporary development doesn't rely on urban supergraphics. Perhaps Dubai-style development is the reason. Dubai's much-derided The Palm and The World developments (Figure 48) function as urban projects and supergraphics that brand the city from the perspective of Google Earth (not coincidentally, Dubai's autocratic ruler, Sheikh Mohammed, is a keen helicopter pilot).[405] The main criticism of such projects is that the actual human experience of residents is overlooked in favour of the branded image from Google Earth, which literally puts the projects on the map.

Perhaps this lineage has led to a reluctance for Australian designers to embed legible supergraphics into their projects. But maybe we have been too quick to dismiss the potential of the urban symbol for both wayfinding and as a community rallying point. Accordingly, this proposal poses the question of whether the open space structure could be elevated from comprising 'soft' green spaces to an encompassing supergraphic, which is the primary driver for the urban morphology (Figure 49).[406] For example, could a large and legible ring of open space assist with orientation and be the rallying symbol that binds together a community in our divisive times?

Commentary

Damien
Yes!

Natasha
Sure, open space is great. But it does seem to come with a lot of sponsorship logos and naming rights more and more often these days. Wouldn't it be great if public open space looked and felt public, not branded?

Rob
Grabbing attention is not enough. Lynch got it wrong when he overstated the importance of legibility over belonging. Legibility matters to tourists. Inhabitants become intimately familiar through inhabitation. This is a solution without

Rachel
Yes! Nice diagram. Start with the logic, character and connectivity of public places, be they parks, plazas or streets, rather than finish with a scratching calculation of 10 per cent 'Vegemite spread' open space left over after optimising yield on a mere quantitative basis.

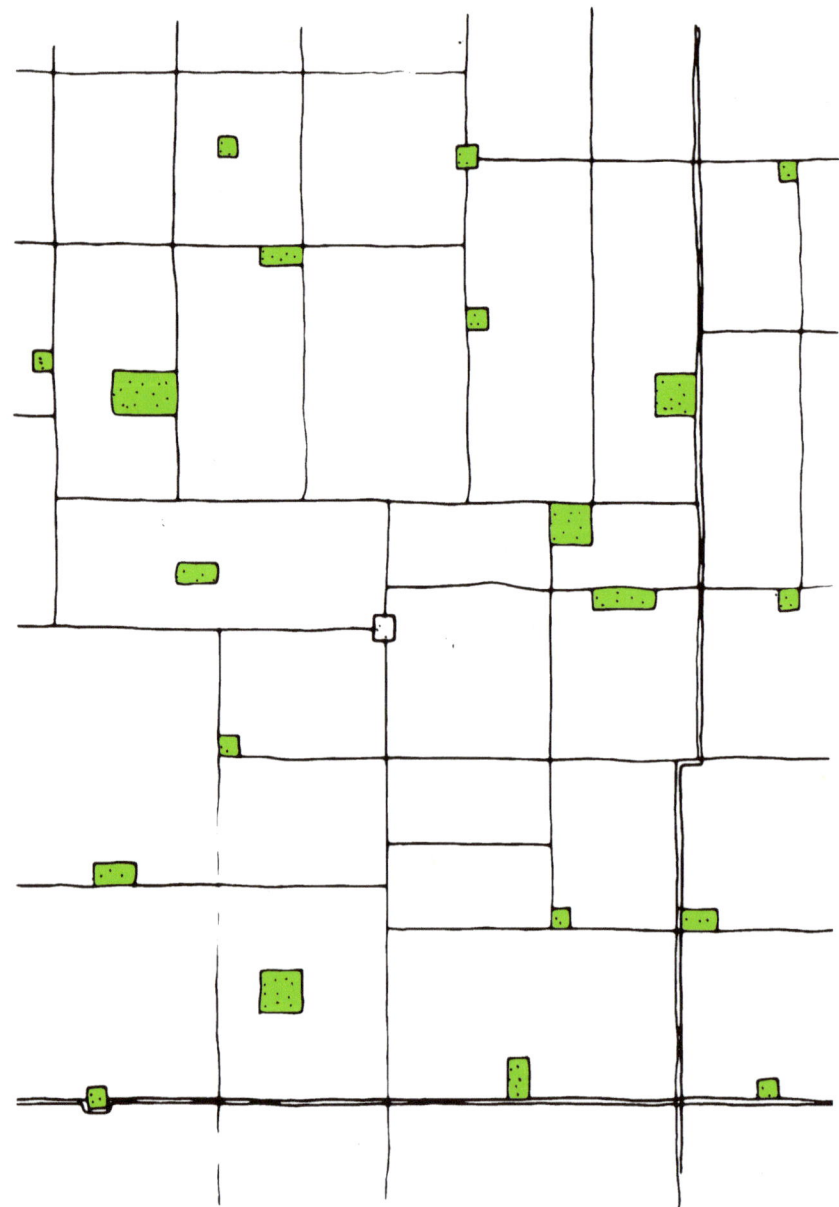

BAU: Urbanism

Figure 49: Supergraphic Urbanism
Site: New suburbs
Scale: Neighbourhood
Method: Recombinant innovation (Suburb + supergraphic)
Relates to: Symbolic Urbanism

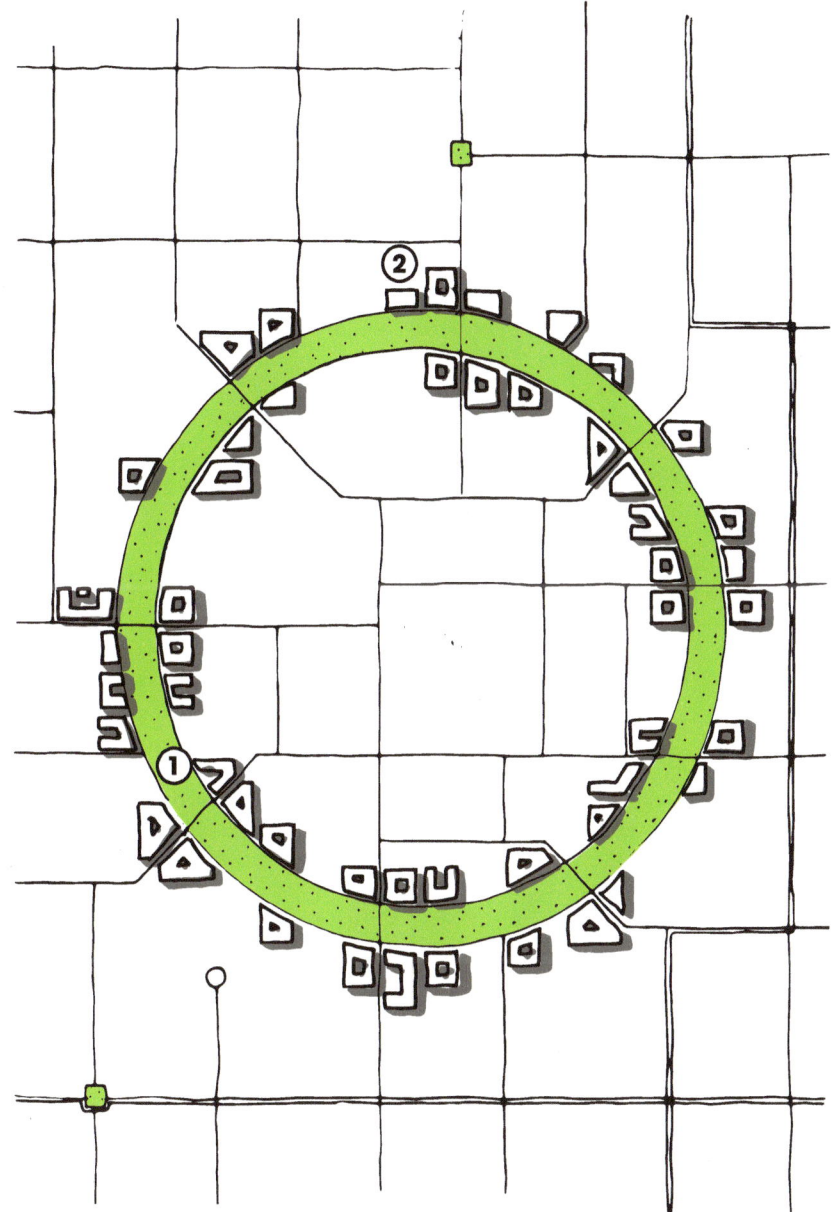

BAUn: Supergraphic Urbanism

Legend:
1. Supergraphic open-space structure
2. Medium-density housing

Symbolic Urbanism

 Do we really think a city is just a thing to move through as easily and efficiently as possible? Is this a complete failure of self-respect? Are we so soulless, so profoundly unromantic in our relations to ourselves and our habitat that we care more about efficiency than delight?[407]
Elizabeth Farrelly

Dating back to Hippodamus's (498–408 BC) city of Miletus, the urban grid has now effectively taken over the globe.[408] Why has the grid been so spectacularly successful? The grid is the fastest, most straightforward way to divide land so speculators can flog it off as real estate. Indeed, rectangular lots are easy to set out, buy, sell and tax.[409] For these reasons, the grid became the preferred system of colonisation worldwide. As an emblem of enlightenment par excellence, administrators and planners flung it across France and the United States with 'revolutionary zeal' in the later eighteenth century.[410] In Australia, the grid was the weapon of choice in forging most of the capital cities (except for Sydney and its wonky street network) and was a conjunction of various ideologies. Beyond sheer convenience was the need for a 'rational ordering of a strange space' and the establishment of 'an idealised European urban space coupled with a distancing of the Aboriginal landscape'.[411] Indeed, rectilinear plans yield a sense of fixity and suggest immutability and permanence,[412] characteristics no doubt appealing to colonial administrators struggling for a foothold in a foreign land.

Regardless of its associations with problematic colonisation, the grid has many defenders. New Urbanists rightly admire the clarity and connectivity that can make gridded neighbourhoods conducive to walking (as opposed to curvilinear cul-de-sac suburbs).[413] Traffic engineers also point out that a regular grid of arterial roads is less vulnerable to the infuriating delays that accidents can cause on dendritic road networks.[414] Moreover, the grid's ubiquitous presence provides a simple, logical and flexible framework for restructured renewal and urban consolidation.[415]

Despite the brutal efficiency and legibility of the grid, Kevin Lynch reminded us that 'there is some value in mystification, labyrinth, or surprise in the environment ... but only where there is no danger of long-term disorientation'.[416] Indeed, the long-term danger of the quest for legibility and efficiency (in which planning is to be seen as a science, not an art) is, as Kim Dovey describes, the 'boredom of formularized urban design', which results in cities as meticulous but soulless machines.[417]

Therefore, this proposal asks why neighbourhood design can't draw on richly symbolic archetypical forms to break away from our fixation with ruthlessly efficient but mute gridded forms (Figure 50). One such form is the inherently dynamic spiral that can suggest potentiality: the unspooling spiral indicates a latent power yet to be released (as well as mimicking the natural growth patterns of mollusc shells).[418] Of course, designers cannot plan urban configurations to achieve a fixed meaning, nor can a meaning be ascribed to them by decree. Instead, they evolve their meanings through people's actions.[419] That said, urban designers can design distinctive forms that collect divergent meanings over time. Indeed, utopian cities have generally had a distinctive geometric order throughout history. As Plato (428–348 BCE) noted, 'the city will never know happiness unless its draughtsman are artists who have the divine as their pattern'.[420]

Commentary

Ian
Urban nature trails. Great idea.

Kamran
The second one is completely impractical. No one would want to live in the middle, as it takes forever to go anywhere. Not to mention what inefficient use of space it is.
It's not happening. Ever.

BAU: Urbanism

Figure 50: *Symbolic Urbanism*
Site: *New suburbs*
Scale: *Street block*
Method: *Assumption reversal (Assumption reversed: 'Efficiency should trump delight')*
Relates to: *Radburn Urbanism 2.0, Car-phobic Urbanism*

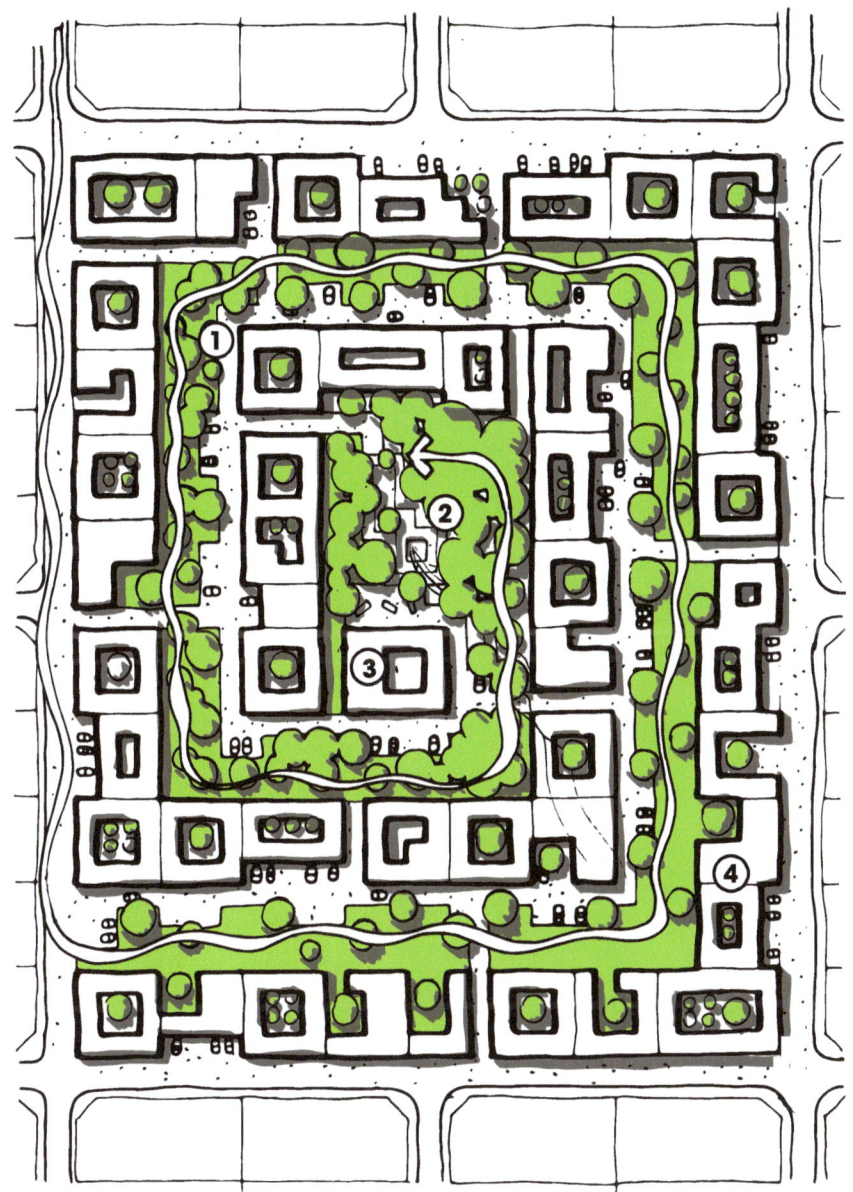

BAUn: Symbolic Urbanism

Legend:
1. *Spiral open-space structure*
2. *Fire pit*
3. *Communal facilities*
4. *Medium-density housing*

Tax-Break Urbanism

Most Australians desire a suburban way of life. Indeed, an entirely 'back to the city' future, as envisioned by some neotraditional urbanists, seems highly improbable short of the imposition of particularly heavy-handed planning regimes.[421] The long history of anti-suburban crusades has shown that such strategies almost always fail.[422]

In Australia and elsewhere, there is a tendency to 'admonish' suburbia for its failure to be urbane.[423] As planning academic Brendan Gleeson points out, an elitist perspective of the Australian urban system has 'construed suburbs as the root of the sustainability crisis'.[424] Indeed, due to the space available, suburban forms may – in some respects – offer more significant advantages than higher-density alternatives, making sustainability 'retrofitting' of suburbia a worthy prospect (Figure 51).[425] Indeed, suburban forests can provide a wide range of benefits, including improvement in human health and well-being and mitigating air pollution, stormwater run-off and the urban heat island effect, and are even linked to decreased crime and noise.[426] Moreover, suburban areas also have ample space for food and energy production.

Nonetheless, urban planners can be blind to opportunities for sustainability at suburban, not urban, densities. This is strange because, as George Seddon explained, historically, the suburban backyard was essentially rural, 'a gesture towards functional self-sufficiency, not complete, but not totally dependent on a web of urban services as we are today'.[427] Indeed, meagre supplies, little refrigeration, patchy services and recurring poverty and shortage, such as in the 1890s and 1930s depressions and the Second World War, meant that suburban dwellers came to rely on their backyard (and sometimes front yard) to supplement meagre diets and even incomes.[428]

So, rather than vilifying suburbia as a wasteful and culturally barren wasteland,[429] this proposal poses the question: What if governments stimulated 'high-performance' suburbia by providing rates and tax breaks for residents whose gardens reap environmental and societal benefits for the surrounding neighbourhood? These could include planting trees to cool microclimates, provide habitats and boost human well-being; renting land to Small Plot Intensive Network (SPIN) farmers to grow fresh food; or installing small, affordable, ancillary dwellings to address chronic housing shortages (Figure 52). Perhaps changes to tax regimes – already used to promote infill development or limit sprawl[430] – are the key to unlocking suburban sustainability. Indeed, as governments respond sluggishly to the looming climate crisis, our house and our garden are one of the limited areas in our lives where we have considerable power to make decisions and put them into practice[431] – at least if given a reasonable financial incentive.

Figure 51: Due to the space available, suburban forms can offer more significant advantages than higher-density alternatives, making sustainability 'retrofitting' of suburbia a worthy prospect.

Commentary

Heather
Criticism of suburbia is wholly legitimate. No matter how good retrofitting the suburbs is, nature is being permanently destroyed and degraded. Species are becoming extinct, be it a spider, an orchid, or a bee. It is not elitist to value all life and to want to fight for it.

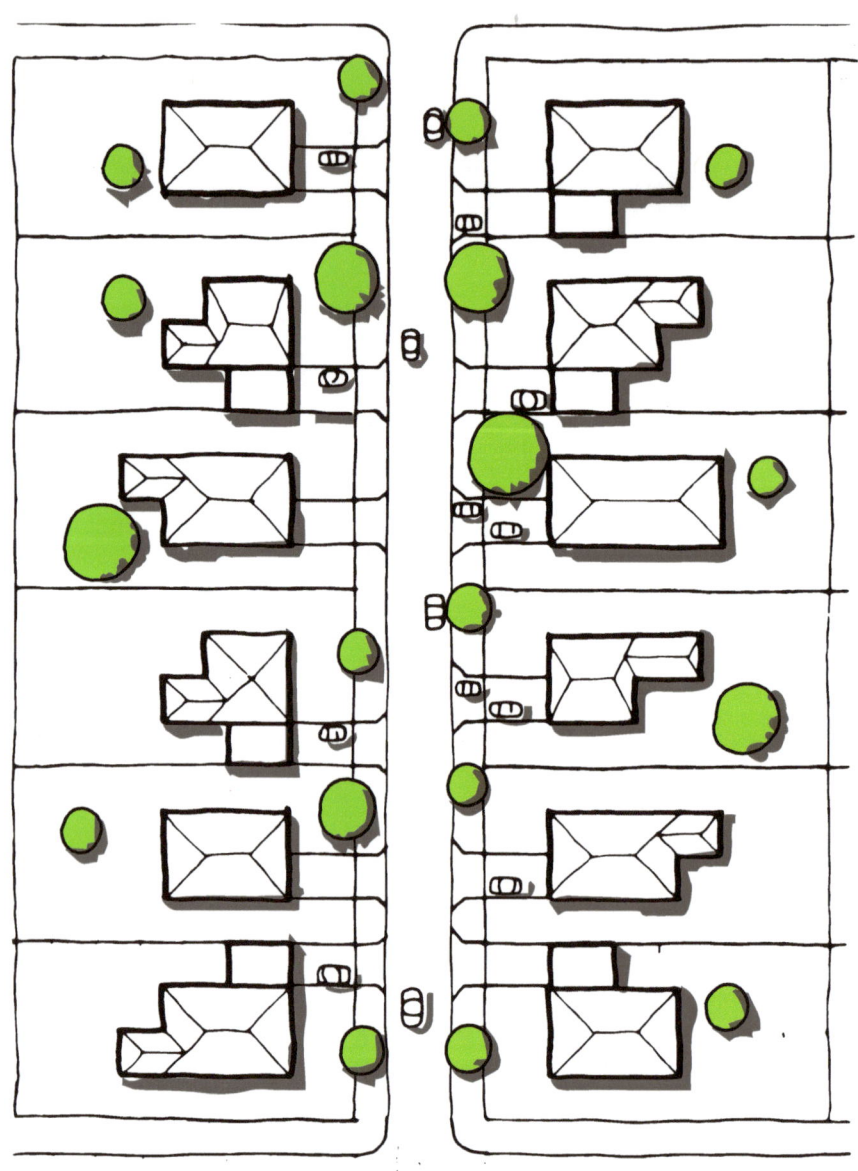

BAU: Urbanism

Figure 52: *Tax-Break Urbanism*
Site: *Existing suburbs*
Scale: *Street block*
Method: *Recombinant Innovation (Suburb + tax breaks)*
Relates to: *Resignation Urbanism*

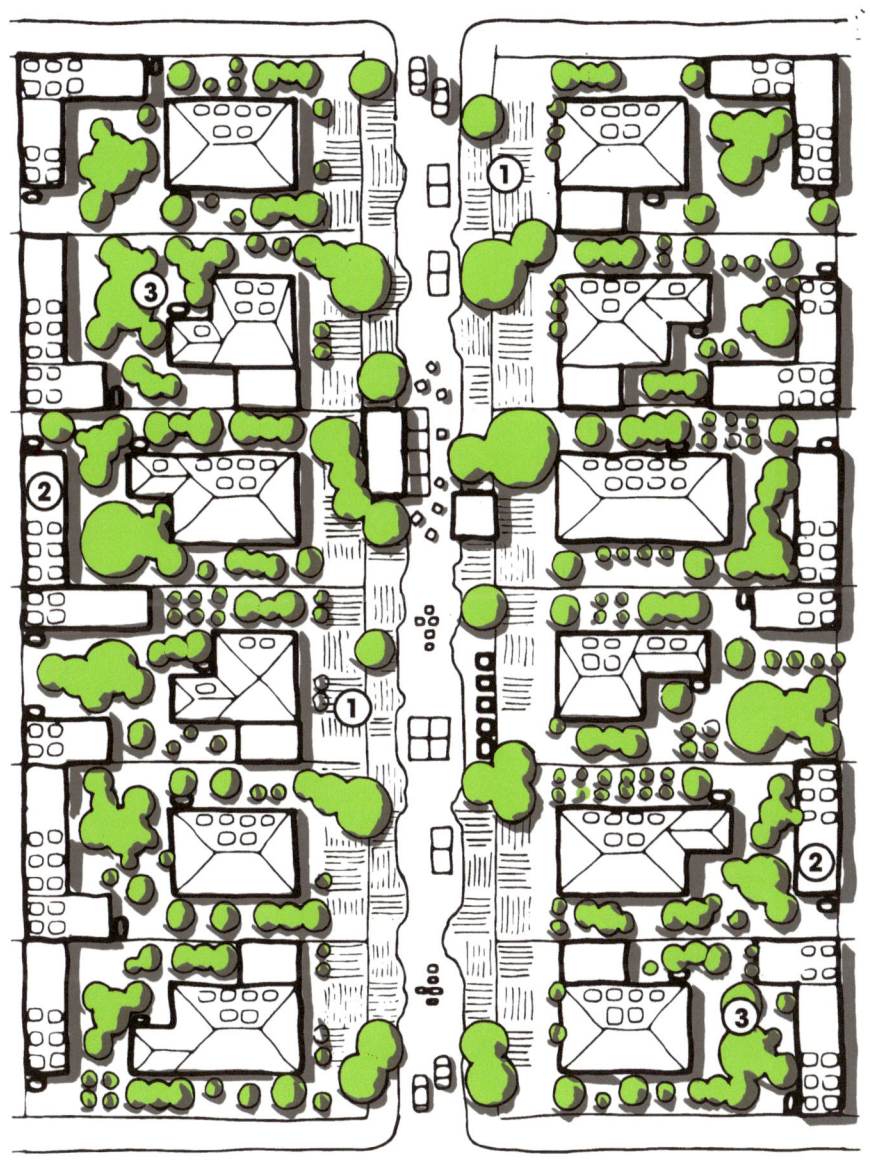

BAUn: Tax-Break Urbanism

Legend:
1. Small Plot Intensive Network (SPIN) farming
2. Ancillary dwellings
3. Urban forest

Tinder Urbanism

 In Chloe, a great city, the people who move through the streets are all strangers. At each encounter, they imagine a thousand things about one another; meetings which could take place between them, conversations, surprises, caresses, bites. But no one greets anyone; eyes lock for a second, then dart away, seeking other eyes, never stopping.[432]
Italo Calvino

Australians are increasingly solitary people.[433] Indeed, almost 15 per cent of Australians, or 3.9 million people, experience social isolation (having few social relationships), and a further 16 per cent, or 4.1 million people, experience loneliness (a painful feeling of a lack of connection to other people).[434] Worryingly, researchers have found a correlation between loneliness, poor physical and mental health, and even premature death.[435]

So why are so many of us so lonely? Shifting demographics provides a clue. The fastest-growing household type in Australia is lone-person households, which undoubtedly reflects and contributes to social isolation and loneliness. At the same time, we rattle around in the world's largest houses (per occupant), and the average total size of new dwellings is a vast 214m².[436] This emergence of lone-person households reflects an ageing and divorcing society, and of lone-person households, 54 per cent contain a widow, 33 per cent a separated or divorced person and 17 per cent an unmarried person.[437]

Countering growing loneliness, compact cities (and their cafes, bars and urban spaces) carry the 'potential for the high-density random social encounter of the crowd',[438] which can spark new social and romantic connections. However, while city life enhances the possibility of contact between people, commentators, such as American social critic James Kunstler, regard the suburb as striving to eliminate precisely that kind of human contact.[439]

This proposal poses the question of whether the ability of urban areas to cultivate social interaction is just about density. Could we design chunks of our suburbs principally for lone-person households (e.g., recent divorcees) as 'social condensers'[440] that spark interactions between varied people, like a physical version of a dating app? Rather than drive-in, lock-up garages that impede interactions (Figure 53), residents would park on the neighbourhood's edge and walk to their modest ~75m² dwellings (equivalent to the UK average house size[441]) along path networks, facilitating spontaneous social encounters (Figure 54). Moreover, small patios adjoining each dwelling would have low-height walls to allow for interactions with passers-by. Communal letterboxes could enable chance encounters, and community gardens could grow food and relationships simultaneously. Given we are amidst a loneliness epidemic, shouldn't we swipe right on social suburbs?

Commentary

Luana
Bring back front porches!

Setayesh
Live alone in your luxury palace and be the King of Walls

Justin
Culture is just as important as design. The diagram on the left is typically suburban. Fill those houses with your stereotypical Aussie family, and then you do have the lack of connection issues noted. 'We' drive home, lock ourselves inside via the garage, and occupy our lounge or backyard (for those lucky enough to have one of usable size). Take that same design somewhere like Iluma Estate in Bennett Springs. With a strong Indian demographic, I've witnessed time and time again (usually late afternoon) tens of families walking up and down the streets/POS, engaging with each other and other community members. Same design, different social outcomes. Design helps, but it is certainly not the silver bullet.

Figure 53: Lock-up, remote-opening garages diminish opportunities for informal social encounters.

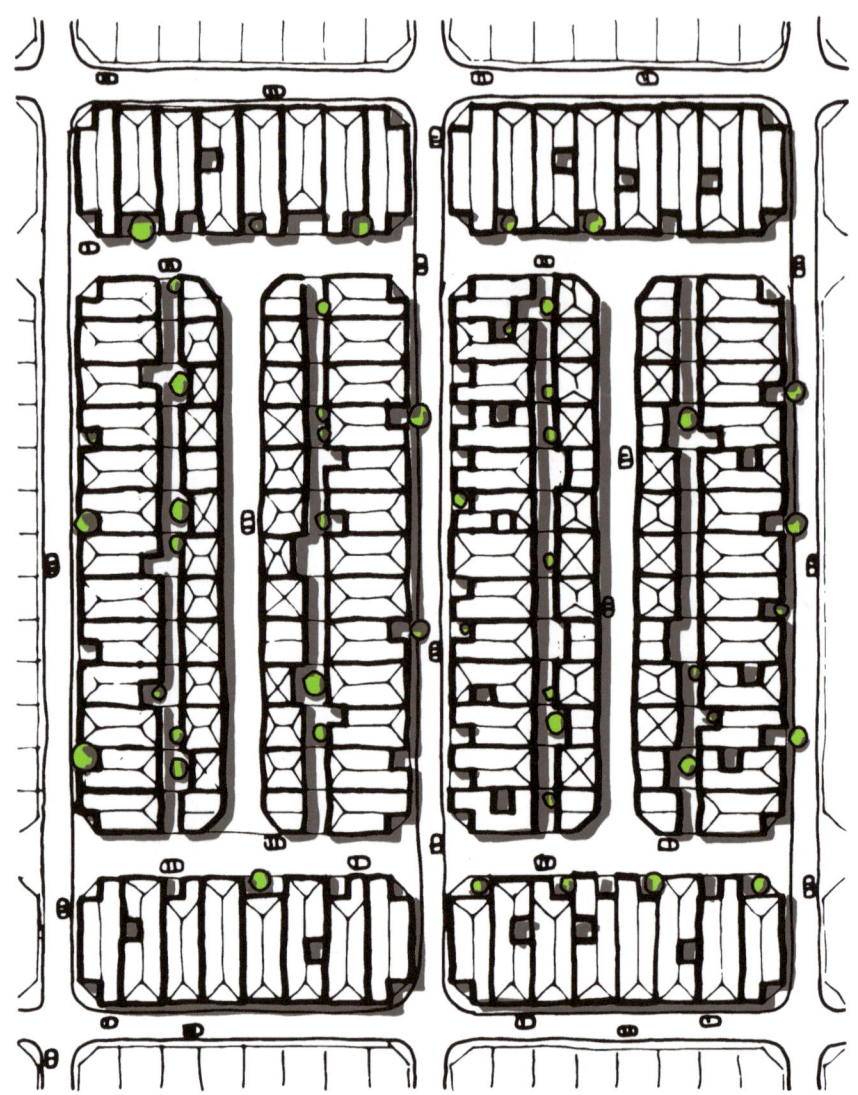

BAU: Urbanism

Figure 54: *Tinder Urbanism*
Site: *New suburbs*
Scale: *Street block*
Method: *Assumption reversal (Assumption reversed: 'Only truly urban areas facilitate high-density random social encounters')*
Relates to: *Kibbutz Urbanism*

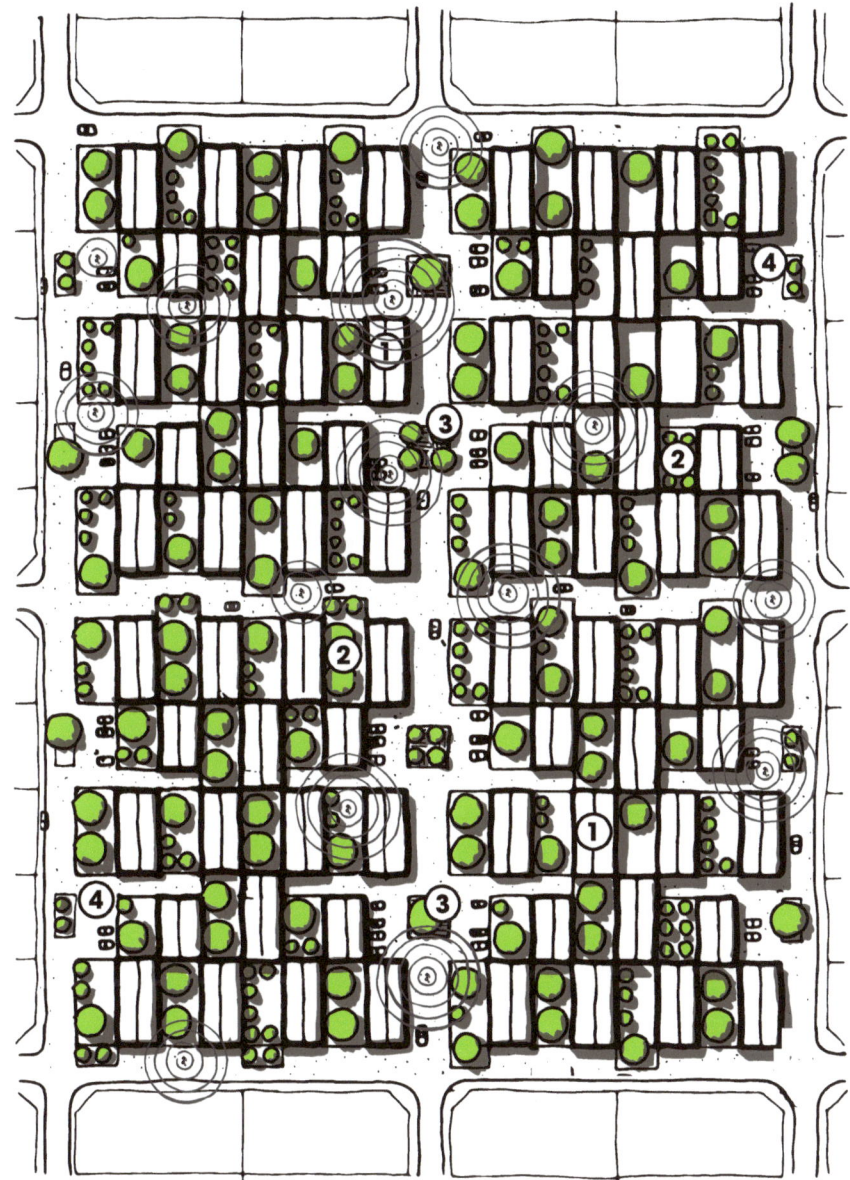

BAUn: Tinder Urbanism

Legend:
1. Modest dwellings
2. Patios with low walls
3. Communal gardens and letterboxes
4. Communal parking

Undercover Urbanism

 To go into the dark with a light is to know the light. To know the dark, go dark. Go without sight, and find that the dark too, blooms and sings, and is travelled by dark feet and dark wings.[442]
Paul Bogard

John Glenn was the third US astronaut to orbit the Earth in 1962. At the behest of the Western Australian State Government, its citizens switched on as many lights as possible on a February evening as a sign of support.[443] As he orbited aboard his spacecraft *Friendship 7*, Glenn admired the twinkling city lights and thanked the people of Perth, and as a result, the city was (for a moment) tagged the 'City of Lights'.[444]

Lighting offers important use, comfort and safety benefits. As a result, governments are introducing lighting systems into previously unlit communities in the Global South, but they are also increasing intensity in already urbanised areas.[445] Fast-forward sixty years on from *Friendship 7*, and light pollution surges at 6 per cent annually globally. Street lighting and light from advertising, buildings, houses and cars all contribute to light pollution at night. However, street lighting is the primary concern as it is generally the most constant and intense lighting in urban areas. As a result, street lighting alone uses a whopping 114-terawatt hours of energy globally per year.[446]

To put the intensity of street lighting into perspective, without artificial light, a clear starry sky gives an illumination of 0.001 lux. In contrast, standard street lighting results in illumination of between 10 and 60 lux.[447] The resulting light pollution has significant ecological implications, including impacts on animals that experience disorientation, attraction, fixation and the rewiring of biological rhythms. This includes nocturnal animals that use subtle moonlight and starlight to forage. Also, patterns of light and darkness regulate circadian rhythms of activity to modulate the behaviour of animals and to initiate seasonal events such as bud burst and flowering.[448] In the human animal, artificial light at night affects circadian rhythms, altering physiological processes, including brain electrical activity, hormone generation and cell regulation (Figure 55). Rewiring the circadian clock relates to multiple medical disorders such as depression, insomnia, cardiovascular disease,[449] breast and prostate cancer, and increased obesity (to name just a few).[450]

Nonetheless, lighting consultants, energy providers and financial experts (not ecologists or public health officials) generally make decisions about streetlighting in our cities because streetlighting is a hefty expense for governments.[451] In response, concerned scientists have established programs such as the International Dark Sky Places to protect natural unlit areas and halt the increasing invisibility of stars due to light pollution.[452] However, these safeguarded areas are often outside our cities and of marginal use to urban biodiversity.

Securing and increasing natural unlit areas is the most effective way to reduce the ecological effects of city lighting.[453] Indeed, the recent development of centrally managed lighting systems allows operators to adjust street lighting schedules remotely in real time.[454] Street lighting can be turned off or dimmed during critical times of high biological activity, such as when foraging, breeding or migratory activities are in process.[455] The introduction of 'adaptive' lighting, in which the movements of people and cars determine the level of street lighting, also has potential.[456]

In response, this proposal asks: given we have historically switched on the lights for orbiting astronauts, could we periodically turn off street lighting (and ideally other lights) in key neighbourhoods at key times of ecological importance to provide refuges of darkness that mobile animals can exploit (Figure 56)?[457] The spin-offs could be limiting a colossal use of energy, a good night's sleep and a clear(er) panorama of the night sky – 'a shared cultural heritage of all humanity'.[458]

Figure 55: In humans artificial light at night affects circadian rhythms, altering physiological processes, including brain electrical activity, hormone generation and cell regulation.

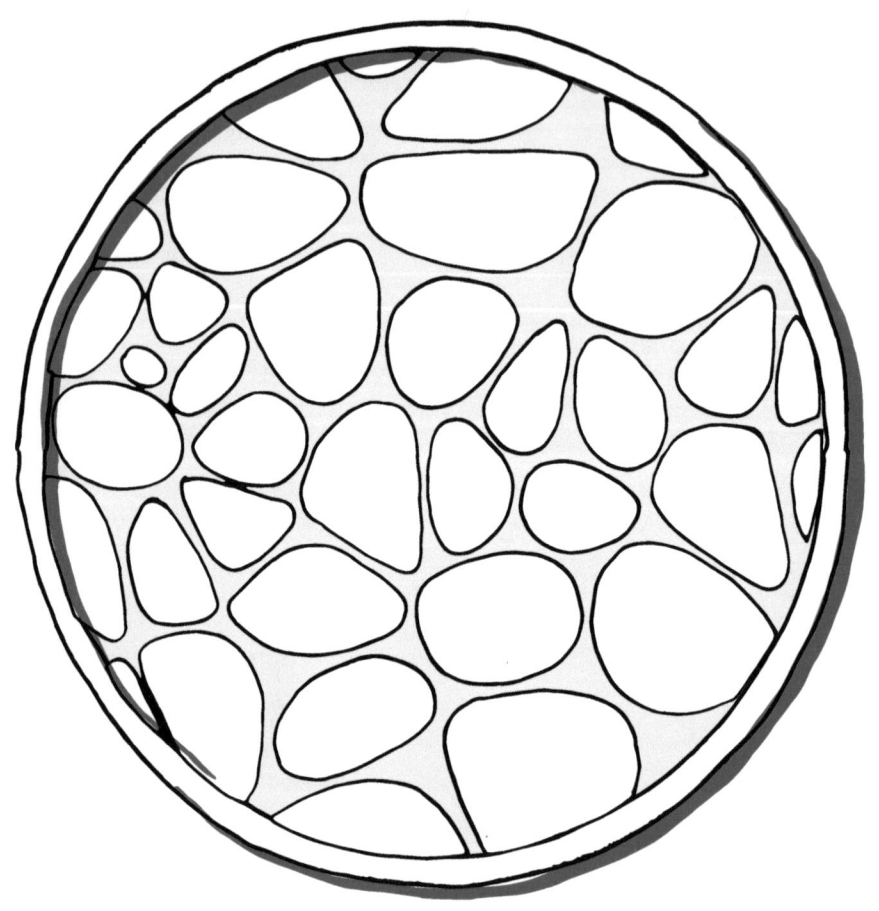

BAU: Urbanism

Figure 56: *Undercover Urbanism*
Site: *Existing suburbs/new suburbs*
Scale: *Neighbourhood*
Method: *Assumption Reversal (Assumption reversed: 'Human use, comfort and safety benefits of lighting should override ecological harm')*
Relates to: *Dumb Urbanism, National Park Urbanism*

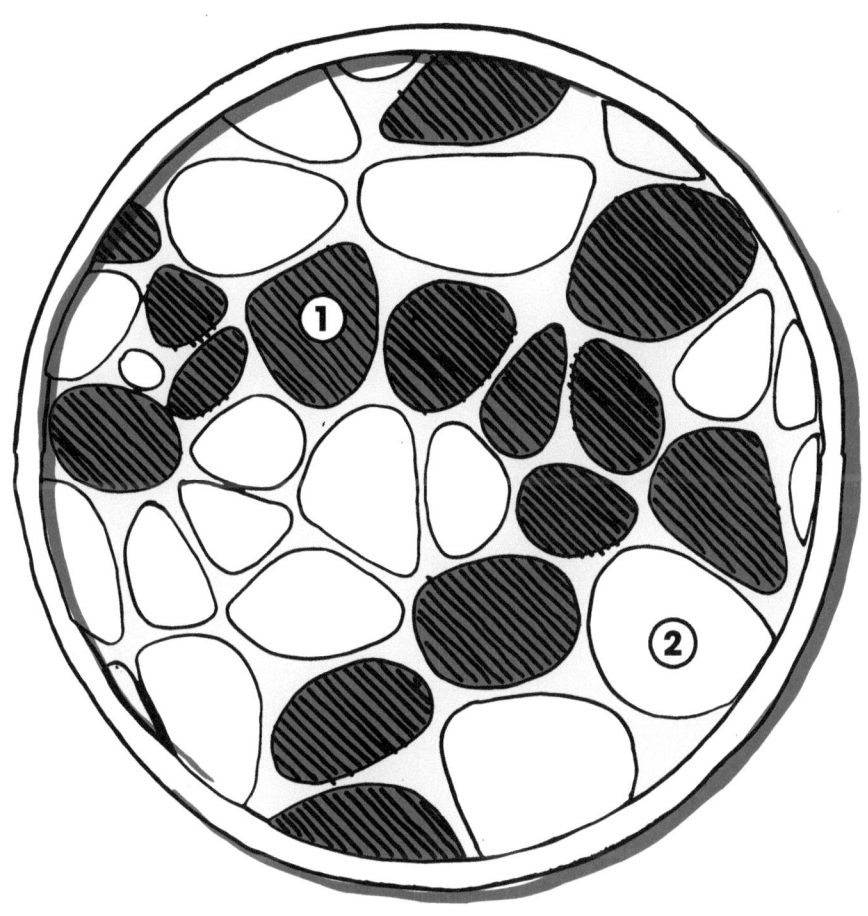

BAUn: Undercover Urbanism

Legend:
1. Lights off
2. Lights on

Woollies-Lite Urbanism

 Ending food waste could, in theory, cut the scale of the agriculture industry in half without any loss of access to the food we presently need. That would allow us to regenerate up to 2.4 billion hectares of land for wildlife habitat and carbon sequestration.[459]
Jason Hickel

Globally, we will require a 70 per cent increase in agricultural production to feed the projected mid-century population.[460] The world is experiencing burgeoning food demand because of this population surge and shifts in developing countries toward Western-style, meat-heavy diets.[461] At the same time, people waste almost half of all the food produced globally – equivalent to an incredible 2 billion tonnes – every year. The Food and Agriculture Organisation estimates that food waste emits 8 per cent of total (human-caused) greenhouse gas emissions annually. Indeed, if food waste were a country, it would be the third largest emitter globally, just trailing the USA.[462] In wealthy nations, food waste is due to supermarkets forcing farmers to discard cosmetically imperfect vegetables, utilising unnecessarily strict sell-by dates on food items and luring in customers with bulk discounts for food items they don't get around to eating. Subsequently, households ditch 30 to 50 per cent of the food[463] they lug home from the shops or a gig-economy slave or diesel truck delivers (Figure 57). This food waste represents an exorbitant ecological cost of energy, land, water and emissions.[464]

Australia is a global food exporter, generating about three times as much food as its population requires, mainly in cereals and meat.[465] However, it would be naive to conclude that food security is not a problem: Australia's population is surging, its scarce water resources are receding, and its agricultural monocultures are highly vulnerable to climate variability.[466] Regardless, according to the Australian Government, Australia wastes 7.6 million tonnes of food annually, costing already-stretched households $2,500 each.[467] Indeed, the land used to grow wasted food in Australia encompasses more than 25 million hectares, a landmass more immense than the state of Victoria.[468] Moreover, based on industry profit margins, supermarkets make $1.2 billion from this waste.[469]

So, how could we address this lamentable situation? Communal camp kitchens, as found in national park campsites, provide a clue. These camp kitchens (with a BBQ, microwave, fridge and seating areas) provide a venue for campers to meet and, more importantly, share food ('We are leaving today, would you like to have our sausages?'). Perhaps one answer to our food-waste crisis would be to build communal camp kitchens (with fridges and hotplates) in suburban streets, where residents can share food, costs and cooking duties (who has time to cook anyway?). The results could be less food waste (slashed greenhouse emissions, reduced animal suffering, freed-up farming land for ecological purposes) and a connected community (Figure 58).[470]

With apologies to Woolworths.

Commentary

Domenic
Perhaps, but having come from a producer background, I'd suggest preventing the problem in the first place by continuing pressure on big supermarket practices. Rationally, consumers don't want to 'waste' produce, but unfortunately, they are often against a rigged system, and it's not 'by chance' that their food has spoilt earlier than expected or not what they should expect.

Figure 57: Households ditch 30 to 50 per cent of the food they lug home from the shops.

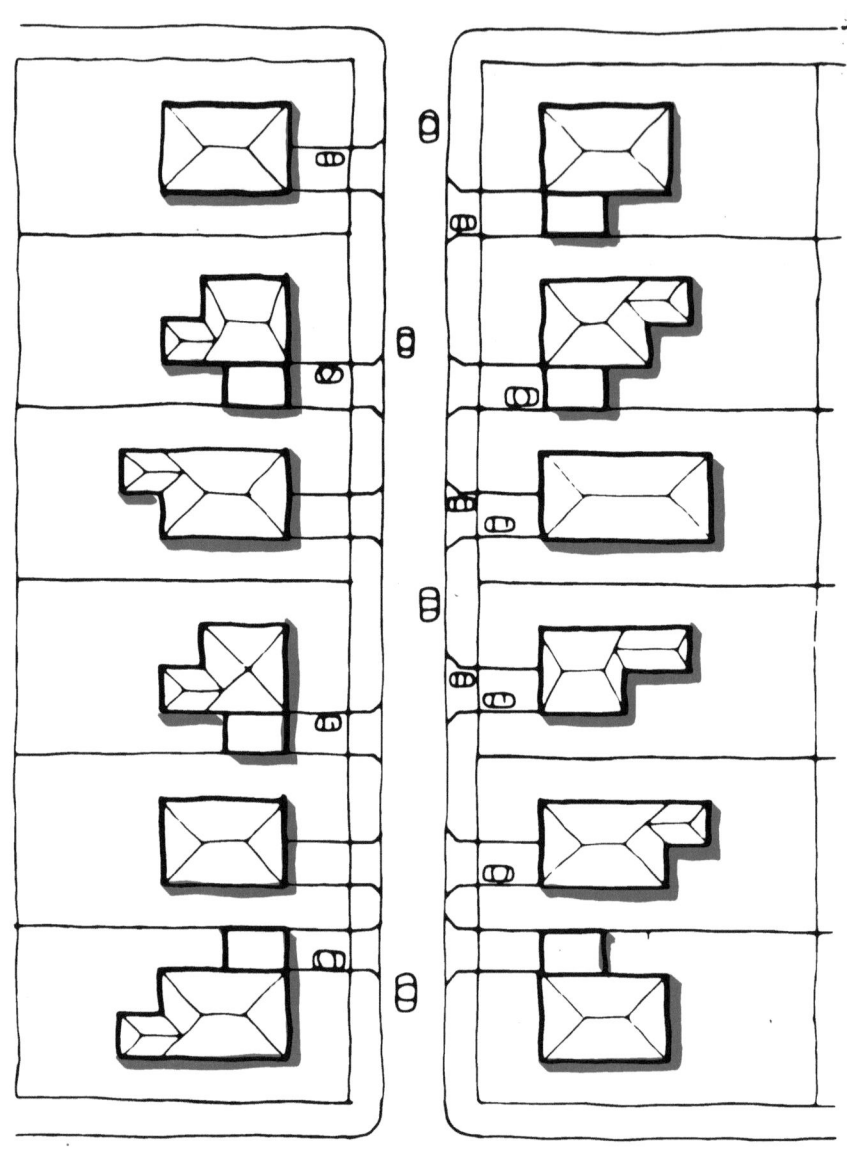

BAU: Urbanism

Figure 58: Woollies-Lite Urbanism
Site: Existing suburbs
Scale: Street
Method: Recombinant innovation (Camp kitchen + suburb)
Relates to: Bunnings-lite Urbanism, Kibbutz Urbanism, Edible Urbanism

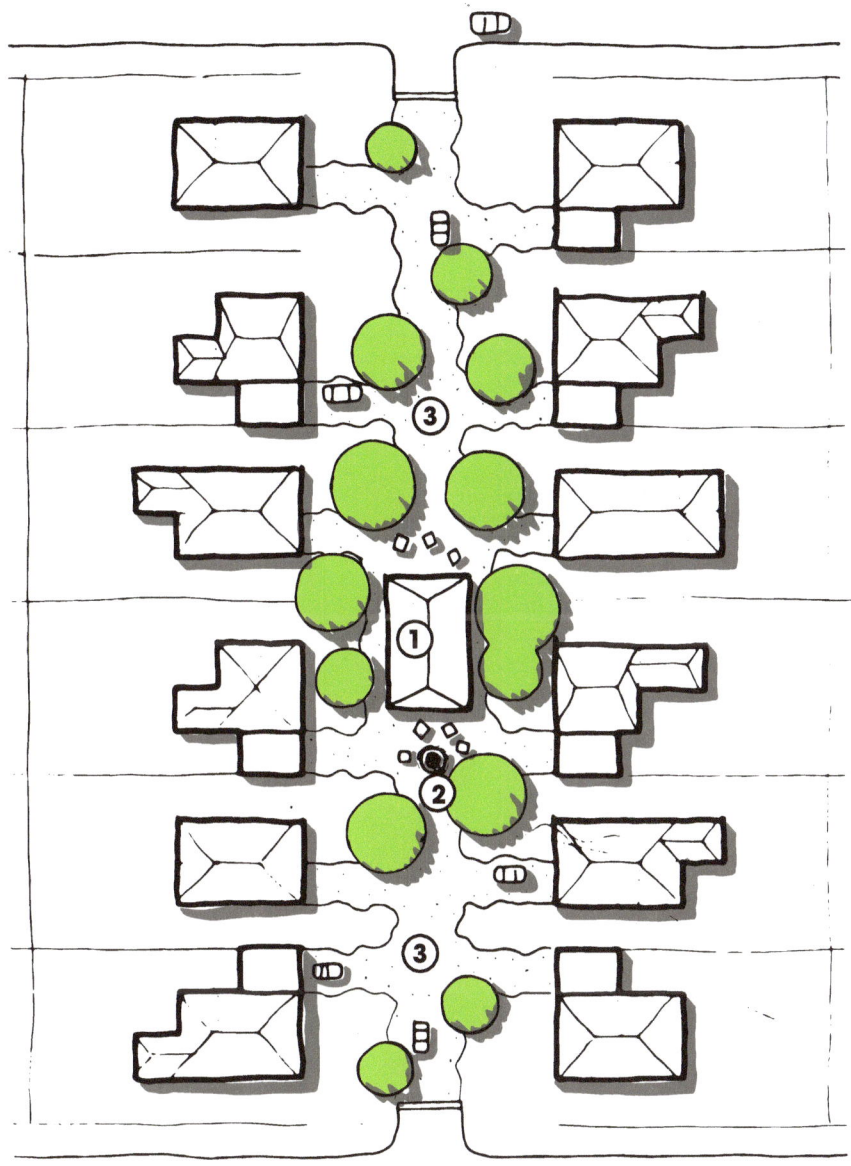

BAUn: Woollies-Lite Urbanism

Legend:
1. *Communal camp kitchen*
2. *BBQ*
3. *Pedestrianised road*

CONCLUSION: TOWARDS BUSINESS AS UNUSUAL

Many of the proposals tabled in this noisy collection range from implementable to polemical, with many shades in between. While I intend this book as a conversation starter and not a manual for implementation, it would be amiss not to suggest how policymakers or the development community could wrestle select proposals into reality. To frame this discussion, I have loosely divided the alternative urbanisms into three categories, which inevitably overlap to some degree. The first category is 'utopias of form', which is primarily spatial and, as such, is (broadly speaking) implementable in that it focuses on urban form rather than the complex underlying processes that generate urban form. The second category is 'utopias of process', which is, to some degree, spatial but also requires some engagement with the bureaucratic, political, societal and economic systems that underpin urban development or management. The third category is 'polemics', which I have intended less as a proposal to be directly implemented and more as a counterbalance, ideally freeing up the rigidity of current modes of BAU thinking.

Utopias of form

Proposals such as Inside Out Urbanism, Laneway Urbanism, Supergraphic Urbanism and Symbolic Urbanism are examples of primarily spatial propositions that conventional developers could deliver within tweaked regulatory frameworks. However, developers only deliver housing for profit; development won't occur without this profit.[471] So, could these proposals deliver such profit? The answer hinges on the willingness of buyers to break away from entrenched housing models (the five-bedroom, two-bathroom home with a double garage and a postage-stamp-sized backyard) for a smaller dwelling with generally a more intimate connection with nature (e.g., as provided in Laneway Urbanism).

The tendency of these proposals to carve out significant swathes of developable land as public or communal open space likely works against development feasibility unless it is attractive and adjacent enough to lure in homebuyers who would pay the premium. Clearly, there is a growing interest in pursuing alternative ways of living closer to nature and within ecological limits – as such, there could be an increasing market for some of the proposals. However, whether the lure of inhabiting a quirky urban experiment can overwhelm real-world pressures for a solid, safe 'bricks and mortar' investment in a suburban home is unclear.

Utopias of process

The urban geographer David Harvey argues that many contemporary urban developments fail to achieve lofty goals for social equity because of their erroneous assumption that spatial form can reshape societal processes.[472] He reasons that the struggle for urban planners and designers ought to lie less with finding novel spatial forms (such as 'utopias of form') than with 'the advancement of a more socially just, politically emancipating and ecologically sane mix of spatiotemporal production processes', challenging the general submission to the forces of 'uncontrolled capital accumulation' (utopias of process).[473] His point is that the processes of urbanisation are more significant for the forging of urban relationships than spatial forms.[474] Examples of proposals that embrace a utopia of process and new 'organising structures' include Bunnings-Lite Urbanism, Woollies-Lite Urbanism, Deregulation Urbanism, Enlightenment Urbanism, Kibbutz Urbanism and Modern Urbanism 2.0. Examples like Bunnings-Lite Urbanism are potentially easily implementable because they are bottom-up[475] proposals that residents could install over a weekend, and utilise mostly existing social networks.

However, as the idea of collaborative consumption scales up, as in Kibbutz Urbanism, more headwinds are experienced, and questions quickly arise as to the processes by which residents could successfully manage and maintain the communally owned land, vegetable gardens, orchards and even small communal buildings. Nonetheless, two opportunities are evident. While not a perfect system, apartments in higher-density developments are subject to a common management agreement governed by an owners' corporation (comprising individual owners) generally responsible for managing communal spaces.[476] Proponents could apply such established governance models to Kibbutz Urbanism (amongst other proposals). Even better, in the *Baugruppen* (translated from German as 'building group') model, a co-housing buyer group leads the development process, allowing the buyers to be directly involved in designing and planning their home and community. This model obviates the need for developers (builders eventually construct the project) and is often not-for-profit, keeping the purchase costs reasonable.[477] Such models also ensure that those buying into the project are committed to co-living, which would be vital in many proposals.

Other proposals, such as Enlightenment Urbanism, Effluent Urbanism or Eternal Urbanism, present problems in asking government departments to step beyond their jurisdictional boundaries to engage with other generally unrelated departments (and the private development industry). German sociologist Max Weber famously argued that people working within bureaucracies live inside an 'iron cage',[478] and such inter-silo collaborations would face inevitable headwinds. For instance, Enlightenment Urbanism would require planning departments to 'up zone' areas around schools and work with housing departments or private developers to deliver family-friendly apartments while also working with education departments to ensure the programming of the school can provide a genuine community hub that appeals to children, parents, grandparents and non-parents alike. Proponents may pursue similar arrangements with cemetery boards to deliver Enlightenment Urbanism. Finally, Effluent Urbanism requires water utilities to work hand-in-hand with planning departments to coordinate water and nutrient resources with planning for open space. Nonetheless, readers should note that TOD requires urban-related planning departments to work together with public transport and road building agencies, so such inter-silo collaborations are not unprecedented.

Finally, proposals such as Modern Urbanism 2.0 are yet more 'aspirational' as they require a fundamental shift away from Neoliberalism, which has been entrenched in Australia and elsewhere since the early 1970s. In Neoliberalism, several critical economic and political realignments occurred, and the government's function pivoted from modest welfare to gross deregulation.[479] Mass housing through Modern Urbanism 2.0 at the scale discussed requires city, state and federal governments to get back in the business of funding, acquiring and building public housing. It sounds far-fetched in Australia, but it is not unprecedented. In state-capitalist Singapore, over 80 per cent of residents from all classes live in public housing. Singapore is not a utopia but it at least demonstrates that some cities already successfully function with mass public ownership.[480]

Polemics

The final suite of proposals, such as Dumb Urbanism, Island Urbanism or Shame Urbanism, function as polemics as much as serious proposals. The word *polemic* comes from the Greek *polemos* or war. Thus, a polemic is a controversial argument, often produced to dispute or refute a widely accepted idea.[481] For instance, Dumb Urbanism challenges the orthodoxy that ubiquitous and unrestricted internet connectivity is fundamentally healthy for society. Shame Urbanism challenges the slightly naive idea that people need to be 'inspired' for ethical reasons to curtail their consumption – and instead adopts less of a carrot and more of a stick approach. Clearly, polemical urbanisms hit a nerve in social media. Not without some reason, too. Many people don't like polemics because a polemic is not seeking the 'truth' (i.e. being objective, fair or balanced) but instead aims to change the opinion of others by consciously overstating its case.[482]

Nonetheless, polemics can perform an important function. Swiss psychologist Jean Piaget identified two processes of cognitive development: assimilation and accommodation.[483] Assimilation is the process of integrating new chunks of information into existing cognitive structures (like fitting a piece into a puzzle).[484] Conversely, accommodation is triggered when existing cognitive structures prove inadequate in comprehending new ideas, forcing people to adjust their thinking (like realizing that the puzzle piece doesn't fit and modifying the puzzle to make it work).[485] At their best, polemics can be the puzzle pieces that don't fit, thus ushering in new ways of thinking.

Conclusion

 The inability to imagine a world in which things are different is evidence only of a poor imagination, not of the impossibility of change.[486]
Rutger Bregman

Although it can be challenging to see beyond the limitations of our current urban system (as some comments on social media would attest), something must give. Due to climate change alone, we are witnessing the 'radical destabilization of life on Earth'.[487] Due to climate change and dizzying technological advancement,[488] our cities are all grappling with 'novel uncertainties'[489] and will be unimaginably different one hundred years from now. That change will occur is definite.[490] Indeed, the past reinforces a simple but pertinent lesson that things will be different. How our world evolves is not the preordained result of some self-evident progression.[491]

Indeed, one of the most crucial but now forgotten lessons from the COVID-19 pandemic was revealing how flexible even stubborn, long-standing behaviour is.[492] Within weeks of the pandemic's arrival, people pulled their plans to travel.[493] Cars remained parked in carports, aircraft hung around in hangars, cruise ships moored in home ports and in-person meetings flipped over to Zoom.[494] While it was distressing at times, the enormous power of creativity is hidden in this very instability of life that the pandemic revealed. In such change processes, many new forms, possibilities and expressions of urban design and planning potentially arise,[495] and as a result the city can change dramatically.[496]

What is Business-As-Unusual now can indeed become Business-As-Usual.

Acknowledgements

This book and its diagrams grew from a series of LinkedIn posts from 2022 to 2024. Thanks to the many people who wrote constructive comments responding to my sometimes-unhinged ideas. The intelligence, insightfulness and wit of the comments have restored my faith in social media.

Well, almost.

I am grateful to my exceptional colleagues from the Australian Urban Design Research Centre (AUDRC) at the University of Western Australia's School of Design: Dr Maassoumeh Barghchi, Wala Beliah, Dr Robert Cameron, Dr Nicole Edwards, Nicolas Mojica Gonzalez, Bill Grace and Jill Penter. Dr Cameron provided a highly constructive yet combative review of an early draft, precisely what the book needed. Thanks to Head of School Dr Kate Hislop for her support over the years.

Thanks to AUDRC's funding partners, the Western Australian Planning Commission, DevelopmentWA and the Department of Communities for supporting AUDRC and making it all possible (noting the opinions in this book are my own and do not necessarily reflect the views of funding agencies...). In particular, I am grateful to AUDRC Advisory Board chairs David MacLennan and Fred Chaney for their contributions and counsel through the years.

Finally, thanks to my family: my dad, Ross Bolleter, for wading through a draft of the book (while apparently on holiday) and helping to nudge the book along with steady praise and encouragement. My sister, Amanda Bolleter, for her excellent guidance in navigating the perils of office politics and middle management. Finally, to my daughter, Rose Bolleter, and wife, Dr Sally Appleton, for supporting yet another book project, particularly as it inevitably spilled into family evenings – scratching away with my drawing pens and tracing paper to the soundtrack of *Young Sheldon*, *Lark Rise to Candleford* and *Slow Horses*.

BIBLIOGRAPHY

Abram, D 1997, *The spell of the sensuous: perception and language in a more-than-human world*, Vintage Books, New York.

Abu-Lughod, JL 1980, 'Contemporary relevance of Islamic urban principles', *Ekistics*, vol. 47, no. 280, pp. 6-10.

Al Maktoum, MbR 2012, *My vision: challenges in the race for excellence*, Motivate Publishing, Dubai.

Alexander, C 1977, *A pattern language: towns, buildings, construction*, Oxford University Press, Oxford.

AlSayyad, N & Guvenc, M 2015, 'Virtual uprisings: On the interaction of new social media, traditional media coverage and urban space during the "Arab Spring"', *Urban Studies*, vol. 52, no. 11, pp. 2018-34.

Amirahmadi, H & Razavi, M 1993, 'Urban development in the Muslim world: Encounter with modernity and implications for planning', *Urban Development in the Muslim World*, pp. 1-36.

Andrews, FJ, Warner, E & Robson, B 2019, 'High-rise parenting: experiences of families in private, high-rise housing in inner city Melbourne and implications for children's health', *Cities & Health*, vol. 3, no. 1-2, pp. 158-68.

Auster, M 1988, 'Colonial beginnings: building a better world?', *Australian Planner*, vol. 26, no. 3, p. 6.

Australian Academy of Science 2021, *The risks to Australia of a 3°c warmer world*, Canberra.

Australian Bureau of Statistics 2013, *Population projections, Australia, 2012 to 2101*.

—— 2021, *Household and family projections, Australia*, Australian Government, viewed 24 07 2024, <https://www.abs.gov.au/statistics/people/population/household-and-family-projections-australia/2021-2046>.

—— 2023, *Labour force status of families*, Australian Government, viewed 24 07 2024, <https://www.abs.gov.au/statistics/labour/employment-and-unemployment/labour-force-status-families/latest-release>.

Australian Conservation Foundation 2020, *New report reveals extinction crisis in the suburbs*, Australian Conservation Foundation, viewed 19 10 2023, <https://www.acf.org.au/new_report_reveals_extinction_crisis_in_the_suburbs>.

Australian Golf Industry Council 2022, *Water and the Australian Golf Industry*.

Australian Institute of Family Studies 2015, Demographics of living alone, Australian Government, viewed 04 04 2025, <https://aifs.gov.au/research/research-reports/demographics-living-alone>.

Australian Institute of Health and Welfare 2023, *Mental health*, Australian Government, viewed 25 07 2024, <https://www.aihw.gov.au/mental-health/topic-areas/mental-health-prescriptions>.

Barlow, M & Levy-Bencheton, C 2019, *Smart cities, smart future*, Wiley, New Jersey.

Barnett, J & Bouw, M 2022, *Managing the climate crisis: Designing and building for floods, heat, drought, and wildfire*, Island Press.

Basar, S 2007, 'Twelve ultimate critical steps to sudden urban success', in *Vision plus money plus historical circumstance equals 'cities from zero' unapologetic expressions of new- found economic and therefore political- prowess in the 21st century*, Architectural Association Publishing, London, pp. 73-95.

Bar-Yosef, E 2013, 'New cities for new Jews: Haifa as futuristic urban fantasy in Theodor Herzl's Altneuland and Violet Guttenberg's A Modern Exodus', *Journal of Modern Jewish Studies*, vol. 12, no. 2, pp. 162-83.

Bengston, D, Fletcher, J & Nelson, K 2004, 'Public policies for managing urban growth and protecting open space: Policy instruments and lessons learned in the United States', *Landscape and Urban Planning*, vol. 69, pp. 271-86.

Berger, A, Kotkin, J & Guzman, C 2017, 'Introduction', in A Berger, J Kotkin & C Guzman (eds), *Infinite suburbia*, MIT, Boston, pp. 10-23.

Bhoge, R, Nolan, H & Pojani, D 2020, 'Designing the subtropical city: an evaluation of climate-sensitive policy effects in Brisbane, Australia', *Journal of Environmental Planning and Management*, vol. 63, no. 10, pp. 1880-901.

Bhowmik, A 2020, 'Flight shaming: how to spread the campaign that made Swedes give up flying for good', *The Conversation*, viewed 25 07 2024, <https://theconversation.com/flight-shaming-how-to-spread-the-campaign-that-made-swedes-give-up-flying-for-good-133842>.

Bicudo de Castro, V & Kober, R 2018, 'The principality of Hutt River: A territory marooned in the Western Australian outback', *Shima (Sydney, N.S.W.)*, vol. 12, no. 1.

Biggs, JD, Fouché, T, Bilki, F & Zadnik, MG 2012, 'Measuring and mapping the night sky brightness of Perth, Western Australia', *Monthly notices of the Royal Astronomical Society*, vol. 421, no. 2, pp. 1450-64.

Bogard, P 2019, The End of Night: Searching for Natural Darkness in an Age of Artificial Light, HarperCollins, New York.

Bolleter, J 2015, *Scavenging the suburbs: Auditing Perth for 1 million infill dwellings*, University of Western Australia Publishing, 2015.

—— 2019, *Desert paradises: Surveying the landscapes of Dubai's urban model*, Routledge, London.

Bolleter, J, Myers, Z & Hooper, P 2020, 'Delivering medium-density infill development through promoting the benefits and limiting background infill', *Journal of Urban Design*, pp. 1-26.

Bregman, R 2018, *Utopia for realists*, Bloomsbury Publishing.

Bullen, J & Tarasov, n 2016, 'Australians spend eight times more hours per week looking at screens than with loved ones: survey', *ABC News,* viewed 21 05 2017, <http://mobile.abc.net.au/news/2016-08-11/australians-spend-46-hours-per-week-with-screens-six-with-family/7718930>.

Burgess, R & Jenks, M 2000, 'The compact city debate: A global perspective', in M. Jenks & R Burgess (eds), *Compact cities, sustainable urban form for developing countries,* Routledge, pp. 21-36.

Burns, C 1944, 'Athens had more housing conscience than us', *The Argus*, 19.08, p. 2.

Burton, P 2017, 'South East Queensland: Change and continuity in planning', in R Freestone & S Hamnett (eds), *Planning Metropolitan Australia*, Routledge, Abingdon, pp. 156-77.

Calvino, I 1978, *Invisible cities*, Houghton Mifflin Harcourt, Boston.

Cameron, R 2020, 'Constructing authenticity: Location based social networks, digital placemaking, and the design of centralized urban spaces', in L Rajendran & N Dellé Odeleye (eds), *Mediated Identities in the Futures of Place: Emerging Practices and Spatial Cultures*, Springer International Publishing, pp. 133-51.

Carlton, I 2009, 'Histories of transit-oriented development: Perspectives on the development of the TOD concept', *Institute of Urban & Regional Development*.

Carmichael, CE & McDonough, MH 2019, 'Community stories: Explaining resistance to street tree-planting programs in Detroit, Michigan, USA', *Society & Natural Resources*, vol. 32, no. 5, pp. 588-605.

Chan, G 2018, *Rusted off: why country Australia is fed up* Vintage Australia, Sydney.

Congress of New Urbanism 2016, *The charter of the New Urbanism*, Congress of New Urbanism, viewed 15 08 2016, <https://www.cnu.org/who-we-are/charter-new-urbanism>.

Coole, D 2018, *Should we control world population?*, Polity Press, Cambridge.

Cooper, JAG & Lemckert, C 2012, 'Extreme sea-level rise and adaptation options for coastal resort cities: a qualitative assessment from the Gold Coast, Australia', *Ocean & Coastal Management*, vol. 64, pp. 1-14.

Corner, J 2003, 'Landscape urbanism', in *Landscape urbanism a manual for the machine landscape*, Architectural Association, London, pp. 58-62.

Davison, G 2003, 'Fatal attraction? The lure of technology and the decline of rural Australia 1890-2000', *Tasmanian Historical Studies*, vol. 8, no. 2, p. 40.

—— 2016, *City dreamers: the urban imagination in Australia*, NewSouth Publishing, Sydney.

Department of Climate Change, Energy, the Environment and Water 2024, *Reducing*

Australia's food waste, Australian Government, viewed 06 01 2024, <https://www.dcceew.gov.au/environment/protection/waste/food-waste#:~:text=Each%20year%20Australians%20waste%20around,Australia's%20annual%20greenhouse%20gas%20emissions>.

Diamond, J 2011, *Collapse: How societies choose to fail or survive*, Penguin Books, London.

—— 2019, *Upheaval: How nations cope with crisis and change*, Penguin, New York.

Doherty, G 2008, 'The landscape of Dubai's urbanism', in *Instant cities; emergent trends in architecture and urbanism in the Arab world*, CSAAR, Amman, pp. 103-11.

Dondero, J 2020, *Supercities on, under, and beyond the earth: housing, feeding, powering, and transporting the urban crowds of the future*, Rowman & Littlefield, London.

Dovey, K 2005, *Fluid city: transforming Melbourne's urban waterfront*, Routledge, London, New York.

—— 2016, *Urban design thinking*, Bloomsbury Academic, London.

Dovey, K & Sandercock, L 2005, 'Riverscapes 1- overview', in *Fluid city: transforming Melbourne's urban waterfront*, Routledge, London, New York.

Duany, A & Plater-Zyberk, E 2015, 'The neighbourhood, the district, and the corridor', in RT LeGates & F Stout (eds), *The City Reader*, Routledge, London, pp. 207- 26.

Duany, A & Talen, E 2013, *Looking backward: Notes on a cultural episode*, New Society Publishers, Gabriola Island.

Dunham-Jones, E 2011, *Retrofitting urban solutions for redesigning suburbs*, Wiley, New Jersey.

Elliot, R 2017, 'Australia's misplaced war on the Australian Dream', in A Berger & J Kotkin (eds), *Infinite suburbia*, MIT, Boston, pp. 104-13.

Fairchild, C 2014, 'Driverless cars a boon for working moms?', *Fortune,* viewed 25 11 2014, <http://transact.org/>.

Farr, D 2008, *Sustainable urbanism: Urban design with nature*, John Wiley and Sons, New Jersey`.

Farrelly, E 2021, *Killing Sydney: The fight for a city's soul*, Picador, Sydney.

Fishman, R 2003, 'Urban utopias: Ebenezer Howard, Frank Lloyd Wright, and Le Corbusier', in S Campbell & S Fainstein (eds), *Readings in planning theory*, Blackwell Publishing, Oxford, Melbourne, pp. 21-60.

Fitzpatrick, JF & Jian, Z 2016, 'Using China's experience to speculate upon the future possibility of Special Economic Zones (SEZ) within the planned development of northern Australia', *Flinders LJ*, vol. 18, p. 29.

Flannery, T 2020, *The climate cure: Solving the climate emergency in the era of COVID-19*, Text Publishing.

Forman, R 2010, *Urban regions: ecology and planning beyond the city*, Cambridge University Press, Cambridge.

Forrest, J, Poulsen, M & Johnston, R 2006, 'A "multicultural model" of the spatial assimilation of ethnic minority groups in Australia's major immigrant-receiving cities', *Urban Geography*, vol. 27, no. 5, pp. 441-63.

Forster, C 2006, 'The challenge of change: Australian cities and urban planning in the new millennium', *Geographical Research*, vol. 44, no. 2, pp. 173-82.

Fox, M & Wang, A *Symbols: A handbook for seeing*, The Monacelli Press.

Francis, J, Wood, LJ, Knuiman, M & Giles-Corti, B 2012, 'Quality or quantity? Exploring the relationship between Public Open Space attributes and mental health in Perth, Western Australia', *Social Science & Medicine*, vol. 74, no. 10, pp. 1570-7.

Franzen, J 2021, *What if we stopped pretending?*, 4th Estate, London.

Freestone, R, Davison, G & Hu, R 2019, *Design the global city: Design excellence, competitions and the remaking of central Sydney*, Palgrave Macmillan.

Freestone, R, Garnaut, C & Iwanicki, I 2011, 'Cold War heritage and the planned community: Woomera Village in outback Australia', *International Journal of Heritage Studies*, vol. 18, no. 6, pp. 541-63.

Freestone, R & Nichols, D 2012, 'Reinvigorating 20th-century residential pocket parks for the 21st century', paper presented to 5th Healthy Cities: Working Together to Achieve Liveable Cities, Geelong.

García-Haro, A, Arellano, B & Roca, J 2023, 'Quantifying the influence of design and location on the cool island effect of the urban parks of Barcelona', *Journal of Applied Remote Sensing*, vol. 17, no. 3, pp. 034512-.

Gaston, KJ, Davies, TW, Bennie, J & Hopkins, J 2012, 'Reducing the ecological consequences of night-time light pollution: options and developments', *The Journal of Applied Ecology*, vol. 49, no. 6, pp. 1256-66.

Giblett, R 1996, *Postmodern wetlands: Culture, history, ecology*, Edinburgh University Press, Edinburgh.

Gilbert, P 2017, *Living like crazy*, Anwyn House, Derbyshire.

Gillen, M 2006, 'The challenge of attaining a sustainable urban morphology for South East Queensland', *Planning, Practice & Research*, vol. 21, no. 3, pp. 291-308.

Gleeson, B 2006, 'Waking from the dream: Towards urban resilience in the face of sudden threat', *Griffith University Urban Research Program*.

—— 2010, *Lifeboat cities*, UNSW Press, Sydney.

—— 2015, *The urban condition*, Routledge, London.

Goodman, R 2017, 'Melbourne: Growing pains for the liveable city', in R Freestone & S Hamnett (eds), *Planning metropolitan Australia*, Routledge, Abingdon, pp. 59-83.

Goodman, R & Moloney, S 2004, 'Activity centre planning in Melbourne revisited', *Australian Planner*, vol. 41, no. 2.

Goodspeed, R 2020, *Scenario planning for cities and regions. Managing and envisioning uncertain futures*, Lincoln Institute of Land Policy, Cambridge.

Graham, S & Marvin, S 2001, *Splintering Urbanism: Networked infrastructures, technological mobilities and the urban condition*, Routledge, London.

Gray, R, Gleeson, B & Burke, M 2010, 'Urban consolidation, household greenhouse emissions and the role of planning', *Urban Policy and Research*, vol. 28, no. 3, pp. 335-46.

Grose, M 2017, 'Designing backward for suburbia', in A Berger, J Kotkin & C Guzman (eds), *Infinite suburbia*, MIT, Boston, pp. 496-505.

Gunder, M 2010, 'Planning as the ideology of (neoliberal) space', *Planning Theory*, vol. 9, no. 4, pp. 298-314.

Haaland, C & van den Bosch, CK 2015, 'Challenges and strategies for urban green-space planning in cities undergoing densification: a review', *Urban Forestry & Urban Greening*, vol. 14, no. 4, pp. 760-71.

Hall, P 2014, *Cities of tomorrow: An intellectual history of urban planning and design since 1880*, 4th edn, Blackwell, Oxford.

Hamouche, M 2004, 'The changing morphology of the Gulf cities in the age of globalisation: the case of Bahrain', *Habitat International*, no. 28, pp. 521-40.

Harvey, D 2002, *Spaces of hope*, Cromwell Press, Edinburgh.

—— 2015, 'Contested cities: social process and spatial form', in RT LeGates & F Stout (eds), *The city reader*, Routledge, London, pp. 227-34.

Healey, P 2001, 'Planning theory: Interaction with institutional contexts'.

Hickel, J 2020, *Less is more: How DEGROWTH WILL SAVE THE WORLD*, Penguin Books, Dublin.

Hill, S, Cumpston, Z & Vigiola, GQ 2021, *Australia state of the environment: Urban*, Commonwealth of Australia.

Hills, P 1994, *Sustainable development and urban form*. M.J. Breheny, (Ed.) (1992) 292pp. London, Pion Limited (European Research in Regional Science, No.2) ISBN 085086 160 8 £28.00 paperback [book review], *Sustainable Development*, vol. 2, no. 1, p. 31.

Holling, C & Haslam McKenzie, F 2010, 'Integrated transit orientated development: Is it Appropriate for Perth?', in I Alexander, S Greive & D Hedgcock (eds), *Planning perspectives from Western Australia: A reader in theory and practice*, Fremantle Press, Perth, pp. 274-88.

Hopkins, R 2019, *From what is to what if: Unleashing the power of imagination to create the future we want*, Chelsea Green Publishing, London.

Horsfield, A & Elborough, T 2016, *Atlas of improbable places: A journey to the world's most unusual corners*.

Hurley, J, Taylor, E & Dodson, J 2017, 'Why has urban consolidation been so difficult?', in N Sipe & K Vella (eds), *The Routledge handbook of Australian urban and regional planning*, Routledge, New York, pp. 123-35.

Infrastructure Australia 2018, *Future cities: Planning for our growing population (summary report)*, Australian Government, Canberra.

IPCC 2022, *IPCC Working Group 2 Sixth Assessment Report*.

Ives, C 2015, *Do urban green corridors "work"?*, The Nature of Cities, viewed 11 01 2016, <https://www.google.com.au/search?q=Do+urban+green+corridors+%22work%22%3F&ie=utf-8&oe=utf-8&gws_rd=cr&ei=aQKTVu7-HYTI0ASijaiQBQ>.

Iwanicki, I & Jones, D 2012, 'Learning from arid planning and design history and practice: from Woomera to creating the new Roxby Downs communities', in *PIA 2012: Planning for a sunburnt country: Building resilient communities through planning: Proceedings of the Planning Institute of Australia 2012 National Congress*, pp. 1-19.

Kelly, J-F, Breadon, P & Reichl, J 2011, *Getting the housing we want*, Grattan Institute, Melbourne.

Kelly, J-F & Donegan, P 2015, *City limits: why Australian cities are broken and how we can fix them*, Melbourne University Press, Melbourne.

Kelly, J-F, Weldmann, B & Walsh, M 2011, *The housing we'd choose*, Grattan Institute.

Kohler, A 2024, 'Australia's housing mess and how to fix it', *The Quarterly*.

Kornfield, J 2009, *A path with heart: A guide through the perils and promises of spiritual life*, Bantam, New York.

Kullmann, K 2011, 'Thin parks/thick edges: towards a linear park typology for (post) infrastructural sites', *Journal of Landscape Architecture*, vol. 6, no. 2, pp. 70-81.

Kunstler, J 1993, *The geography of nowhere: The rise and decline of America's man-made landscape*, Simon & Schuster, New York.

Le Corbusier 1947, *The city of tomorrow*, MIT Press, Cambridge.

Lenzholzer, S 2015, *Weather in the city: How design shapes the urban climate*, nai010, Rotterdam.

Lowe, T 2017, *The new nature*, Penguin, Australia.

Lynch, K 1960, *The image of the city*, The MIT Press, Cambridge.

Maginn, PJ & Hamnett, S 2016, 'Multiculturalism and Metropolitan Australia: demographic change and implications for strategic planning', *Built Environment*, vol.

42, no. 1, pp. 120-44.

Mars, R & Kohlstedt, K 2020, *The 99% invisible city: A field guide to the hidden world of everyday design*, Houghton Mifflin, Boston.

Martin, M 2004, 'Designing the next Radburn: A green-hearted American neighbourhood for the 21st century', paper presented to Open Space/People Space: An International Conference on Inclusive Environments, Edinburgh: Research Centre for Inclusive Access to Outdoor Environments.

Marx, P 2022, *Road to nowhere: what Silicon Valley gets wrong about the future of transportation*, Verso Books, London.

Matsumoto, T, Sanchez-Serra, D & Ostry, A 2012, *Compact city policies: a comparative assessment*, OECD, viewed 04 04 2025, <https://www.oecd.org/content/dam/oecd/en/publications/reports/2012/05/compact-city-policies_g1g191f1/9789264167865-en.pdf>.

McClinton, B 2007, 'A defence of polemics', *Humani*, no. 105, pp. 12-3.

McDonald, R 2015, *Conservation for cities: How to plan and build natural infrastructure*, Island Press, Washington.

McLanahan, S & Sandefur, G 1995, *Growing up with a single parent: What hurts, what helps*, Harvard University Press, Boston.

McLaren, D & Agyeman, J 2015, *Sharing cities: A case for truly smart and sustainable cities*, MIT Press.

McLeod, S 2024, *Understanding accommodation and assimilation in psychology*, Simply Psychology, viewed 02 11 2024, <https://www.simplypsychology.org/what-is-accommodation-and-assimilation.html#:~:text=While%20accommodation%20seeks%20to%20create,schemas%20based%20on%20familiar%20concepts>.

McNee, G & Pojani, D 2021, 'NIMBYism as a barrier to housing and social mix in San Francisco', *Journal of Housing and the Built Environment*, pp. 1-21.

Mittermeier, R, Turner, W, Larsen, F, Brooks, T & Clascon, C 2011, 'Global biodiversity conservation: The critical role of hotspots', in F Zachos & JC Habel (eds), *Biodiversity hotspots: Distribution and protection of conservation priority areas*, Springer-Verlag, Berlin.

Montgomery, C 2013, *Happy cities: Transforming our lives through urban design*, Penguin, St Ives.

Morris, A 2013, *History of urban form before the industrial revolutions*, Longman Scientific and Technical, New York.

Mumford, L 1961, *The City in History*, Harcourt, San Diego, New York, London.

Mundell, M 2019, 'From hotbeds of depravity to hidden treasures: The narrative evolution of Melbourne's laneways', *TEXT*, vol. 23, no. Special 55, pp. 1-16.

Murphy, K 2009, '"The modern idea is to bring the country into the city": Australian urban reformers and the ideal of rurality, 1900–1918', *Rural History*, vol. 20, no. 1, pp. 119-36.

Murphy, P 2012, 'The metropolis', in P Maginn & S Thompson (eds), *Planning Australia: An Overview of Urban and Regional Planning*, Cambridge University Press, Melbourne, pp. 155-79.

Murray, S, Bertram, N, Khor, L-A, Rowe, D, Meyer, B, Newton, P, Glackin, S, Alves, T & McGauran, R 2015, 'Processes for developing affordable and sustainable medium density housing models for Greyfield precincts', *Melbourne: AHURI*.

Neuman, M 2005, 'The compact city fallacy', *Journal of Planning Education and Research*, vol. 25, no. 1, pp. 11-26.

Newman, P, Beatley, T & Boyer, H 2009, *Resilient cities*, Island Press, Washington.

Newton, P 2010, 'Beyond Greenfield and Brownfield: the challenge of regenerating Australia's greyfield suburbs', *Built Environment*, vol. 36, no. 1, pp. 81-104.

Newton, PW 1985, 'Planning new towns for harsh arid environments: an evaluation of Shay Gap and Newman mining towns, Australia', *Ekistics*, vol. 52, no. 311, pp. 180-8.

Ng, ES & Metz, I 2015, 'Multiculturalism as a strategy for national competitiveness: The case for Canada and Australia', *Journal of Business Ethics*, vol. 128, no. 2, pp. 253-66.

O'Neil, C & Watts, T 2015, *Two futures: Australia at a critical moment*, Text Publishing.

Office for Metropolitan Architecture, Koolhaas, R & Mau, B 1995, *S, M, L, XL*, Monacelli Press, Inc, New York.

Orchard, L 1999, 'Shifting visions in national urban and regional policy 2: The Whitlam Program, the backlash and the Keating revival', *Australian Planner*, vol. 36, no. 4, pp. 200-9.

Pacione, M 2004, 'Where will the people go?—assessing the new settlement option for the United Kingdom', *Progress in Planning*, vol. 62, no. 2, pp. 73-129.

Park, BJ, Tsunetsugu, Y, Kasetani, T, Kagawa, T & Miyazaki, Y 2010, 'The physiological effects of Shinrin-yoku (taking in the forest atmosphere or forest bathing): Evidence from field experiments in 24 forests across Japan', *Environmental Health and Preventive Medicine*, vol. 15, no. 1, pp. 18-26.

Popenoe, D 2009, *Families without fathers fathers, marriage and children in American society*, Transaction Publishers, New Brunswick, N.J.

Putnam, R 2000, *Bowling alone*, Touchstone, New York.

Qadeer, M 1997, 'Pluralistic planning for multicultural cities', in E Birch (ed.), *The urban and regional planning reader*, Routledge, New York, pp. 30-40.

Randolph, B 2006, *Delivering the compact city in Australia: current trends and future implications*, 0811-1146, City Futures Research Centre, Sydney.

Randolph, B, Freestone, R & Bunker, R 2017, 'Sydney: Growth, globalization and governance', in R Freestone & S Hamnett (eds), *Planning metropolitan Australia*, Routledge, Abingdon, pp. 84-108.

Raupach, M, McMichael, A, Alford, K, Fulton, E, Finnigan, J, Grigg, N, Leves, F, Manderson, L & Walker, B 2012, 'Living scenarios for Australia as an adaptive system', in M Raupach, A McMichael, J Finnigan, L Manderson & B Walker (eds), *Negotiating our future: Living scenarios for Australia to 2050*, Australian Academy of Science, Canberra, pp. 1-53.

Rhodes, A 2017, *Screen time and kids: What's happening in our homes?*, The Royal Children's Hospital Melbourne, viewed 16 10 2023, <https://www.rchpoll.org.au/wp-content/uploads/2017/06/ACHP-Poll7_Detailed-Report-June21.pdf>.

Romer, P 2010, *Technologies, rules, and progress: The case for charter cities*. Center for Global Development, viewed 04 04 2025, <https://www.files.ethz.ch/isn/113646/1423916_file_TechnologyRulesProgress_FINAL.pdf>.

Rossant, J & Baker, S 2019, *Hop, skip, go: How the mobility revolution will transform our lives and our planet*, HarperCollins, London.

Rowley, S & Phibbs, P 2012, *Delivering diverse and affordable housing on infill development sites*, Australian Housing and Urban Research Institute, Melbourne.

Salthammer, T, Uhde, E, Schrippa, T, Schieweck, A, Morawska, L, Mazaheri, M, Clifford, S, He, C, Buonanno, G, Querol, X, Viana, M & Kumar, P 2016, 'Children's well-being at schools: Impact of climatic conditions and air pollution', *Environment International*, vol. 94, no. 2016, pp. 196-210.

Sandercock, L 1998, *Towards cosmopolis: planning for multicultural cities*, John Wiley and Sons, Chichester.

Sarkissian, W 2013, *Wendy Sarkissian on NIMBYism, Community resistance and housing density*, The Fifth Estate, viewed 17.12 2015, <http://www.thefifthestate.com.au/spinifex/nimbyism-community-resistance-and-housing-density/45397>.

Seamer, P 2019, *Breaking POINT: The future of Australian cities*, Nero, Melbourne.

Seddon, G 1994, 'The Australian back yard', in I Craven (ed.), *Australian popular culture*, Cambridge University Press, Cambridge, pp. 22-35.

Seddon, G & Ravine, D 1986, *A city and its setting: Images of Perth, Western Australia*, Fremantle Arts Centre Press, Perth.

Sedlak, D 2024, *Water for all: Global solutions for a changing climate*, Yale University Press, New Haven.

Sennett, R & Sendra, P 2020, *Designing disorder: Experiments and disruptions in the city*, Verso Books.

Sharifi, E, Sivam, A & Boland, J 2016, 'Resilience to heat in public space: a case study of Adelaide, South Australia', *Journal of Environmental Planning and Management*, vol. 59, no. 10, pp. 1833-54.

Smith, K 1999, 'Linear landscapes: Corridors, conduits, strips, edges, and segues', *Harvard Design Magazine*, p. 77.

Spilhaus, A 1967, 'The experimental city', *Science*, no. 159, pp. 710-5.

Stannage, CT 1979, *The people of Perth: A social history of Western Australia's capital city*, Perth City Council, Perth.

Stein, S 2019, *Capital city: Gentrification and the real estate state*, Verso, London.

Stevenson, A & Sutton, R 2011, 'There's no place like a refugee camp? Urban planning and participation in the camp context ', *Refuge,* vol. 28, no. 1, pp. 137-46.

Strandell, A & Hall, CM 2015, 'Impact of the residential environment on second home use in Finland–Testing the compensation hypothesis', *Landscape and Urban Planning*, vol. 133, pp. 12-23.

Syed, M 2019, *Rebel ideas: The power of diverse thinking*, John Murray, London.

Taleb, N 2010, *The black swan: The impact of the highly improbable*, Penguin Books, London.

Talen, E 2012, *Design for diversity*, Routledge, Abingdon.

—— 2013, *The social apathy of landscape urbanism*, New Society Publishers, Gabriola Island.

Tan, AJ, Mancini, V, Gross, JJ, Goldenberg, A, Badcock, JC, Lim, MH, Becerra, R, Jackson, B & Preece, DA 2022, 'Loneliness versus distress: A comparison of emotion regulation profiles', *Behaviour Change*, vol. 39, no. 3, pp. 180-90.

The Australia Institute 2023, *Research reveals $1.2 billion profit from food waste*, The Australia Institute, viewed 06 01 2024, <https://australiainstitute.org.au/post/research-reveals-1-2-billion-profit-from-food-waste/>.

The Carbon Alamanac Network 2022, *The carbon alamanac*, Penguin, Glasgow.

Troy, P 2004, 'Saving our cities with suburbs', in J Schultz (ed.), *Griffith Review: Dreams of land*, Griffith University, Brisbane.

Troy, PN 1996, *The perils of urban consolidation: A discussion of Australian housing and urban development policies*, Federation Press, Sydney.

Twill, J 2017, *Supersized cities: Residents band together to push back against speculative development pressures*, The Conversation, viewed 03 11 2024, <https://theconversation.com/supersized-cities-residents-band-together-to-push-back-against-speculative-development-pressures-77553>.

Van Leynseele, Y & Bontje, M 2019, *Visionary cities or spaces of uncertainty? Satellite cities and new towns in emerging economies*, Routledge, 1356-3475.

Van Noorloos, F & Kloosterboer, M 2017, 'Africa's new cities: The contested future of urbanisation', *Urban Studies*, vol. 55, no. 6, pp. 1-19.

Varoufakis, Y 2017, *Talking to my daughter about the economy: A brief history of capitalism*, Random House, Rochester.

—— 2024, *Technofeudalism: What killed capitalism*, Melville House, New Jersey.

Ward Thompson, C 2002, 'Urban open space in the 21st century', *Landscape and Urban Planning*, vol. 60, pp. 59-72.

Wassmer, RW & Wahid, I 2019, 'Does the likely demographics of affordable housing justify NIMBYism?', *Housing Policy Debate*, vol. 29, no. 2, pp. 343-58.

Water Corporation 2019, *A move to buffertopia strategic resource precincts*, Water Services of Australia, viewed 03 10 2024, <https://www.wsaa.asn.au/sites/default/files/publication/download/Case%20study%2019%20A%20move%20to%20buffertopia.pdf>.

Watson, D 2014, *The bush*, Hamish Hamilton, Sydney.

Weller, R 2015, 'World Park', *LA+*, vol. Wild, pp. 10-9.

—— 2017, 'The city Is not an egg: Western urbanization in relation to changing conceptions of nature', in F Steiner, G Thompson & A Carbonell (eds), *Nature and cities: The ecological imperative in urban design and planning*, Lincoln Institute of Land Policy, Cambridge, pp. 31-49.

—— 2024, *To the ends of the earth: A grand tour for the 21st century*, Birkhauser, Basel.

Wennersten, JR & Robbins, D 2017, *Rising tides: Climate refugees in the twenty-first century*, Indiana University Press, Bloomington.

Westbury, M 2008, 'Fluid cities create', in J Schultz (ed.), *Griffith Review: Cities on the edge*, Griffith University, Brisbane, pp. 171-83.

Wheeler, T 2010, 'Garden cities of tomorrow: Upside down, inside out and back to front', *Griffith Review 29: Prosper or perish*, pp. 46-56.

Wilkinson, S 2015, 'A Psychological perspective on Landscape', *Landscape Architecture Australia*, no. 148, pp. 15-8.

Willing, R & Pojani, D 2017, 'Is the suburban dream still alive in Australia? Evidence from Brisbane', *Australian Planner*, vol. 54, no. 2, pp. 67-79.

Wolfe, T 1981, *From Bauhaus to our house*, Picador, London.

World population review 2024, *House size by country 2024*, World population review, viewed 06 01 2024, <https://worldpopulationreview.com/country-rankings/house-size-by-country>.

Yalom, ID 2008, *Staring at the sun: Overcoming the terror of death*, Jossey-Bass, New Jersey.

ENDNOTES

1. David Harvey, *Spaces of hope* (Edinburgh: Cromwell Press, 2002), 155.

2. Rutger Bregman, *Utopia for realists* (Bloomsbury Publishing, 2018).

3. Samuel Stein, *Capital City: Gentrification and the Real Estate State* (London: Verso, 2019).

4. Jonathan Franzen, *What if we stopped pretending?* (London: 4th Estate, 2021), 20.

5. P Seamer, *Breaking Point: The Future of Australian Cities* (Melbourne: Nero, 2019).

6. Jane-Frances Kelly and Paul Donegan, *City limits: why Australian cities are broken and how we can fix them* (Melbourne: Melbourne University Press, 2015).

7. Elizabeth Farrelly, *Killing Sydney: the fight for a city's soul* (Sydney: Picador, 2021).

8. Sarah Hill, Zena Cumpston, and Gabriela Quintana Vigiola, *Australia State of the Environment: Urban*, Commonwealth of Australia (Commonwealth of Australia, 2021), https://soe.dcceew.gov.au/about-soe/downloads.

9. Kelly and Donegan, *City limits: why Australian cities are broken and how we can fix them*.

10. Kelly and Donegan, *City limits: why Australian cities are broken and how we can fix them*.

11. Farrelly, *Killing Sydney: the fight for a city's soul*, 303.

12. Mike Gillen, "The challenge of attaining a sustainable urban morphology for South East Queensland," *Planning, Practice & Research* 21, no. 3 (2006).

13. Christine Haaland and Cecil Konijnendijk van den Bosch, "Challenges and strategies for urban green-space planning in cities undergoing densification: a review," *Urban Forestry & Urban Greening* 14, no. 4 (2015).

14. Ross Elliot, "Australia's misplaced war on the Australian Dream," in *Infinite suburbia*, ed. Alan Berger and Joel Kotkin (Boston: MIT, 2017).

15. The 2018 ACT planning strategy has a 70:30 ratio infill to sprawl, the 30-year plan for Greater Adelaide an 85:15 ratio, Plan Melbourne 2017–2050 75:35, the South East Queensland plan 2017 (2017–2031) a 60:40 ratio, the Perth and Peel @3.5million plan 47:53, the Greater Sydney Region Plan: a metropolis of three cities (2018) a 70:30 ratio and the Southern Tasmania regional land use strategy 2010–2035, which targets a 50:50 ratio Hill, Cumpston, and Vigiola, *Australia State of the Environment: Urban*.

16. Anna Strandell and C Michael Hall, "Impact of the residential environment on second home use in Finland– Testing the compensation hypothesis," *Landscape and Urban Planning* 133 (2015).

17. Clive Forster, "The challenge of change: Australian cities and urban planning in the new millennium," *Geographical research* 44, no. 2 (2006): 180.

18. Gillen, "The challenge of attaining a sustainable urban morphology for South East Queensland."

19. Gillen, "The challenge of attaining a sustainable urban morphology for South East Queensland."; Rowan Gray, Brendan Gleeson, and Matthew Burke, "Urban Consolidation, Household Greenhouse Emissions and the Role of Planning," *Urban Policy and Research* 28, no. 3 (2010).

20. Kelly and Donegan, *City limits: why Australian cities are broken and how we can fix them*; Robin Goodman and Susie Moloney, "Activity Centre Planning in Melbourne Revisited," *Australian Planner* 41, no. 2 (2004); Paul Burton, "South East Queensland: Change and Continuity in Planning," in *Planning Metropolitan Australia*, ed. Robert Freestone and Stephen Hamnett (Abingdon: Routledge, 2017); Robin Goodman, "Melbourne: Growing pains for the liveable city," in *Planning Metropolitan Australia*, ed. Robert Freestone and Stephen

Hamnett (Abingdon: Routledge, 2017); Bill Randolph, Robert Freestone, and Raymond Bunker, "Sydney: Growth, Globalization and Governance," in Planning Metropolitan Australia, ed. Robert Freestone and Stephen Hamnett (Abingdon: Routledge, 2017); Gillen, "The challenge of attaining a sustainable urban morphology for South East Queensland."

21. Peter Murphy, "The metropolis," in *Planning Australia: An Overview of Urban and Regional Planning,* ed. Paul Maginn and Susan Thompson (Melbourne: Cambridge University Press, 2012).

22. Joe Hurley, Elizabeth Taylor, and Jago Dodson, "Why has urban consolidation been so difficult?," in *The Routledge handbook of Australian urban and regional planning,* ed. Neil Sipe and Karen Vella (New York: Routledge, 2017).

23. Jason Twill, "Supersized cities: residents band together to push back against speculative development pressures," *The Conversation,* 2017, accessed 03.11, 2024, https://theconversation.com/supersized-cities-residents-band-together-to-push-back-against-speculative-development-pressures-77553.

24. Twill, "Supersized cities: residents band together to push back against speculative development pressures."

25. Elliot, "Australia's misplaced war on the Australian Dream."

26. Elliot, "Australia's misplaced war on the Australian Dream," 111.

27. Haaland and van den Bosch, "Challenges and strategies for urban green-space planning in cities undergoing densification: a review."

28. Tadashi Matsumoto, Daniel Sanchez-Serra, and Adam Ostry, *Compact City Policies: A Comparative Assessment* (OECD, 2012), http:/ldx.doi.org/10.1787/9789264167865-en.

29. Haaland and van den Bosch, "Challenges and strategies for urban green-space planning in cities undergoing densification: a review."

30. Peter Hills, "Sustainable development and urban form. M.J. Breheny, (Ed.) (1992) 292pp. London, Pion Limited (European Research in Regional Science, No.2) ISBN 085086 160 8 £28.00 paperback," in *Sustainable Development* (Chichester, UK: John Wiley & Sons, Ltd, 1994); Patrick Nicol Troy, *The perils of urban consolidation: a discussion of Australian housing and urban development policies* (Sydney: Federation Press, 1996); Rod Burgess and Mike Jenks, "The Compact City Debate: A Global Perspective," (Routledge, 2000).

31. Michael Neuman, "The Compact City Fallacy," *Journal of planning education and research* 25, no. 1 (2005), https://doi.org/10.1177/0739456x04270466.

32. Gillen, "The challenge of attaining a sustainable urban morphology for South East Queensland," 303.

33. Strandell and Hall, "Impact of the residential environment on second home use in Finland–Testing the compensation hypothesis," 13.

34. Strandell and Hall, "Impact of the residential environment on second home use in Finland–Testing the compensation hypothesis."

35. Strandell and Hall, "Impact of the residential environment on second home use in Finland–Testing the compensation hypothesis."

36. Seamer, Breaking Point: The Future of Australian Cities, 144.

37. Yanis Varoufakis, *Talking to my daughter about the economy: A brief history of capitalism* (Rochester: Random House, 2017), 100..

38. I use the term urban planning herein as inclusive of urban design and other related disciplines.

39. Renuka Bhoge, Hannah Nolan, and Dorina Pojani, "Designing the subtropical city: an evaluation of climate-sensitive policy effects in Brisbane, Australia," *Journal of environmental planning and management* 63, no. 10 (2020).

40. In Matthew Syed, *Rebel Ideas: The Power of Diverse Thinking* (London: John Murray, 2019), 231.

41. Bhoge, Nolan, and Pojani, "Designing the subtropical city: an evaluation of climate-sensitive policy effects in Brisbane, Australia."
42. Charles Montgomery, *Happy Cities: Transforming Our Lives Through Urban Design* (St Ives: Penguin, 2013).
43. Syed, *Rebel Ideas: The Power of Diverse Thinking*.
44. Bregman, *Utopia for realists*.
45. Syed, *Rebel Ideas: The Power of Diverse Thinking*.
46. Harvey in Michael Gunder, "Planning as the ideology of (neoliberal) space," *Planning theory* 9, no. 4 (2010).
47. Scott and Roweis in Gunder, "Planning as the ideology of (neoliberal) space."
48. Jason Hickel, *Less is More: How Degrowth Will Save the World* (Dublin: Penguin Books, 2020).
49. Harvey, *Spaces of hope*, 150.
50. Jeffrey F. Fitzpatrick and Zhang Jian, "Using China's experience to speculate upon the future possibility of Special Economic Zones (SEZ) within the planned development of northern Australia," *Flinders LJ* 18 (2016).
51. Bregman, *Utopia for realists*, 54.
52. Naomi Klein in Rob Hopkins, *From what is to what if: unleashing the power of imagination to create the future we want* (London: Chelsea Green Publishing, 2019), 14.
53. Syed, *Rebel Ideas: The Power of Diverse Thinking*.
54. Syed, *Rebel Ideas: The Power of Diverse Thinking*.
55. Kim Dovey, *Urban design thinking* (London: Bloomsbury Academic, 2016), 259.
56. For more about the drawing process you can check out the YouTube video here: https://tinyurl.com/4ctah4ch
57. Nassim Taleb, *The Black Swan: The Impact of the Highly Improbable* (London: Penguin Books, 2010).
58. Taleb, *The Black Swan: The Impact of the Highly Improbable,* 167.
59. Emily Talen, "The Social Apathy of Landscape Urbanism," ed. Andres Duany and Emily Talen, *Landscape Urbanism and its Discontents: Dissimulating the Sustainable City* (Gabriola Island: New Society Publishers, 2013); Andres Duany and Emily Talen, "Looking Backward: Notes on a Cultural Episode," ed. Andres Duany and Emily Talen, Landscape Urbanism and its Discontents: Dissimulating the Sustainable City (Gabriola Island: New Society Publishers, 2013).
60. P Healey, "Planning theory: Interaction with institutional contexts," (2001).
61. Robert Fishman, "Urban Utopias: Ebenezer Howard, Frank Lloyd Wright, and Le Corbusier," in *Readings in Planning Theory,* ed. Scott Campbell and Susan Fainstein (Oxford Melbourne: Blackwell Publishing, 2003), 23.
62. Emily Talen, *Design for diversity* (Abingdon: Routledge, 2012).
63. M. Auster, "Colonial beginnings: building a better world?," *Australian Planner* 26, no. 3 (1988).
64. Bregman, *Utopia for realists,* 41.
65. Harvey, *Spaces of hope,* 159.
66. Harvey, *Spaces of hope,* 189.
67. E.g., Douglas Farr, *Sustainable Urbanism: Urban Design with Nature* (New Jersey`: Jon Wiley and Sons, 2008).
68. I note also that the proposals are not mutually exclusive, which is an unavoidable byproduct of the way they were developed.
69. The ideas also have potential application in larger regional cities.
70. Peter Newton, "Beyond Greenfield and Brownfield: the challenge of regenerating Australia's greyfield suburbs," *Built Environment* 36, no. 1 (2010), http://www.ingentaconnect.com/content/alex/benv/2010/00000036/00000001/art00006 http://dx.doi.org/10.2148/benv.36.1.81.
71. Australian Bureau of Statistics, Population Projections, Australia, 2012 to 2101, (2013).

72. Hopkins, *From what is to what if: unleashing the power of imagination to create the future we want*, 51.
73. Jack Kornfield, *A path with heart: A guide through the perils and promises of spiritual life* (New York: Bantam, 2009).
74. Montgomery, *Happy Cities: Transforming Our Lives Through Urban Design*.
75. Montgomery, *Happy Cities: Transforming Our Lives Through Urban Design*.
76. Montgomery, *Happy Cities: Transforming Our Lives Through Urban Design*.
77. Montgomery, *Happy Cities: Transforming Our Lives Through Urban Design*, 10.
78. Farrelly, *Killing Sydney: the fight for a city's soul*.
79. Montgomery, *Happy Cities: Transforming Our Lives Through Urban Design*.
80. Kornfield, *A path with heart: A guide through the perils and promises of spiritual life*, 16.
81. Farrelly, *Killing Sydney: the fight for a city's soul*.
82. Montgomery, *Happy Cities: Transforming Our Lives Through Urban Design*.
83. Duncan McLaren and Julian Agyeman, *Sharing Cities: A Case for Truly Smart and Sustainable Cities* (MIT Press, 2015), 317.
84. Robert Putnam, *Bowling Alone* (New York: Touchstone, 2000), 210.
85. Hickel, *Less is More: How Degrowth Will Save the World*.
86. Hickel, *Less is More: How Degrowth Will Save the World*.
87. Farrelly, *Killing Sydney: the fight for a city's soul*, 55.
88. Paris Marx, *Road to nowhere: what Silicon Valley gets wrong about the future of transportation* (London: Verso Books, 2022), 11.
89. Marx, *Road to nowhere: what Silicon Valley gets wrong about the future of transportation*, 11.
90. Hopkins, *From what is to what if: unleashing the power of imagination to create the future we want*, 20.
91. Dovey, *Urban design thinking*.
92. John Rossant and Stephen Baker, *Hop, Skip, Go: How the Mobility Revolution Will Transform Our Lives and Our Planet* (London: HarperCollins, 2019), xvii.
93. Rossant and Baker, *Hop, Skip, Go: How the Mobility Revolution Will Transform Our Lives and Our Planet*, xii.
94. James Kunstler, *The Geography of Nowhere: The Rise and Decline of America's Man-Made Landscape* (New York: Simon & Schuster, 1993).
95. Montgomery, *Happy Cities: Transforming Our Lives Through Urban Design*.
96. Marx, *Road to nowhere: what Silicon Valley gets wrong about the future of transportation*.
97. Rossant and Baker, *Hop, Skip, Go: How the Mobility Revolution Will Transform Our Lives and Our Planet*.
98. Montgomery, *Happy Cities: Transforming Our Lives Through Urban Design*.
99. Athelstan Spilhaus, "The experimental city," *Science*, no. 159 (1967): 713.
100. Farrelly, *Killing Sydney: the fight for a city's soul*, 67.
101. Le Corbusier, *The city of tomorrow* (Cambridge: MIT Press, 1947), 12.
102. Syed, *Rebel Ideas: The Power of Diverse Thinking*.
103. Yves Van Leynseele and Marco Bontje, "Visionary cities or spaces of uncertainty? Satellite cities and new towns in emerging economies," (Routledge, 2019).
104. Paul Romer, *Technologies, Rules, and Progress: The Case for Charter Cities* (Centre for Global Development, 2010), 8.
105. Femke Van Noorloos and Marjan Kloosterboer, "Africa's new cities: The contested future of urbanisation," *Urban Studies* 55, no. 6 (2017).
106. Dovey, *Urban design thinking*.
107. Van Leynseele and Bontje, "Visionary cities or spaces of uncertainty? Satellite cities and new towns in emerging economies," 210.
108. Alan Horsfield and Travis Elborough, *Atlas of improbable places: a journey*

to the world's most unusual corners (2016), 20.

109 Richard Sennett and Pablo Sendra, *Designing Disorder: Experiments and Disruptions in the City* (Verso Books, 2020).

110 Vicente Bicudo de Castro and Ralph Kober, "The Principality Of Hutt River: A Territory Marooned in the Western Australian Outback," *Shima* (Sydney, N.S.W.) 12, no. 1 (2018), https://doi.org/10.21463/shima.12.1.13.

111 Syed, *Rebel Ideas: The Power of Diverse Thinking*, 174.

112 Syed, *Rebel Ideas: The Power of Diverse Thinking*.

113 Dovey, *Urban design thinking*, 52.

114 Andres Duany and Elizabeth Plater-Zyberk, "The neighbourhood, the district, and the corridor," in *The City Reader*, ed. Richard T LeGates and Frederic Stout (London: Routledge, 2015), 211.

115 Graeme Davison, *City dreamers: the urban imagination in Australia* (Sydney: NewSouth Publishing, 2016).

116 Davison, *City dreamers: the urban imagination in Australia*.

117 Davison, *City dreamers: the urban imagination in Australia*, 76.

118 Farrelly, *Killing Sydney: the fight for a city's soul*, 57.

119 Davison, *City dreamers: the urban imagination in Australia*.

120 In Davison, *City dreamers: the urban imagination in Australia*, 95.

121 Talen, *Design for diversity*, 194.

122 Sennett and Sendra, *Designing Disorder: Experiments and Disruptions in the City*.

123 Farrelly, *Killing Sydney: the fight for a city's soul*.

124 Kelly and Donegan, *City limits: why Australian cities are broken and how we can fix them*.

125 Mustapha Hamouche, "The changing morphology of the Gulf cities in the age of globalisation: the case of Bahrain," *Habitat International*, no. 28 (2004).

126 Hamouche, "The changing morphology of the Gulf cities in the age of globalisation: the case of Bahrain."

127 Talen, *Design for diversity*.

128 Talen, *Design for diversity*.

129 Marcus Westbury, "Fluid cities create," in *Griffith Review: Cities on the edge*, ed. Julianne Schultz (Brisbane: Griffith University, 2008).

130 Catharine Ward Thompson, "Urban open space in the 21st century," *Landscape and Urban Planning* 60 (2002): 69.

131 Sennett and Sendra, *Designing Disorder: Experiments and Disruptions in the City*.

132 Sennett and Sendra, *Designing Disorder: Experiments and Disruptions in the City*.

133 Dovey, *Urban design thinking*, 242.

134 Dovey, *Urban design thinking*, 173.

135 Dovey, *Urban design thinking*.

136 Tim Flannery, *The Climate Cure: Solving the Climate Emergency in the Era of COVID-19* (Text Publishing, 2020).

137 Jess Dondero, *Supercities on, under, and beyond the earth: housing, feeding, powering, and transporting the urban crowds of the future* (London: Rowman & Littlefield, 2020).

138 Dovey, *Urban design thinking*, 241.

139 Sennett and Sendra, *Designing Disorder: Experiments and Disruptions in the City*.

140 Anne Stevenson and Rebecca Sutton, "There's No Place Like A Refugee Camp? Urban Planning and Participation in the Camp Context " 28, no. 1 (2011).

141 Spilhaus, "The experimental city."

142 Hopkins, *From what is to what if: unleashing the power of imagination to create the future we want*.

143 Yanis Varoufakis, *Technofeudalism: What killed capitalism* (New Jersey: Melville House, 2024), 179.

144 Mike Barlow and Cornelia Levy-Bencheton, *Smart cities, smart future* (New Jersey: Wiley, 2019), xxi.

145. Dondero, *Supercities on, under, and beyond the earth: housing, feeding, powering, and transporting the urban crowds of the future.*

146. Dondero, *Supercities on, under, and beyond the earth: housing, feeding, powering, and transporting the urban crowds of the future.*

147. Jared Diamond, *Collapse: How Societies Choose to Fail or Survive* (London: Penguin Books, 2011), 504.

148. Anthea Rhodes, "Screen time and kids: What's happening in our homes?," The Royal Children's Hospital Melbourne, 2017, accessed 16.10, 2023, https://www.rchpoll.org.au/wp-content/uploads/2017/06/ACHP-Poll7_Detailed-Report-June21.pdf.

149. Dondero, *Supercities on, under, and beyond the earth: housing, feeding, powering, and transporting the urban crowds of the future.*

150. David Abram, *The spell of the sensuous: perception and language in a more-than-human world* (New York: Vintage Books, 1997), 41.

151. Robert Cameron, "Constructing authenticity: Location based social networks, digital placemaking, and the design of centralized urban spaces," in *Mediated Identities in the Futures of Place: Emerging Practices and Spatial Cultures,* ed. L Rajendran and N Dellé Odeleye (Springer International Publishing, 2020).

152. In Kunstler, *The Geography of Nowhere: The Rise and Decline of America's Man-Made Landscape,* 10.

153. James Bullen and nne Tarasov, "Australians spend eight times more hours per week looking at screens than with loved ones: survey," *ABC News,* 2016, accessed 21.05, 2017, http://mobile.abc.net.au/news/2016-08-11/australians-spend-46-hours-per-week-with-screens-six-with-family/7718930.

154. Hill, Cumpston, and Vigiola, *Australia State of the Environment: Urban.*

155. Hopkins, *From what is to what if: unleashing the power of imagination to create the future we want.*

156. Don Watson, *The bush* (Sydney: Hamish Hamilton, 2014), 299.

157. Watson, *The bush,* 291.

158. Hill, Cumpston, and Vigiola, *Australia State of the Environment: Urban.*

159. Hill, Cumpston, and Vigiola, *Australia State of the Environment: Urban.*

160. Watson, *The bush,* 299.

161. Bregman, *Utopia for realists.*

162. Hopkins, *From what is to what if: unleashing the power of imagination to create the future we want.*

163. Andres Duany in Ellen Dunham-Jones, *Retrofitting urban solutions for redesigning suburbs* (New Jersey: Wiley, 2011), xxi.

164. A Morris, *History of urban form before the industrial revolutions* (New York: Longman Scientific and Technical, 2013).

165. Hopkins, *From what is to what if: unleashing the power of imagination to create the future we want.*

166. Roxanne Willing and Dorina Pojani, "Is the Suburban Dream Still Alive in Australia? Evidence from Brisbane," *Australian Planner* 54, no. 2 (2017): 68.

167. Rob Giblett, *Postmodern wetlands: culture, history, ecology* (Edinburgh: Edinburgh University Press, 1996), 82.

168. George Seddon and David Ravine, *A City and Its Setting: Images of Perth, Western Australia* (Perth: Fremantle Arts Centre Press, 1986), 70.

169. Hickel, *Less is More: How Degrowth Will Save the World,* 173.

170. C.T Stannage, *The People of Perth: A Social History of Western Australia's Capital City* (Perth: Perth City Council, 1979).

171. Stannage, *The People of Perth: A Social History of Western Australia's Capital City.*

172. Lionel Orchard, "Shifting Visions in National Urban and Regional Policy 2: The Whitlam Program, the Backlash and the Keating Revival," *Australian Planner* 36, no. 4 (1999).

173. Jonathan Barnett and Matthijs Bouw, *Managing the Climate Crisis: Designing and Building for Floods, Heat, Drought, and Wildfire* (Island Press, 2022).

174. David Sedlak, *Water for all: global solutions for a changing climate* (New Haven: Yale University Press, 2024).

175. Barnett and Bouw, *Managing the Climate Crisis: Designing and Building for Floods, Heat, Drought, and Wildfire.*

176. Water Corporation, "A move to buffertopia Strategic resource precincts," Water Services of Australia, 2019, accessed 03.10, 2024, https://www.wsaa.asn.au/sites/default/files/publication/download/Case%20study%2019%20A%20move%20to%20buffertopia.pdf.

177. Giblett, *Postmodern wetlands: culture, history, ecology,* 82.

178. Stephen Graham and Simon Marvin, *Splintering Urbanism: Networked Infrastructures, Technological Mobilities and the Urban Condition* (London: Routledge, 2001), 12.

179. Patrick Troy, "Saving our cities with suburbs," in *Griffith Review: Dreams of Land,* ed. Julianne Schultz (Brisbane: Griffith University, 2004).

180. This proposal builds on innovative work done by the Water Corporation in Western Australia, entitled 'Buffertopia' Water Corporation, "A move to buffertopia Strategic resource precincts.".

181. Ellwood Cubberley (1916) in Syed, *Rebel Ideas: The Power of Diverse Thinking,* 157.

182. Australian Bureau of Statistics, "Labour Force Status of Families," Australian Government, 2023, accessed 24.07, 2024, https://www.abs.gov.au/statistics/labour/employment-and-unemployment/labour-force-status-families/latest-release.

183. Australian Bureau of Statistics, "Household and Family Projections, Australia," Australian Government, 2021, accessed 24.07, 2024, https://www.abs.gov.au/statistics/people/population/household-and-family-projections-australia/2021-2046.

184. Kelly and Donegan, *City limits: why Australian cities are broken and how we can fix them.*

185. Putnam, *Bowling Alone.*

186. Caroline Fairchild, "Driverless cars a boon for working moms?," Fortune, 2014, accessed 25.11, 2014, http://transact.org/.

187. Sara McLanahan and Gary Sandefur, *Growing Up with a Single Parent: What Hurts, What Helps.* (Boston: Harvard University Press, 1995).

188. David Popenoe, *Families without fathers fathers, marriage and children in American society* (New Brunswick, N.J: Transaction Publishers, 2009).

189. Fiona J Andrews, Elyse Warner, and Belinda Robson, "High-rise parenting: experiences of families in private, high-rise housing in inner city Melbourne and implications for children's health," *Cities & health* 3, no. 1-2 (2019).

190. Andrews, Warner, and Robson, "High-rise parenting: experiences of families in private, high-rise housing in inner city Melbourne and implications for children's health."

191. Andrews, Warner, and Robson, "High-rise parenting: experiences of families in private, high-rise housing in inner city Melbourne and implications for children's health."

192. Commuting times are increasing and 10 per cent of parents spend more time commuting than they do with their children Andrews, Warner, and Robson, "High-rise parenting: experiences of families in private, high-rise housing in inner city Melbourne and implications for children's health.".

193. Tunga Salthammer et al., "Children's well-being at schools: Impact of climatic conditions and air pollution," *Environment International* 94, no. 2016 (2016), http://dx.doi.org/10.1016/j.envint.2016.05.009.

194. Kornfield, *A path with heart: A guide through the perils and promises of spiritual life,* 23.

195. Irvin D Yalom, *Staring at the sun: Overcoming the terror of death* (New Jersey: Jossey-Bass, 2008).

196 Yalom, *Staring at the sun: Overcoming the terror of death.*

197 Roman Mars and Kurt Kohlstedt, *The 99% Invisible City: A field guide to the hidden world of everyday design* (Boston: Houghton Mifflin, 2020).

198 Lewis Mumford, *The City in History* (San Diego, New York, London: Harcourt, 1961), 40.

199 Kornfield, *A path with heart: A guide through the perils and promises of spiritual life,* 23.

200 Yalom, *Staring at the sun: Overcoming the terror of death.*

201 Kornfield, *A path with heart: A guide through the perils and promises of spiritual life,* 323.

202 Yalom, *Staring at the sun: Overcoming the terror of death,* 9.

203 Yalom, *Staring at the sun: Overcoming the terror of death.*

204 Yalom, *Staring at the sun: Overcoming the terror of death,* 115.

205 Yalom, *Staring at the sun: Overcoming the terror of death.*

206 Abram, *The spell of the sensuous: perception and language in a more-than-human world.*

207 Abram, *The spell of the sensuous: perception and language in a more-than-human world,* 15.

208 Abram, *The spell of the sensuous: perception and language in a more-than-human world,* 15.

209 Leonie Sandercock, *Towards cosmopolis: planning for multicultural cities* (Chichester: John Wiley and Sons, 1998).

210 Clare O'Neil and Tim Watts, *Two Futures: Australia at a Critical Moment* (Text Publishing, 2015).

211 Alan Kohler, "Australia's Housing Mess and How to Fix It," *The Quarterly,* 2024.

212 Kohler, "Australia's Housing Mess and How to Fix It."

213 The Organisation for Economic Co-operation and Development.

214 O'Neil and Watts, *Two Futures: Australia at a Critical Moment,* 44.

215 Kohler, "Australia's Housing Mess and How to Fix It."

216 Kohler, "Australia's Housing Mess and How to Fix It."

217 Kelly and Donegan, *City limits: why Australian cities are broken and how we can fix them.*

218 Julian Bolleter, Zoe Myers, and Paula Hooper, "Delivering medium-density infill development through promoting the benefits and limiting background infill," *Journal of Urban Design* (2020), https://doi.org/10.1080/13574809.2020.1851594.

219 C Holling and F Haslam McKenzie, "Integrated Transit Orientated Development: Is it Appropriate for Perth?," in *Planning Perspectives from Western Australia: A Reader in Theory and Practice,* ed. I Alexander, S Greive, and D Hedgcock (Perth: Fremantle Press, 2010).

220 Australian Golf Industry Council, *Water and the Australian Golf Industry* (Australian Golf Industry Council, 2022), https://archive.golf.org.au/wp-content/uploads/2020/11/00035025-source.pdf.

221 Julian Bolleter, *Scavenging the suburbs: Auditing Perth for 1 million infill dwellings* (2015: University of Western Australia Publishing, 2015). https://uwap.uwa.edu.au/products/scavenging-the-suburbs-auditing-perth-for-1-million-infill-dwellings?variant=6295015747.

222 Spilhaus, "The experimental city," 710.

223 Graeme Davison, "Fatal attraction? The lure of technology and the decline of rural Australia 1890-2000," *Tasmanian Historical Studies* 8, no. 2 (2003).

224 In Putnam, *Bowling Alone,* 207.

225 Peter Newman, Timothy Beatley, and Heather Boyer, *Resilient Cities* (Washington: Island Press, 2009), 38.

226 Diana Coole, *Should We Control World Population?* (Cambridge: Polity Press, 2018).

227 Montgomery, *Happy Cities: Transforming Our Lives Through Urban Design.*

228. Gabrielle Chan, *Rusted off: why country Australia is fed up* (Sydney: Vintage Australia, 2018).

229. Paul Gilbert, *Living like crazy* (Derbyshire: Anwyn House, 2017).

230. Gilbert, *Living like crazy*.

231. Fishman, "Urban Utopias: Ebenezer Howard, Frank Lloyd Wright, and Le Corbusier."

232. Fishman, "Urban Utopias: Ebenezer Howard, Frank Lloyd Wright, and Le Corbusier," 31.

233. Michael Pacione, "Where will the people go?—assessing the new settlement option for the United Kingdom," *Progress in Planning* 62, no. 2 (2004).

234. Kate Murphy, "'The modern idea is to bring the country into the city': Australian urban reformers and the ideal of rurality, 1900–1918," *Rural History* 20, no. 1 (2009).

235. Auster, "Colonial beginnings: building a better world?."

236. Abram, *The spell of the sensuous: perception and language in a more-than-human world*, 272.

237. Bregman, *Utopia for realists*.

238. Hickel, *Less is More: How Degrowth Will Save the World*, 72.

239. Flannery, *The Climate Cure: Solving the Climate Emergency in the Era of COVID-19*.

240. J-F Kelly, B Weldmann, and M Walsh, *The Housing We'd Choose*, Grattan Institute (2011), https://grattan.edu.au/wp-content/uploads/2014/04/090_cities_report_housing_market.pdf.

241. Wendy Sarkissian, "Wendy Sarkissian on NIMBYism, Community Resistance and Housing Density," The Fifth Estate, 2013, accessed 17.12, 2015, http://www.thefifthestate.com.au/spinifex/nimbyism-community-resistance-and-housing-density/45397.

242. Kelly and Donegan, *City limits: why Australian cities are broken and how we can fix them*, 129.

243. Sarkissian, "Wendy Sarkissian on NIMBYism, Community Resistance and Housing Density."

244. Barlow and Levy-Bencheton, Smart cities, smart future, 101.

245. In Sarkissian, "Wendy Sarkissian on NIMBYism, Community Resistance and Housing Density."

246. Jared Diamond, *Upheaval: How Nations Cope with Crisis and Change* (New York: Penguin, 2019).

247. Shane Murray et al., "Processes for developing affordable and sustainable medium density housing models for Greyfield precincts," *Melbourne: AHURI* (2015): 112.

248. J-F Kelly, P Breadon, and J Reichl, *Getting the Housing We Want*, Grattan Institute (Melbourne, 2011), https://grattan.edu.au/wp-content/uploads/2014/04/117_report_getting_the_housing_we_want.pdf.

249. Infrastructure Australia, *Future Cities: Planning for our growing population* (summary report), Australian Government (Canberra, 2018).

250. Stein, *Capital City: Gentrification and the Real Estate State*.

251. Jacinta Francis et al., "Quality or quantity? Exploring the relationship between Public Open Space attributes and mental health in Perth, Western Australia," *Social science & medicine* 74, no. 10 (2012).

252. Ward Thompson, "Urban open space in the 21st century."

253. Sandercock, *Towards cosmopolis: planning for multicultural cities*.

254. John R Wennersten and Denise Robbins, *Rising tides: Climate refugees in the twenty-first century* (Bloomington: Indiana University Press, 2017).

255. Paul J Maginn and Stephen Hamnett, "Multiculturalism and Metropolitan Australia: demographic change and implications for strategic planning," *Built environment* 42, no. 1 (2016).

256. H Amirahmadi and MR Razavi, "Urban Development in the Muslim World: Encounter with Modernity and Implications for Planning," *Urban Development in the Muslim World* (1993).

257. Janet L Abu-Lughod, "Contemporary relevance of Islamic urban principles," *Ekistics* 47, no. 280 (1980).
258. Hill, Cumpston, and Vigiola, *Australia State of the Environment: Urban*.
259. Tone Wheeler, "Garden cities of tomorrow: Upside down, inside out and back to front," *Griffith Review* 29: Prosper or Perish (2010).
260. Hill, Cumpston, and Vigiola, *Australia State of the Environment: Urban*.
261. Sandercock, *Towards cosmopolis: planning for multicultural cities*.
262. Shumon Basar, "Twelve Ultimate Critical Steps to Sudden Urban Success," in *Vision Plus Money Plus Historical Circumstance Equals 'Cities From Zero' Unapologetic Expressions of New- Found Economic and Therefore Political- Prowess in the 21st Century* (London: Architectural Association Publishing, 2007), 87.
263. Talen, *Design for diversity*, 32.
264. James Forrest, Michael Poulsen, and Ron Johnston, "A 'multicultural model' of the spatial assimilation of ethnic minority groups in Australia's major immigrant-receiving cities," *Urban Geography* 27, no. 5 (2006).
265. Forrest, Poulsen, and Johnston, "A 'multicultural model' of the spatial assimilation of ethnic minority groups in Australia's major immigrant-receiving cities," 445.
266. Talen, *Design for diversity*.
267. Forrest, Poulsen, and Johnston, "A 'multicultural model' of the spatial assimilation of ethnic minority groups in Australia's major immigrant-receiving cities," 442.
268. Forrest, Poulsen, and Johnston, "A 'multicultural model' of the spatial assimilation of ethnic minority groups in Australia's major immigrant-receiving cities."
269. Eddy S Ng and Isabel Metz, "Multiculturalism as a strategy for national competitiveness: The case for Canada and Australia," *Journal of Business Ethics* 128, no. 2 (2015).
270. Mohammad Qadeer, "Pluralistic Planning for Multicultural Cities," in *The Urban and Regional Planning Reader*, ed. Eugenie Birch (New York: Routledge, 1997).
271. Talen, *Design for diversity*.
272. Ng and Metz, "Multiculturalism as a strategy for national competitiveness: The case for Canada and Australia."
273. Talen, *Design for diversity*, 45.
274. Talen, *Design for diversity*, 18.
275. Qadeer, "Pluralistic Planning for Multicultural Cities."
276. Talen, *Design for diversity*, 45.
277. Christopher Alexander, *A pattern language: towns, buildings, construction* (Oxford: Oxford University Press, 1977).
278. Talen, *Design for diversity*, 43.
279. Yalom, *Staring at the sun: Overcoming the terror of death*, 113.
280. Farrelly, *Killing Sydney: the fight for a city's soul*.
281. Putnam, *Bowling Alone*, 27.
282. Putnam, *Bowling Alone*, 27.
283. Farrelly, *Killing Sydney: the fight for a city's soul*.
284. Marx, *Road to nowhere: what Silicon Valley gets wrong about the future of transportation*.
285. Farrelly, *Killing Sydney: the fight for a city's soul*.
286. Putnam, *Bowling Alone*, 210.
287. Putnam, *Bowling Alone*.
288. McLaren and Agyeman, *Sharing Cities: A Case for Truly Smart and Sustainable Cities*.
289. Putnam, *Bowling Alone*.
290. Yalom, *Staring at the sun: Overcoming the terror of death*.
291. Montgomery, *Happy Cities: Transforming Our Lives Through Urban Design*.
292. Hickel, *Less is More: How Degrowth Will Save the World*.
293. A kibbutz is an intentional community in Israel that was traditionally based on agriculture.
294. Eitan Bar-Yosef, "New Cities for New Jews: Haifa as Futuristic Urban Fantasy

294. in Theodor Herzl's Altneuland and Violet Guttenberg's A Modern Exodus," *Journal of Modern Jewish Studies* 12, no. 2 (2013).
295. Robert Freestone and David Nichols, "Reinvigorating 20th-century residential pocket parks for the 21st century" (5th Healthy Cities: Working Together to Achieve Liveable Cities, Geelong, Healthy Cities, 2012).
296. Stein, *Capital City: Gentrification and the Real Estate State.*
297. Freestone and Nichols, "Short Reinvigorating 20th-century residential pocket parks for the 21st century." 10.
298. Montgomery, Happy Cities: Transforming Our Lives Through Urban Design. 299 Hill, Cumpston, and Vigiola, *Australia State of the Environment: Urban.*
299. Hill, Cumpston, and Vigiola, *Australia State of the Environment: Urban.*
300. Hill, Cumpston, and Vigiola, *Australia State of the Environment: Urban.*
301. Australian Conservation Foundation, "New report reveals extinction crisis in the suburbs," Australian Conservation Foundation, 2020, accessed 19.10, 2023, https://www.acf.org.au/new_report_reveals_extinction_crisis_in_the_suburbs.
302. Richard Weller, "The city Is not an egg: western urbanization in relation to changing conceptions of nature," in *Nature and cities: the ecological imperative in urban design and planning,* ed. Frederick Steiner, George Thompson, and Armando Carbonell (Cambridge: Lincoln Institute of Land Policy, 2017), 48.
303. Robert McDonald, *Conservation for Cities: How to Plan and Build Natural Infrastructure* (Washington: Island Press, 2015).
304. Richard Weller, "World Park," *LA+*, 2015, 13.
305. Chris Ives, "Do urban green corridors "work"?," The Nature of Cities, 2015, accessed 11.01, 2016, https://www.google.com.au/search?q=Do+urban+green+corridors+%22work%22%3F&ie=utf-8&oe=utf-8&gws_rd=cr&ei=aQKTVu7-HYTIOASijaiQBQ.
306. Meg Mundell, "From hotbeds of depravity to hidden treasures: The narrative evolution of Melbourne's laneways," *TEXT* 23, no. Special 55 (2019).
307. Robert Freestone, Gethin Davison, and Richard Hu, *Design The Global City: Design Excellence, competitions and the remaking of central Sydney* (Palgrave Macmillan, 2019).
308. Line from the film 'The Castle.'
309. Seamer, *Breaking Point: The Future of Australian Cities,* 169.
310. Robert W Wassmer and Imaez Wahid, "Does the likely demographics of affordable housing justify NIMBYism?," *Housing Policy Debate* 29, no. 2 (2019), Talen, *Design for diversity.*
311. Georgina McNee and Dorina Pojani, "NIMBYism as a barrier to housing and social mix in San Francisco," *Journal of Housing and the Built Environment* (2021), 3.
312. Brendan Gleeson, *Lifeboat cities* (Sydney: UNSW Press, 2010), 131.
313. Brendan Gleeson, *The Urban Condition* (London: Routledge, 2015), 125.
314. Sandercock, *Towards cosmopolis: planning for multicultural cities,* 26.
315. Clayton Burns, "Athens had more housing conscience than us," *The Argus* (Melbourne), 19.08 1944, 6.
316. Kohler, "Australia's Housing Mess and How to Fix It."
317. Kohler, "Australia's Housing Mess and How to Fix It."
318. Kelly and Donegan, *City limits: why Australian cities are broken and how we can fix them.*
319. Stein, *Capital City: Gentrification and the Real Estate State.*
320. Kohler, "Australia's Housing Mess and How to Fix It."
321. Kohler, "Australia's Housing Mess and How to Fix It."
322. Kohler, "Australia's Housing Mess and How to Fix It."
323. Freestone, Davison, and Hu, *Design*

The Global City: Design Excellence, competitions and the remaking of central Sydney.

324 Kohler, "Australia's Housing Mess and How to Fix It."

325 Shafir in Bregman, *Utopia for realists*, 57.

326 George Orwell in Bregman, *Utopia for realists*, 95.

327 Bregman, *Utopia for realists*.

328 Bregman, *Utopia for realists*.

329 Bregman, *Utopia for realists*.

330 Burns, "Athens had more housing conscience than us," 2.

331 Stein, *Capital City: Gentrification and the Real Estate State.*

332 Tom Wolfe, *From Bauhaus to our house* (London: Picador, 1981).

333 Stein, *Capital City: Gentrification and the Real Estate State.*

334 Stein, *Capital City: Gentrification and the Real Estate State.*

335 Duany and Plater-Zyberk, "The neighbourhood, the district, and the corridor."

336 Jacobs in Stevenson and Sutton, "There's No Place Like A Refugee Camp? Urban Planning and Participation in the Camp Context " 138.

337 Sandercock, *Towards cosmopolis: planning for multicultural cities.*

338 The National Park City Foundation declared London a National Park City by with the support of the Mayor of London and 260 partner organisations.

339 Hopkins, *From what is to what if: unleashing the power of imagination to create the future we want*, 68.

340 Russell Mittermeier et al., "Global Biodiversity Conservation: The Critical Role of Hotspots," in *Biodiversity Hotspots: Distribution and Protection of Conservation Priority Areas*, ed. Frank Zachos and Jan Christian Habel (Berlin: Springer-Verlag, 2011).

341 Mittermeier et al., "Global Biodiversity Conservation: The Critical Role of Hotspots," 19.

342 Mittermeier et al., "Global Biodiversity Conservation: The Critical Role of Hotspots."

343 Hill, Cumpston, and Vigiola, *Australia State of the Environment: Urban.*

344 Richard Forman, *Urban regions: ecology and planning beyond the city* (Cambridge: Cambridge University Press, 2010).

345 Forman, *Urban regions: ecology and planning beyond the city.*

346 Forman, *Urban regions: ecology and planning beyond the city.*

347 Hopkins, *From what is to what if: unleashing the power of imagination to create the future we want.*

348 David Harvey, "Contested cities: social process and spatial form," in *The city reader*, ed. Richard T LeGates and Frederic Stout (London: Routledge, 2015), 234.

349 Harvey, "Contested cities: social process and spatial form."

350 Bregman, *Utopia for realists.*

351 Hopkins, *From what is to what if: unleashing the power of imagination to create the future we want.*

352 Hopkins, *From what is to what if: unleashing the power of imagination to create the future we want.*

353 Abram, *The spell of the sensuous: perception and language in a more-than-human world.*

354 McDonald, *Conservation for Cities: How to Plan and Build Natural Infrastructure.*

355 Rhodes, "Screen time and kids: What's happening in our homes?."

356 Abram, *The spell of the sensuous: perception and language in a more-than-human world.*

357 Abram, *The spell of the sensuous: perception and language in a more-than-human world*, ix.

358 Sophie Wilkinson, "A Psychological perspective on Landscape," *Landscape Architecture Australia*, 2015, 16.

359 McDonald, *Conservation for Cities: How to Plan and Build Natural Infrastructure.*

360 Tim Lowe, *The New Nature* (Australia: Penguin, 2017), 313.

361 Robert Freestone, Christine Garnaut, and Iris Iwanicki, "Cold War heritage and the planned community: Woomera Village in outback Australia," *International Journal of Heritage Studies* 18, no. 6 (2011).

362 Iris Iwanicki and David Jones, "Learning from arid planning and design history and practice: from Woomera to creating the new Roxby Downs communities" (paper presented at the PIA 2012: Planning for a Sunburnt Country: Building resilient communities through planning: Proceedings of the Planning Institute of Australia 2012 National Congress, 2012).

363 Michael Martin, "Designing the Next Radburn: A Green-hearted American Neighbourhood for the 21st Century" (Open Space/People Space: An International Conference on Inclusive Environments, Edinburgh: Research Centre for Inclusive Access to Outdoor Environments, 2004); Martin, "Short Designing the Next Radburn: A Green-hearted American Neighbourhood for the 21st Century."

364 Ken Smith, "Linear Landscapes: Corridors, Conduits, Strips, Edges, and Segues," *Harvard Design Magazine* (1999).

365 In Karl Kullmann, "Thin parks/thick edges: towards a linear park typology for (post) infrastructural sites," *Journal of Landscape Architecture* 6, no. 2 (2011): 72.

366 Talen, *Design for diversity*.

367 Freestone and Nichols, "Short Reinvigorating 20th-century residential pocket parks for the 21st century."

368 Talen, *Design for diversity*.

369 Bum Jin Park et al., "The physiological effects of Shinrin-yoku (taking in the forest atmosphere or forest bathing): Evidence from field experiments in 24 forests across Japan," *Environmental health and preventive medicine* 15, no. 1 (2010), https://doi.org/10.1007/s12199-009-0086-9.

370 Franzen, *What if we stopped pretending?*, 61.

371 IPCC, *IPCC Working Group 2 Sixth Assessment Report* (International Panel on Climate Change, 2022), 98, https://www.ipcc.ch/report/ar6/wg2/.

372 Australian Academy of Science, *The risks to Australia of a 3°c warmer world* (Canberra: Australian Academy of Science, 2021), www.science.org.au/warmerworld.

373 Australian Academy of Science, *The risks to Australia of a 3°c warmer world*.

374 Ehsan Sharifi, Alpana Sivam, and John Boland, "Resilience to heat in public space: a case study of Adelaide, South Australia," *Journal of Environmental Planning and Management* 59, no. 10 (2016): 1834.

375 Flannery, *The Climate Cure: Solving the Climate Emergency in the Era of COVID-19*.

376 Hill, Cumpston, and Vigiola, *Australia State of the Environment: Urban*.

377 J. A. G. Cooper and Charles Lemckert, "Extreme sea-level rise and adaptation options for coastal resort cities: a qualitative assessment from the Gold Coast, Australia," *Ocean & Coastal Management* 64 (2012).

378 Australian Academy of Science, *The risks to Australia of a 3°c warmer world*; IPCC, *IPCC Working Group 2 Sixth Assessment Report*.

379 Ian Carlton, "Histories of Transit-Oriented Development: perspectives on the development of the TOD concept," *Institute of Urban & Regional Development* (2009).

380 Carlton, "Histories of Transit-Oriented Development: perspectives on the development of the TOD concept."

381 Sharifi, Sivam, and Boland, "Resilience to heat in public space: a case study of Adelaide, South Australia."

382 Franzen, *What if we stopped pretending?*, 36.

383 Flannery, *The Climate Cure: Solving the Climate Emergency in the Era of COVID-19*.

384. Sanda Lenzholzer, *Weather in the City: How Design Shapes the Urban Climate* (Rotterdam: nai010, 2015).
385. Lenzholzer, *Weather in the City: How Design Shapes the Urban Climate.*
386. Alan García-Haro, Blanca Arellano, and Josep Roca, "Quantifying the influence of design and location on the cool island effect of the urban parks of Barcelona," *Journal of Applied Remote Sensing* 17, no. 3 (2023).
387. O'Neil and Watts, *Two Futures: Australia at a Critical Moment,* 120.
388. Hopkins, *From what is to what if: unleashing the power of imagination to create the future we want.*
389. Coole, *Should We Control World Population?*
390. Basar, "Twelve Ultimate Critical Steps to Sudden Urban Success."
391. Marx, *Road to nowhere: what Silicon Valley gets wrong about the future of transportation.*
392. Coole, *Should We Control World Population?*
393. Montgomery, *Happy Cities: Transforming Our Lives Through Urban Design,* 8.
394. Montgomery, *Happy Cities: Transforming Our Lives Through Urban Design.*
395. Bregman, *Utopia for realists,* 10.
396. Avit Bhowmik, "Flight shaming: how to spread the campaign that made Swedes give up flying for good," The Conversation, 2020, accessed 25.07, 2024, https://theconversation.com/flight-shaming-how-to-spread-the-campaign-that-made-swedes-give-up-flying-for-good-133842.
397. Bhowmik, "Flight shaming: how to spread the campaign that made Swedes give up flying for good."
398. Mohammed bin Rashid Al Maktoum, *My vision: challenges in the race for excellence* (Dubai: Motivate Publishing, 2012), 155.
399. Kevin Lynch, *The image of the city* (Cambridge: The MIT Press, 1960), 4.
400. Lynch, *The image of the city,* 4.
401. Talen, *Design for diversity.*
402. Lynch, *The image of the city.*
403. Mark Fox and Angie Wang, *Symbols: A Handbook for Seeing* (The Monacelli Press).
404. Peter W. Newton, "Planning new towns for harsh arid environments: an evaluation of Shay Gap and Newman mining towns, Australia," *Ekistics* 52, no. 311 (1985).
405. Julian Bolleter, *Desert paradises: Surveying the landscapes of Dubai's urban model* (London: Routledge, 2019).
406. Gareth Doherty, "The Landscape of Dubai's Urbanism," in *Instant Cities; Emergent Trends in Architecture and Urbanism in the Arab World* (Amman: CSAAR, 2008).
407. Farrelly, *Killing Sydney: the fight for a city's soul,* 107.
408. Weller, "The city Is not an egg: western urbanization in relation to changing conceptions of nature."
409. Montgomery, *Happy Cities: Transforming Our Lives Through Urban Design.*
410. Weller, "The city Is not an egg: western urbanization in relation to changing conceptions of nature," 36.
411. Kim Dovey and Leonie Sandercock, "Riverscapes 1- overview," in *Fluid city: transforming Melbourne's urban waterfront* (London, New York: Routledge, 2005), 30.
412. Fox and Wang, *Symbols: A Handbook for Seeing,* 193.
413. Congress of New Urbanism, "The charter of the New Urbanism," Congress of New Urbanism, 2016, accessed 15.08, 2016, https://www.cnu.org/who-we-are/charter-new-urbanism.
414. Montgomery, *Happy Cities: Transforming Our Lives Through Urban Design.*
415. Morris, *History of urban form before the industrial revolutions.*
416. Lynch, *The image of the city,* 5.
417. Dovey, *Urban design thinking,* 81.

418 Fox and Wang, *Symbols: A Handbook for Seeing.*

419 Nezar AlSayyad and Muna Guvenc, "Virtual Uprisings: On the Interaction of New Social Media, Traditional Media Coverage and Urban Space during the 'Arab Spring'," *Urban Studies* 52, no. 11 (2015): 2022.

420 In Richard Weller, *To the Ends of the Earth: A Grand Tour for the 21 st Century* (Basel: Birkhauser, 2024), 33.

421 Alan Berger, Joel Kotkin, and Celina Guzman, "Introduction," in *Infinite suburbia,* ed. Alan Berger, Joel Kotkin, and Celina Guzman (Boston: MIT, 2017), 10.

422 Berger, Kotkin, and Guzman, "Introduction."

423 Weller, "The city Is not an egg: western urbanization in relation to changing conceptions of nature," 39.

424 Brendan Gleeson, "Waking from the Dream: Towards Urban Resilience in the Face of Sudden Threat," *Griffith University Urban Research Program* (2006): 18.

425 Gleeson, "Waking from the Dream: Towards Urban Resilience in the Face of Sudden Threat," 18.

426 Christine E Carmichael and Maureen H McDonough, "Community stories: Explaining resistance to street tree-planting programs in Detroit, Michigan, USA," *Society & Natural Resources* 32, no. 5 (2019).

427 George Seddon, "The Australian Back Yard," in *Australian Popular Culture,* ed. Ian Craven (Cambridge: Cambridge University Press, 1994), 24.

428 Seddon, "The Australian Back Yard.".

429 Gleeson, "Waking from the Dream: Towards Urban Resilience in the Face of Sudden Threat."

430 David Bengston, Jennifer Fletcher, and Kristen Nelson, "Public Policies for Managing Urban Growth and Protecting Open Space: Policy Instruments and Lessons Learned in The United States," *Landscape and Urban Planning* 69 (2004).

431 Seddon, "The Australian Back Yard."

432 Italo Calvino, *Invisible cities* (Boston: Houghton Mifflin Harcourt, 1978), 44.

433 Montgomery, *Happy Cities: Transforming Our Lives Through Urban Design.*

434 Australian Institute of Health and Welfare, "Mental health," Australian Government, 2023, accessed 25.07, 2024, https://www.aihw.gov.au/mental-health/topic-areas/mental-health-prescriptions; Alyssa J. Tan et al., "Loneliness Versus Distress: A Comparison of Emotion Regulation Profiles," *Behaviour change* 39, no. 3 (2022), https://doi.org/10.1017/bec.2022.18.

435 Australian Institute of Health and Welfare, "Mental health."

436 World population review, "House Size by Country 2024," World population review, 2024, accessed 06.01, 2024, https://worldpopulationreview.com/country-rankings/house-size-by-country.

437 Australian Institute of Family Studies, "Demographics of living alone," Australian Government, 2015, accessed 04.04, 2025, https://aifs.gov.au/research/research-reports/demographics-living-alone.

438 Kim Dovey, *Fluid city: transforming Melbourne's urban waterfront* (London, New York: Routledge, 2005), 16.

439 Kunstler, *The Geography of Nowhere: The Rise and Decline of America's Man-Made Landscape.*

440 Office for Metropolitan Architecture, Rem Koolhaas, and Bruce Mau, *S, M, L, XL* (New York: Monacelli Press, Inc), 921.

441 World population review, "House Size by Country 2024."

442 Paul Bogard, *The End of Night: Searching for Natural Darkness in an Age of Artificial Light* (New York: Back Bay Books, 2014).

443 James D. Biggs et al., "Measuring and mapping the night sky brightness of Perth, Western Australia," *Monthly notices of the Royal Astronomical Society* 421, no. 2 (2012), https://doi.org/10.1111/j.1365-2966.2012.20416.x.

444 Biggs et al., "Measuring and mapping the night sky brightness of Perth, Western Australia," 1450.

445 Kevin J. Gaston et al., "Reducing the ecological consequences of night-time light pollution: options and developments," *The Journal of applied ecology* 49, no. 6 (2012), https://doi.org/10.1111/j.1365-2664.2012.02212.x.

446 Gaston et al., "Reducing the ecological consequences of night-time light pollution: options and developments."

447 Gaston et al., "Reducing the ecological consequences of night-time light pollution: options and developments."

448 Gaston et al., "Reducing the ecological consequences of night-time light pollution: options and developments.

449 Biggs et al., "Measuring and mapping the night sky brightness of Perth, Western Australia."

450 Margaret Grose, "Designing backward for suburbia," in *Infinite suburbia,* ed. Alan Berger, Joel Kotkin, and Celina Guzman (Boston: MIT, 2017).

451 Grose, "Designing backward for suburbia."

452 Gaston et al., "Reducing the ecological consequences of night-time light pollution: options and developments."

453 Gaston et al., "Reducing the ecological consequences of night-time light pollution: options and developments."

454 Gaston et al., "Reducing the ecological consequences of night-time light pollution: options and developments."

455 Gaston et al., "Reducing the ecological consequences of night-time light pollution: options and developments."

456 Gaston et al., "Reducing the ecological consequences of night-time light pollution: options and developments."

457 Gaston et al., "Reducing the ecological consequences of night-time light pollution: options and developments."

458 Biggs et al., "Measuring and mapping the night sky brightness of Perth, Western Australia.".

459 Hickel, *Less is More: How Degrowth Will Save the World.*

460 Coole, *Should We Control World Population?*

461 Michael Raupach et al., "Living scenarios for Australia as an adaptive system," in *Negotiating our future: living scenarios for Australia to 2050,* ed. Michael Raupach et al. (Canberra: Australian Academy of Science, 2012).

462 The Carbon Alamanac Network, *The Carbon Alamanac* (Glasgow: Penguin, 2022).

463 Hickel, *Less is More: How Degrowth Will Save the World.*

464 Hickel, *Less is More: How Degrowth Will Save the World.*

465 Raupach et al., "Living scenarios for Australia as an adaptive system."

466 Raupach et al., "Living scenarios for Australia as an adaptive system."

467 Department of Climate Change, Energy, the Environment and Water, "Reducing Australia's food waste," Australian Government, 2024, accessed 06.01, 2024, https://www.dcceew.gov.au/environment/protection/waste/food-waste#:~:text=Each%20year%20Australians%20waste%20around,Australia's%20annual%20greenhouse%20gas%20emissions.

468 Department of climate change, "Reducing Australia's food waste."

469 The Australia Institute, "Research Reveals $1.2 Billion Profit from Food Waste," The Australia Institute, 2023, accessed 06.01, 2024, https://australiainstitute.org.au/post/research-reveals-1-2-billion-profit-from-food-waste/.

470 Hickel, *Less is More: How Degrowth Will Save the World.*

471 Steven Rowley and Peter Phibbs, *Delivering Diverse and Affordable Housing on Infill Development Sites,* Australian Housing and Urban Research Institute (Melbourne: Australian Housing and Urban Research Institute, 2012), https://www.ahuri.edu.au/__data/assets/pdf_file/0014/2066/AHURI_Final_

472 Harvey in James Corner, "Landscape Urbanism," in *Landscape Urbanism A Manual for the Machine Landscape* (London: Architectural Association, 2003).

473 Harvey in Corner, "Landscape Urbanism," 61.

474 Corner, "Landscape Urbanism." 475 Peter Hall, Cities of Tomorrow: An Intellectual History of Urban Planning and Design since 1880, 4th ed. (Oxford: Blackwell, 2014).

476 Bill Randolph, *Delivering the compact city in Australia: current trends and future implications,* City Futures Research Centre (Sydney: University of New South Wales Faculty of the Built Environment, 2006).

477 Twill, "Supersized cities: residents band together to push back against speculative development pressures."

478 In Sennett and Sendra, *Designing Disorder: Experiments and Disruptions in the City,* 11.

479 Stein, *Capital City: Gentrification and the Real Estate State.*

480 Stein, *Capital City: Gentrification and the Real Estate State.*

481 Brian McClinton, "A defence of polemics," Humani, no. 105 (2007).

482 McClinton, "A defence of polemics."

483 Saul McLeod, "Understanding Accommodation JAnd Assimilation In Psychology," Simply Psychology, 2024, accessed 02.11, 2024, https://www.simplypsychology.org/what-is-accommodation-and-assimilation.html#:~:text=While%20accommodation%20seeks%20to%20create,schemas%20based%20on%20familiar%20concepts.

484 McLeod, "Understanding Accommodation JAnd Assimilation In Psychology."

485 McLeod, "Understanding Accommodation JAnd Assimilation In Psychology."

486 Bregman, *Utopia for realists,* 199.

487 Franzen, *What if we stopped pretending?,* 20.

488 Robert Goodspeed, *Scenario Planning for Cities and Regions. Managing and Envisioning Uncertain Futures* (Cambridge: Lincoln Institute of Land Policy, 2020).

489 Goodspeed, *Scenario Planning for Cities and Regions. Managing and Envisioning Uncertain Futures,* 5.

490 Stein, *Capital City: Gentrification and the Real Estate State.*

491 Bregman, *Utopia for realists.*

492 Flannery, *The Climate Cure: Solving the Climate Emergency in the Era of COVID-19.*

493 Flannery, *The Climate Cure: Solving the Climate Emergency in the Era of COVID-19.*; Although I note the subsequent massive bounce back in travel.

494 Flannery, *The Climate Cure: Solving the Climate Emergency in the Era of COVID-19.*

495 Kornfield, *A path with heart: A guide through the perils and promises of spiritual life.*

496 Montgomery, *Happy Cities: Transforming Our Lives Through Urban Design.*

First published in 2025 by
UWA Publishin
Crawley, Western Australia 6009
www.uwap.uwa.edu.au

UWAP is an imprint of UWA Publishing,
a division of The University of Western Australia.

THE UNIVERSITY OF WESTERN AUSTRALIA

This book is copyright. Apart from any fair dealing for the purpose of private study, research, criticism or review, as permitted under the Copyright Act 1968, no part may be reproduced by any process without written permission. Enquiries should be made to the publisher.

Copyright Julian Bolleter © 2025
The moral right of the author has been asserted.

ISBN: 978-1-76080-330-8
Design by Melinda Penn
Printed by Lightning Source

www.ingramcontent.com/pod-product-compliance
Lightning Source LLC
Chambersburg PA
CBHW041610220426
43667CB00004B/62